D0730608

DANCING ON THE WI

THE **SUNY** SERIES

CULTURAL STUDIES IN CINEMA/VIDEO

WHEELER WINSTON DIXON | EDITOR

Dancing on the White Page

Black Women Entertainers Writing Autobiography

Kwakiutl L. Dreher

STATE UNIVERSITY OF NEW YORK PRESS

Cover photo: Eartha Kitt circa 1954. Courtesy of Photofest.

Published by
State University of New York Press, Albany

For information, contact State University of New York Press, Albany, NY
www.sunypress.edu

Production by Marilyn P. Semerad
Marketing by Anne M. Valentine

Library of Congress Cataloging in Publication Data

Dreher, Kwakiutl L., 1957-
    Dancing on the white page : Black women entertainers writing
autobiography / Kwakiutl L. Dreher.
       p. cm. — (SUNY series, cultural studies in cinema/video)
    Includes bibliographical references and index.
    ISBN 978-0-7914-7283-5 (hardcover : alk. paper) — ISBN 978-0-7914-
7284-2 (pbk. : alk. paper) 1. African American women entertainers—Biography. 2. Autobiography—African American authors. 3. Autobiography—
Women authors. I. Title.

PN2286.D74 2008
791.092'396073--dc22
[B]

                                                    2007001925

                        10 9 8 7 6 5 4 3 2 1

Dedicated to:

My mother,
Mrs. Tyratha Patricia Bellamy Dreher
"Learn to type and sew; you'll always have a job.
Someone will need something typed up and you can
take in sewing on the sly."

My father,
Mr. Ulysses William Dreher
March 4, 1928–October 30, 2002
"Get your education so you won't have to ask a soul
for a !@#$ thing!"

*My parents who gave me the gifts of industry and
diligence, and who developed in me the strong will
to work and to learn about the world.*

—

Reverend Roscoe C. Wilson, Pastor Emeritus
St. John Baptist Church, Columbia, South Carolina
Reverend Wilson issued a mandate to the congregation to
mentor its youth. I am a product of that mentoring.

Contents

Acknowledgments

It takes villages to breathe life into an idea, and I have been blessed with a cornucopia of villagers—colleagues, mentors, and friends—with whom I have the pleasure to sup, eat, and break bread during this most meticulous process. *Dancing on the White Page* was watered and brought to life in a most nurturing academic village, to include the Department of English at the University of Nebraska-Lincoln, specifically Linda Pratt (former chair), Wheeler Winston Dixon, Gwendolyn Audrey Foster, Kalenda Eaton, Marco Abel, Amelia M. Montes, Nicholas Spencer, Hilda Raz, Fran Kaye, and Susan Belasco (English); the Institute for Ethnic Studies, Marcela Raffaelli, Director; Oyekan Owomoyela, Coordinator, African American and African Studies Program; Jeannette Eileen Jones and Dawne Y. Curry (History); the University of Nebraska Research Council; and the University of Nebraska Humanities Center (defunct). I am appreciative of the valuable insights Maureen Honey and Joy Ritchie (Chair) provided on women in popular culture and women's rhetoric respectively.

I am especially grateful to my academic village of friends, at the UN-L to include M. Colleen Jones (Business Administration); Stephanie G. Adams (Engineering); Harriet McLeod (Textiles, Clothing and Design); George E. Wolf and James McShane (Ret., English); and, Gerald David Shapiro, Judith Carol Slater and Jonis Agee (Creative Writing). I appreciate the support of Venetria K. Patton (Purdue University), Elizabeth Nunez (Medgar Evers College, Brooklyn, New York), Wendy Smooth (Ohio State University), Merida Grant (Vanderbilt), and Thadious Davis (University of Pennsylvania).

ix

I also wish to thank the Administrative Staff in the department, especially, Linda Rossiter, LeAnn Messing, Elaine Dvorak, Susan Hart, and Janet Carlson.

Dancing demanded the migration to a village of film and television libraries on the West coast. Many thanks to two librarians in southern California: Barbara Hall, Head Librarian at the Margaret Herrick Library of the Academy of Motion Picture Arts and Sciences and Ned Comstock, librarian at the Cinema Television Library at the University of Southern California. Much appreciation to several other librarians, to include Charlene Maxey-Harris (UN-L); Beth Howse (Fisk University); Francine I. Henderson (Auburn Avenue Research Library on African American Culture, Atlanta, Georgia); and Sunshine Tucker, archivist (Fox Theatre, Atlanta, Georgia).

Roxanne Gay and Lisa Metzger are two readers whose organizational skills helped to order the content of the manuscript *before* it moved to SUNY.

Other villagers who made possible the success of this project include Emory Elliott, Katherine Kinney, Marguerite Waller, Josh Kun (English); Sterling Stuckey (History); and Ralph Crowder (Ethnic Studies) at the University of California, Riverside. Thank you to Shannon Bush, Ph.D. my research assistant, for combing the stacks and organizing an abundance of materials.

I am indebted to Antonette Toney, database analyst, who arranged for me my own writing studio at the *Center for Ideas and Society* in Riverside, California. Thanks to Laura Lozon and Marilyn Davis also at the *Center for Ideas and Society.*

Much appreciation to my colleagues Cathy Cuchinella and Michelle "Cheli" Reutter for listening to me read to them certain parts of the manuscript and for dialoguing with me on these women in entertainment.

I offer my deepest gratitude to my Elder Sisters . . . my mentors from Clark Atlanta University in Atlanta, Georgia whom, I believe the ancestors entrusted with my well-being when I entered academia. These are the women whose arms embrace and uplift me:

Phyllis Briggs-Emmanuel, (retired, CAU) affirms the scholar in me that I now have become. Her tutelage, sprinkled with encouragement, always gives me a safe place to land no matter the situation. When weariness come to visit, she reminds me to trust life and the work I am doing therein; and I, thus, harvest an inner strength to keep on.

Mary Arnold Twinning (retired, CAU) walks with me while I am on this journey. A flower-child at heart, she encourages me to remember the life strides I have made since taking this journey and be renewed by the power and grace of the universe.

To Janice Liddell, also at CAU, thank you for your support and advice.

A host of members in my spiritual village have walked with me on this path, and they are Inez L. Able, Nelda Thomas Canada, Harriett Green, Anita Terraine Cooper Adams, Cheryl Elaine Johnson, Lydia Sandiford, the late Clara Davenport, Conchita B. Edens, Jeryl Salmond, John Logan Heyward, and Mark Stewart (Columbia, South Carolina); Rev. Barbara Hurd, Sharon West, Myra Crawford, Virginia "Ginny" Albert, Audrey Jackson, Harold and Alice Wyatt; Joseph Beck, Esq. (Atlanta, Georgia); Ustaine Talley (Topeka, Kansas); Jermaine Archer (Long Island, New York); Rahel Kassahun (Washington, D.C.); Anne and Leroy Stokes, Rev. Carol Lunde, Mary Lou Meier, and Jana Holzmeier (Lincoln, Nebraska). Special thanks for encouragement Michael W. Tyler Esq. (Atlanta, Georgia).

To my sisters and brother, Shu-yan, Y. Karlton Zantc, and Tywatha, thank you for keeping our sister- and brotherhood strong.

Finally, I pay homage to the ancestors who are an awesome presence and constant force in my life and who have given me the right people and the right place to grow. Thank you for watching over me, protecting me, and, most of all for fiercely loving me into the wild wise woman I have come to be. Thank you for enfolding me in your spirit, and thank you for giving me enough sense to let you do it.

Introduction

Are We Listening to the Footsteps of the Dance on the White Page?

On June 30, 1995, Phyllis Hyman, one of the most talented soulful jazz/R&B vocalists of the twentieth century, commits suicide in her one-bedroom apartment in New York just hours before her scheduled performance at the Apollo Theatre in Harlem. July 6 of that year would have marked her forty-sixth birthday.

In the assessment of this Phyllis Hyman moment, I ask, dear reader, your patience, because emphasizing the various ways in which black female entertainers go to great lengths to tell us their stories is crucial. More important, I really want to underscore the urgency of listening to each of them. We cannot allow what happens to Phyllis Hyman's call to be heard to happen to the women in this study: Lena Horne, Dorothy Dandridge, Eartha Kitt, Diahann Carroll, Mary Wilson, and Whoopi Goldberg. "It is in the end," Alice Walker reminds us, "the saving of lives that we writers are about. . . .We do it because we care" (14). We save lives by listening . . . We have to care.

The news of Hyman's death overwhelms me as poignant memories of her concert performance and television appearances flash in my mind. I attended her concert December 31, 1991, at the Fox Theater in Atlanta, Georgia. At the Fox, her voice drapes lyrics in deep maroon velvet with the grace of a teardrop, and the crowd assembles in the palm of her hand. She catches the spirit of the night, and the six-foot one-inch

1

diva takes her shoes off to feel more at one with the audience. A year later, on November 4, 1992, Hyman appears on *The Arsenio Hall Show*. She talks with Hall about having lived a life filled with loneliness, but she remains hopeful of finding someone with whom to share it. She is working on the production of new songs, and their lyrics reflect the interior health she has come to realize after years of isolation. Yet, in 1995, she is dead.

The words "Fans and Friends Mourn the Tragic Death of Singer Phyllis Hyman" became a blur as I read excerpts of her obituary in the July 24, 1995 issue of one of the most popular black periodicals, *Jet* magazine. Through teary eyes, I wonder: Phyllis, with all that you had—a successful career and a voice as fluid as honey that told me how to feel during my most desperate times—what in the world would enter your mind and convince you to take yourself out of here? Her voice whirls through my head as does the dance of her words on the white pages in previous issues of *Jet*. I realize then that Hyman has given me all along her *own story* for almost fifteen years in *Jet* and, more revealing, through her music. *I just was not listening.*

In an October 1981 *Jet* article, "Phyllis Hyman Wants Love to Match Records, Stage Success," the singer brings to light that her professional success belies the absence of a personal life. She says:

> I try to avoid even thinking about it . . . [b]ecause there is nothing to balance. There's only the professional. . . . And I really want people to know that what they think and read about entertainers's [sic] lives being so glamorous—hell, no! That is far from the truth and *especially for female performers*. Men seem to be in awe of you and feel you can't be approached. (62, my emphasis)

Hyman discerns early in her career how the circulation of the glamorous image in the mainstream of popular culture compromises the private life. The compromise forms a tension between the public and private spheres. The act of performance, she also recognizes, mandates a separation between performer and spectator. The spectator, in turn, marvels at this untouchable phenomenon doing something beyond the everyday. This separation, according to Hyman, frustrates the performer's efforts to form viable nourishing communities and partnerships. Hyman believes, moreover, the weight of the tension falls more heavily on the shoulders of women in entertainment. *Were we listening?*

The album *Living All Alone* (Capitol Records, 1986) is the song stylist's siren call to her audience that all is not well in her "glamorous" world. In the song "Living All Alone," for example, the listener enters an apartment once shared by two lovers. Now, a single voice echoes throughout the rooms. Hyman wails for five minutes and fifteen seconds that she just cannot stand living all alone, especially after having been somebody's baby. She mourns the times she was held tight and loved right. Who will mend this devastating break in her life accompanied by long and lonely nights? With a glass of milk in one hand and a pint of chocolate Häagen-Dazs in my lap, I nod. I know what you're talking about, girl. "You Just Don't Know" continues the theme of unbearable loneliness and chronicles the tears she cries planning her nights by the *TV Guide* as well as how the telephone becomes her partner while she waits for a call. Do you know what being lonely feels like? You do not know; I do not know. Girl, sing your song. *But I just wasn't listening.*

In 1991 she again confided to *Jet,* "[t]here is a deep connection between part of my loneliness with my music *if you listen* to some of the words to my songs. I sing about a lot of pain, which is something I know a lot about" ("Phyllis Hyman Says" 58; my emphasis). *Did we listen?*

Finally, on June 29, 1995, she allegedly confesses to her former boyfriend before taking an overdose of sleeping pills, "I'm unhappy. The only bright light is to die. . . . I have no personal life and no energy. All I want to do is go" ("Ex-boyfriend of Phyllis Hyman" 60). *Did he listen?*

The CD entitled *I Refuse to Be Lonely* is a posthumous release and is just as revealing as Hyman's dance on the white page. Her haunting interpretation of these lyrics, her disconsolate feelings, and the story she tells on *The Arsenio Hall Show* and in *Jet* magazine are pieces of her autobiography that affirm not only her internal suffering, but also verify the story of Hyman's extreme isolation and her lack of a nurturing community, the one she fails to realize in the culture of celebrity. *I just was not listening.*

In a way, I did listen but those glamour shots of Hyman on the cover of *Jet* magazine distract me from her narrative dance. She *looks* good. She *looks* radiant. She *looks* healthy. The inside photos show her laughing heartily and having a grand time with fans and other entertainers such as Bill Cosby, Natalie Cole, Barry Manilow, and saxophonist Ronnie Laws. The dance on the white page accompanying those photos, nevertheless, speak of "fear of rejection," "living alone," "withdrawal from the social scene," and destructive impulses. Hyman's suicide charges me with the responsibility to listen to the voices of black female entertainers.

Dancing on the White Page, then, pays attention to the written narratives of six acclaimed black women in entertainment. Each woman beckons to us to listen to her dance on the white page. Dancing is

performance art no matter the venue, and it requires the body, coordi-
nation, rhythm and style, choreography and practice, and moments for
improvisation. Dancing, according to Eartha Kitt, "set[s] the spirit
free[; it is] a celebration of life and of the soul" (*Alone* 63). As we listen
to each woman's story, we can hear the dance steps of her narrative on
the white page. We ascertain how each woman improvises the choreography of her life to survive and thrive in the formidable film, television,
and music industries with their attendant celebrity cultures. We also can
see the black community as an important aspect of how well each
woman thrives.

The title of my book, *Dancing on the White Page,* refers to the written record of the life Phyllis Hyman left as well as that of each of the
entertainers in my study. The dance on the white page by black female
entertainers explored here offers us the opportunity to grasp each
woman's full meaning in American culture at large and in American
entertainment culture in particular. *Dancing on the White Page*'s study
of black female entertainers writing autobiography coaxes us to see
them through myriad lenses, rather than through a single lens fixed on
the glamour image of popular culture. Using autobiography as a tool for
discovery, as a lens for seeing, we can learn the real stories of Horne,
Dandridge, Carroll, Wilson, Kitt, and Goldberg as wife, (single) mother,
widow, world traveler and wanderer, battered child/battered woman,
divorcee, drug abuser, banished and exiled woman, activist/renegade
and, ultimately, storyteller. They are our griottes carrying the history of
our visual culture. By recounting their life stories via the written word,
each of these black female entertainers asks to be recognized as a storyteller in the community of black women writing.

Herein I combine a personal voice and the academic as in the spirit
of three black feminist cultural critics: Patricia J. Williams, bell hooks,
and Alice Walker. Academia generally directs the trained scholar to close
off the personal from examination of a chosen subject matter to not
compromise the scholar's "authority." The writing styles of Williams,
hooks, and Walker, as well as my own style, challenge the parameters of
this traditional scholarship. Each of these Black writers takes advantage
of everyday life occurrences and her feelings that form around them to
unearth the stealth elements of racism and sexism and to critique race
relations, class issues, and women's rights and domestic matters. Patricia
J. Williams, a critical race theorist and attorney, for example, uses autobiography to critique traditional legal scholarship. Williams considers
the ways in which legalese deployed by the power majority is exclusionary, and inevitably muffles the voices of those without access to the
"magic words" legal discourse requires. Williams believes the intermix-

ing of her own life story with the legal discourse she has mastered allows her to "highlight . . . factors that would otherwise go unremarked [and to] describe a community of context for those social actors whose traditional legal status has been the isolation of oxymoron, of oddity, of outsider" (7). To that end, Williams anecdotally highlights her own everyday life occurrences, family, and subject position as a black female lawyer to give voice to those community contexts and voices "othered" by traditional legal scholarship.

bell hooks works in a similar fashion. Although widely known as a scholar of critical theory, hooks liberally references her own daily battles with racism and sexism with language that is direct and personal. In her book of essays, *Killing Rage: Ending Racism* (1995), hooks analyzes the ways in which the presence and denial of racism can drive a black woman to extremes, even to think of committing murder. An airline refuses to acknowledge a mistake in a seat assignment, for example, which results in hooks's friend being forced to give up her seat to a white man. The very first line of hooks's opening chapter, "Militant Resistance," reads, "I'm writing this essay sitting beside an anonymous white male that I long to murder" (8).

On a related note, the critical scholarship of *In Search of Our Mother's Gardens: Womanist Prose* is based on Walker's growth as a black woman coming of age in the South during the 1960s as a feminist and as a mother. In this collection of essays, speeches, and letters she relays a particularly telling personal anecdote to discuss the challenge of writing and motherhood. She writes:

> Another writer and I were discussing the difficulty of working immediately after the birth of our children. "I wrote nothing for a year," I offered, "that didn't sound as though a baby were screaming right through the middle of it." "And I," she said, [. . .] "was so stricken with melancholia whenever I tried to think of writing that I spent months in a stupor." (66)

This very personal conversation between two writers who are also mothers launches Walker into an inquiry and critique of "traditional Western ideas about how art is produced" (69).

These excerpts demonstrate the writer's presence in the composition of her professional work for these three critics, an approach very much like my own. Williams, hooks, and Walker tell us the writer never is isolated from the world around her. *She is listening.* In this book, as well, my personal voice interacts with the dance on the white page of black female celebrities by making each woman's choreographed story more audible, especially discernible to audiences unfamiliar with her. It also enables me to extend my academic voice for a more inclusive analysis of my chosen subjects. The combination of these two voices—the academic and the personal—in *Dancing on the White Page* creates a hybrid dialogic that extends my range and reach as an academic so I can go beyond the prescribed limits of my profession. I increase my latitude because the personal helps you and me to see black female entertainers not just as *objects* of study—not just as *spectacles* or *things*—but also as *people* like all of us who suffer failures and successes, joys and moments of depression, laughter, and tears. In reality, when you peel back the glamour image, the black female entertainers in this narrative are no different from the rest of us when it comes to *living* the personal life. They certainly have an economic advantage over most of us (at least that is what the glamour shots imply), but that leverage is not much, and I will demonstrate. The fusion of voices I create in this study removes the economic distance between stage/star and audience while constructing a window for that audience to see and hear more clearly the dance on the white page.

Recalling the black female entertainer's place in our popular culture assists the engagement between star and audience. Generally, entertainers are tossed aside and forgotten as the whims of the mass audience, as well as the popular press and the entertainment industry, determine who is worthy of attention. The ephemeral nature of celebrity, moreover, is more pronounced when it comes to black female performers who battle a mélange of issues (for example, domestic abuse, intra-racial politics, economic disparities) within popular culture. This dismissal is what popular culture historian Donald Bogle experiences when he sets out to do a feature story on Butterfly McQueen (Prissy in *Gone with the Wind*; dir. Victor Fleming) while working as a staff writer for *Ebony* magazine in Chicago. "[The editors] dismissed the old-time actors as toms and mammies," Bogle recalls, "and spoke of them with boredom, disgust, and contempt, and even condescension [. . .]" (*Toms, Coons* xxii). What we have to refute the editors' dismissal is Bogle's major contribution to the genre of black film studies: *Toms, Coons, Mulatoes, Mammies, and Bucks: An Interpretive History of Blacks in American Films* (1973) and *Brown Sugar: Eighty Years of America's Black Female Superstars* (1980). Dorothy Dandridge is one of the many black actresses he exhumes, and a major star brought to life by Academy Award winner Halle Berry in her HBO special *Introducing Dorothy Dandridge* (1999). Berry's Golden Globe win for that project helped to solidify a place in our memory of the late great actress.

In essence, *Dancing on the White Page* endeavors to do what Spike Lee, Quentin Tarantino, George Clooney, and others have done for veteran and contemporary black actresses, and to enlarge what Donald Bogle already has accomplished. Lee's films *Do The Right Thing* (1989) and *Jungle Fever* (1991) recover for a savvy hip-hop and rap community civil rights activists and theater and film actors, Ruby Dee and the late Ossie Davis. Similarly, by casting Pam Grier as the lead in his film *Jackie Brown* (1997), Tarantino renews interest in the actress and her work as a black female action star in "blaxploitation" films such as *Coffy* (1973) and *Foxy Brown* (1974). More commendable is the honor Hattie McDaniel receives from Academy Award winner for Best Supporting Actor George Clooney at the Seventy-Eighth Annual Academy Awards, televised March 5, 2006. During his speech, Clooney remarks:

> [the Academy] talked about civil rights when it wasn't really popular. And we, you know, we bring up subjects. This Academy, this group of people gave Hattie McDaniel an Oscar in 1939 when blacks were still sitting in the backs of theaters. I'm proud to be a part of this Academy. Proud to be part of this community.

Journalist Diane Sawyer asks in her post–Academy Award interview with Clooney, "I went back and read Hattie McDaniel's [Academy Award] acceptance speech. What do you think she would've thought where this industry has come?" "It must've been a fascinating thing in 1939 [. . .], answers Clooney"; cut to McDaniel, sans the mammy outfit, lovely in a crepe gown decorated in white flowers and sequins; she wears a flower in her hair, also. McDaniel, the first black woman to win an Academy Award since the Academy handed out its first Oscar May 16, 1929, stands tall and proud behind the podium. She begins with tears in her eyes, "I sincerely hope I shall always be a credit to my race and to the motion picture industry. My heart is too full to tell you just how I feel, and may I say thank you and God bless you." Contrary to Spike Lee's lambaste of Clooney's note of McDaniel ("To use [McDaniel's Academy Award win] as an example of how progressive Hollywood is is ridiculous. Hattie McDaniel played MAMMY in *Gone with the Wind*. That film was basically saying that the wrong side won the Civil War and that black people should still be enslaved"), the Oscar winner's interpolation of her in his speech makes evident the *actress*—really, an ancestral colleague he apparently feels had been overlooked ("Spike"). Clooney's admiration and praise for the community within he works may appear extravagant (McDaniel earned that Oscar); however, invoking civil rights, Hattie McDaniel, her Oscar, and segregation in the United States to his colleagues in this celebrated community and to the viewing audience make visible the black actress's presence in that community—regardless of her roles on the silver screen. Together, these historians, directors, and actors introduce a new generation of film audiences to forgotten or dismissed black actresses, to such an extent that Diane Sawyer went back to review (black) Hollywood history. *Dancing on the White Page* encourages others to follow.

Although this project complements these cinematic (re)introductions, career revivals, and scholarly gestures, *Dancing on the White Page* departs from these important recovery efforts. First, it launches an inquiry into *both* the literature black women in entertainment write *and* the visual images of these women as seen in popular culture. In addition, I incorporate personal anecdotes not only to reveal my own introduction to these women, but also to discover the ways the visual, the literary, and the personal coalesce to produce a more holistic evaluation of black female entertainers and the world in which they and I live(d). For example, much is known of the (international) impact the music of Motown has on popular music during the 1960s. *Dancing on the White Page* foregrounds the influence Mary Wilson and the Supremes—a girl group with attractive and refined eighteen- and nineteen-year-old young adult black women—has on black girls on the elementary school playground when blue-eyed blonde women in popular culture loom large on the landscape as *the* standard of beauty.

Another contribution I make to the resurrection of black actresses filmmakers, scholars, and actors already have begun is to (re)open discussion of what counts as literature. Whether a narrative told to a hired pen by the author or a story written solely by the author herself, the genre of black women's autobiography—beginning in the eighteenth century with "Belinda, or the Cruelty of Men Whose Faces Were Like the Moon" (1787) as black feminist critic Joanne Braxton tells us (2)—is an integral part of the African-American literary canon. The autobiographical narrative black female celebrities write assumes a place on that continuum of written black expression in that black female celebrity autobiography is a formidable subgenre in its own right. *Dancing on the White Page,* furthermore, draws out an awareness of the autobiographical voices silenced in an iron-clad African-American literary canon that authorizes the inclusion of only a particular chorus of black literary voices, namely the beloved autobiographies of Zora Neale Hurston, Maya Angelou, and others.

If some critics overlook black celebrity autobiographies for inclusion in the African-American literary canon, for various literary reasons, I must admit that I initially harbored my own misgivings about black female entertainers' writing. My apprehensions toward these black female entertainers have to do with the sociocultural political lens through which I viewed them. *Batman* and *Julia* air in 1966 and 1968 respectively; *Sanford and Son* in 1972. The black actresses on television clash discordantly with the black women I witness marching, singing, and raising fists in the name of freedom and equality in the civil rights and black feminist movements of the 1960s and early 1970s. Like Phyllis Hyman, Lena Horne and the other women in *Dancing on the White Page* enter my life in a problematic way long before I conceive of a scholarly project on them. Horne appears to me first as a guest via television on the popular 1970s black sitcom *Sanford and Son*. Her appearance as a black singer waltzing through Fred Sanford's junkyard door at first, however, does not awaken in me a desire to know more about her. Horne seems to overact; hers is a hyperperformance. Later, on the silver screen, I watch and listen to her sing good luck wishes to Dorothy (Diana Ross) as Glinda, the Good Witch in the forgettable 1978 box office disaster *The Wiz* (which Sidney Lumet, Horne's son-in-law at the time, directed), and I remember feeling relieved when she finishes her number. Three years later, the broadcast news and print media make so much hoopla over her 1981 one-woman show on Broadway, *The Lady and Her Music*, that I rush to buy the album, thinking I would hear a different sound. The award-winning show is the longest running one-woman show in Broadway history at that time, and Horne wins a Grammy for the album. As the vinyl disc rotates on my turntable, however, I only can think of Glinda, the Good Witch—nothing has changed. I promptly give the album to a friend, who looks at me like I just have lost my mind. "You don't know what you're doing or who you're giving away," she remarks with a furrowed brow. But I have cut my teeth on the buttered biscuit, collard greens, and black-eyed pea R&B song stylists such as Gladys Knight, Tammi Terrell, Minnie Ripperton, Stephanie Mills, and Chaka Khan; I cannot appreciate the unfamiliar gourmet sound from a past era of Horne's voice nor the history behind it.

Eartha Kitt, too, receives a shrug from my shoulders. Yes, she keeps Batman (Adam West) on his toes, but her antics fail to keep me interested. She seems obsessed with this masked white man, always trying to outsmart him as she rides around in that tawdry Catmobile of hers. She runs with crazy-looking white men dressed in embarrassing fashions; she even allows them into her flamboyantly distasteful home. What an alley cat! I have no use for her. On a Saturday afternoon trek to a used record store, however, I happen across an old *Eartha Kitt Collectible* album. I buy the album because I admire Kitt's hairstyle and white sequined gown on the cover, and the album costs only 99 cents. I never had heard her sing—only purr like a cat in *Batman*. Imagine my surprise when that same catlike voice floats out of my speakers! What the . . . ? What kind of voice *is* that? Who would want to record a voice like that? I double-check my turntable speed—fine. I check to make sure the name on the album matches the name on the album cover—it does. These sounds are most peculiar—unlike anything I ever have heard in my music listening experiences. Kitt sounds like a gurgling cat singing in the rain with a vibrato that could rival a California earth tremor. And what kind of song is "Uska Dara" anyway? Why would a black woman even think to—no: why would a black woman even *want* to—sing a song in Turkish?

If Horne and Kitt fail to impress me, Diahann Carroll really bites the dust. I hated *Julia*, the television sitcom in which she stars. I curl up in front of the television set to view the premiere episode in 1968, and I am turned off from the sitcom forever. Julia sleeps on a sofa bed in her living room before the entire television viewing audience. On her way to a job interview, this registered nurse leaves her young son, Corey (Marc Copage), in the care of her neighbor, Marie Waggedorn (Betty Beaird), a white stay-at-home mother and her son, Earl (Michael Link). "What black mother would do that?" I ask myself. "Where are Julia's black friends?" I wonder. Suppose Mr. Waggedorn (Hank Brandt) comes home and finds a young black man in the apartment with his wife? What is more, when Julia opens her mouth, her voice comes across as starched and pressed flat to the point of excruciating sterility. Her lips appear partially glued together, and she acts like a robotized black Barbie doll. With the exception of her expression of love and admiration for her son, I conclude in my adolescence that the whole world of *Julia*, especially Julia Baker, is a fake.

The popular culture movement to pique my interest in the black actress and singers of previous eras is the arrival of the peerless *and* single *and* wealthy Dominique Deveraux in 1984, played by none other than Diahann Carroll, who transforms from black Barbie to the first "black bitch" on the most popular, the most glamorous, and the most sensational nighttime soap opera of the 1980s, *Dynasty*. When the perfectly coiffed Miss Deveraux struts through the door of the *Dynasty* mansions (and into my family room) wearing lynx furs, gloves, and red lipstick, when she practically spits out Alexis Carrington's (Joan Collins) "burned" champagne, and when she tussles with Alexis in her own bedroom for calling her a lounge lizard, I fall in love with Diahann Carroll, and by extension, the black celebrity of the past. Lavish! Bodacious! Alexis meets her match. It is about time! Goody-two-shoes blond blue-eyed Krystle Carrington (Linda Evans) just does not cut it.

To add intrigue to the story, in the episode "The Will," Thomas Fizzeminth "Tom" Carrington (Harry Andrews), grand-patriarch and Blake Carrington's (John Forsyth) father, admits to an interracial relationship out of which Miss Deveraux is born. On his deathbed, the senior Carrington affirms his "indiscretion," claims Dominique as his daughter, changes his will, and divides his estate among his son Blake, Alexis and Dominique. Get this: he names Dominique executor. Astonishing! Miss Deveraux unglues Julia Baker's lips and hands, and enters corporate America (indeed a white environment) as a wealthy equal standing on her own merits, not as a clipped-wing Barbie doll. In the episode "The Verdict," for example, she offers CEO Blake Carrington $25 million for control of his company, Denver-Carrington *before* her inheritance from Tom Carrington. Blake counters for $30 million and 40 percent of the share, and forms a Deveraux-Carrington partnership. When his debt to Alexis threatens to crush him, Miss Deveraux offers a $50-million loan to untrammel him from Alexis's monetary stronghold ("Focus"). Powerful! Additionally, she owns *Titania Records*, her record company. I never have seen such a bold black woman on television act in the ways of Dominique Deveraux. Stunning!

Who is *this* Diahann Carroll? Carroll's groundbreaking *Dynasty* role opens my mind to the multidimensionality of black female celebrities. Over time, the life stories of such celebrities fascinate me. The publication of Mary Wilson's *Dreamgirl: My Life as a Supreme* summons me to *read* black female celebrity autobiography rather than just scan the pictures therein. Wilson's book is of great importance because *Dreamgirl* popularizes the genre of black celebrity autobiography. Halle Berry's successful project *Introducing Dorothy Dandridge* brings back memories of my own introduction to Dorothy in the hallway of my high school in the 1970s.

My high school classmates and I inherit from the black arts and civil rights movements the courage, the freedom, and the *permission* to challenge our white teachers' expectation that dead white men and their culture will be the focus of written assignments. Our black history, literature, and culture are the heart of our attention: Frederick Douglass, the Harlem Renaissance, Marcus Garvey, Ralph Ellison, Maya Angelou, and, as I learn in 1974, Dorothy Dandridge. "I'm going to write about our very first black real movie star," my friend Valerie declares with an air of pride. "Who?" I ask trying to align the white notches and numbers with the indent on the silver face of my combination lock. "Dorothy Dandridge . . . our first black movie star. Haven't you heard of her?" As we slam the tin doors of our lockers, hoist our books under our arms, and proceed to study hall, this Dandridge person fails to appear among the images shuffling through my mind. In the 1960s and 1970s, black women with voices worthy of attention in literature, theater, and film are the gun-totin' (Foxy Brown), bandanna-cornrow-Afro-wearin' (Cicely Tyson), "nigga can you kill" (Giovanni) renegade black women. Poets to read and write about were Gwendolyn Brooks, our first black Pulitzer Prize winner; Mari Evans; and Nikki Giovanni. These women secure our attention. They are celebrities.

If a black "celebrity or star" is worthy of discourse, she is the incomparable Angela Davis. In 1974 Random House publishes *Angela Davis: An Autobiography*. Her story not only satisfies "a curious privacy" that attends celebrity status, but the autobiography, in particular the preface, also, indirectly brings home to me that, from the slave revolts to the civil rights and black nationalist movements, the participants have the courage literally to place their lives on the line. They are men and women willing to die for *me*. What can a celebrity do except sit and look pretty?

Meanwhile, on the way to study hall, Valerie abides my curiosity with patience, "Who? What? You're writing about a *movie star* for a *theme paper*???" I ask again, bumping into Ronnie Taylor and John Logan. "I never have heard of her . . . what did she . . . who?" Angela Davis's demure photograph on the dust jacket of her autobiography comes into focus. Valerie gently feeds my developing hunger for knowledge about Dorothy Dandridge as we both huddle together whispering in the corner of study hall; and, I admire her nerve to write about a subject that is so outside of the norm. "Oh, she could act!!!! Momma remembers the large turnouts to see her onscreen. . . . Here, see, here's an article and a picture. . . ." Valerie slides a frayed copy of the *Life* magazine into my hands. I marvel at the November 1, 1954 cover. So *this* is Dorothy Dandridge. Black peasant blouse and red skirt. Short coiffed black hair that frames a face with a single mole. The red rose in line with the hoop earring. The hand on the hip and that coquettish turn to the camera. Dorothy Dandridge.

In spite of my awe of Dorothy Dandridge, the movie star, I have to ask myself: can the sequined-gowned and pampered black woman celebrity who smiles seductively for the Hollywood camera compete with *my star*, Angela Davis, and the others? Memories from that high school event nudge another image of the dreadlocked Whoopi Goldberg, an unlikely black star of the 1980s for whom I have a curiosity. I spy Whoopi Goldberg's *Book* in the San Jose State University's campus bookstore. A cursory reading cues me that Goldberg approaches black celebrity autobiography from a different angle. I wanted to know what that was.

The advent of Miss Deveraux in the 1980s signals for me and for thousands of others the magnetic appeal of the black woman in U.S. popular culture. Hyman's suicide, on the other hand, alerts me to the tension between this powerful public persona and the private lives of black women entertainers. Her tragedy is a warning sign, to those willing to see it, that the strain between public and private spheres can undermine the psychic health of many black female stars. If Hyman experiences this strain, how many others do as well, I wonder. If so, what strategies do black female celebrities employ not only to survive, but also to thrive while in the constant eye of the public? What are Horne, Dandridge, Carroll, Kitt, Wilson, and Goldberg saying about themselves and the world in which they live? What stories do their texts tell that are not accessible in their music, performances, or both? Reading each autobiography as a site of self-revelation concerning such issues, I find stories of black self-determination along with the push for liberation from oppression and racial and gender discrimination in variety of venues. Often the public image compromises the private life, but the revelation of each woman's interior life as she fights for self-preservation is one of the most compelling features of these autobiographies. The experiences of these women as members of their own biological or nuclear families move me beyond the glitter and glamour their images so readily make available to the public into an understanding of what and who produces the public image initially and what that public image manifests for the industry and public.

The Dance Movements

"The Symbol Must Stand for Something" is the first movement in the choreography of the dance on the white page. This first chapter investigates Lena Horne in the era of World War II and Hollywood's desire to present to the film-going public an alternative image of the black American woman onscreen. Horne enters at this stage and agrees to become the first Negro woman to sign a long-term contract with Metro-Goldwyn-Mayer (MGM). Neither conventional stardom nor acceptance from the west coast Negro community of actors accompanies the MGM contract. Grief and anxiety follow Horne as she struggles to come to terms with what it means to be a symbol for the black race in the entertainment industry during her tenure at MGM.

Chapter two, "Dorothy Dandridge: The Dance of the Black Female Child Entertainer" surveys how black matriarchs—Ruby Dandridge, her mother, and Eloise Matthews (also known as Geneva Williams or Auntie

Ma-ma), Ruby's lover—and the black church fashion Little Dottie into Dorothy Dandridge, the star. Hollywood carries much of the blame for the tragedy of Dorothy Dandridge because the film industry fails to make available to her the same kinds of career-making roles afforded to her white colleagues, Ava Gardner and Marilyn Monroe. Dandridge's autobiography *Everything and Nothing: The Tragedy of Dorothy Dandridge*, however, is also an indictment of the most venerated institutions in the black community. Dorothy makes known that while the black family and black church trumped Hollywood in making her a star, the process both institutions put her through as a child to bring her stardom to fruition made her a virtual thing before she enters the film world. Dorothy copes with abandonment, exploitation, and ill-treatment in her own home that began when she is Little Dottie and continues throughout her teenage years.

Chapter three, "Eartha Kitt: The Dance of the Autobiographical Defense," investigates the ways Eartha Kitt "takes up" for herself in a number of spaces, including the nuclear home sphere; in the domain of black dance; and in the American national home, the White House. I draw out how Kitt's autobiographical corpus works in tandem as an antidefamation manifesto as she makes conscious attempts to take up for herself against critics and to defend her reputation—past and present—as a difficult self-absorbed diva. Kitt's texts also reveal her presumed "indecorous behavior" challenges the myth of the film and stage ingénue as well as gendered norms of the 1950s.

Chapter four, "Diahann Carroll: The Recuperation of Black Widow–Single Mother/Womanhood," takes a behind-the-scenes look at Diahann Carroll's decision to accept the role of Julia Baker on the 1968 sitcom *Julia*. Carroll's interaction with Hal Kanter, the sitcom's influential white writer, is of primary concern in this chapter because the majority of the dialogue about her is that she was the first black woman to star in a sitcom. This chapter also examines the importance of her role as Dominique Deveraux on *Dynasty*.

Chapter five, "Mary Wilson: Taking Care of the Business of Girlfriends through Autobiography," is a study of Wilson's text, one that popularizes celebrity autobiography, *Dreamgirl: My Life as a Supreme*. On one hand, Wilson's book is an attempt to refind her self after being displaced as one of the lead singers and the subsequent crowning of Diana Ross as her replacement at the expense of the group. On the other, Wilson's book is a postmortem apology to Florence Ballard. This chapter also deals with discovering along with Wilson how the teenager at the time (re)negotiates an identity adult black men and women in power in the 1960s had formed. How does this renegotiation take place when so much of it is tied up and into the *supreme* image and stardom? What were the *intra*racial dynamics in such a *supreme* organization that introduce to 1960s black teenage culture a hip, cool, kind of black womanhood?

Chapter six, "Whoopi Goldberg: The Black Woman Celebrity Tell-All Iconoclast," is a comparative analysis of Whoopi Goldberg's *Book* with Dorothy Dandridge's *Everything and Nothing* and Diahann Carroll's *Diahann*. Dandridge and Carroll gain popularity during a period in which black women held "ladyhood" in a high, fierce regard, specifically the 1950s and 1960s. "Ladies" practice the utmost discretion, refrain from coarse language, and matters of the boudoir are discussed delicately if at all. Goldberg encourages a novel approach to reading (watching) black women in entertainment.

Dancing with the Stars and They Dance with Me

The stories of these powerful and successful black entertainers dance with me every moment of this project. They accompany me to coffee shops and restaurants; they speak to me in the produce section of the grocery store. Many nights I have to pause during my ritual meditation to silence their voices; they even insert themselves in my personal journal writing. When I briefly step away from the project, these women dance, sing, and act across my mind and pick apart a particular scene that hesitates to reveal itself. Each woman becomes a part of the writing process itself. That is to say, these women teach me what it means to dance on the white page and to choreograph movements in the literary dance. They teach me to negotiate (if not reconcile) my creative sense with that of my trained analytical mind, and thus fashion the hybrid dialogic in the style of Williams, hooks, and Walker.

The act of writing about each of these women proves to be an exhausting challenge. The written word cannot contain the expanse of their lives and the scope of their talents. At times, given the weight and significance of their presence in popular culture, I grapple with the question of what features of their lives deserve focus. Each phase of these entertainers' lives matter, and they entice me to trust that any phase I choose to interrogate only leads the spectator closer to the *person* behind the visual representation.

Dancing on the White Page is an investigation into the negotiations and resistance strategies Lena Horne, Dorothy Dandridge, Eartha Kitt, Diahann Carroll, Mary Wilson, and Whoopi Goldberg choreograph as they gain access to and, most compellingly, defy four formidable communities: the film, television, and music industries, and the politics of the black community, particularly as they are manifested in the National Association for the Advancement of Colored People (NAACP). Generally, what we know about these black women celebrities, in particular Horne, Dandridge, and Carroll, has to do with their being "the first black woman to . . ." attendant to breaking down racial barriers in entertainment venues. The tropes and narrative techniques they exercise in the tradition of black autobiography are of particular interest to me because they talk back to the most influential and powerful men and women in entertainment industries as well as to ethnic and other political communities as they usher in a new image of black womanhood.

The struggle for black women to talk back, bell hooks maintains, "has not been to emerge from silence into speech but to change the nature and direction of our speech, to make a speech that compels listeners, one that is heard" (*Talking Back* 6). The dance on the white page by black female celebrities compels the audience to listen to the footsteps of a dance other than that of a glossy publicity photo. This latter visual discourse imparts a world of social privilege resplendent with leisure, material wealth, and economic prosperity; but the visual is only a partial portrait of an artist's life. More dangerous, stardom's cloak threatens to permanently weld the black female entertainer to the stereotype of the unapproachable hypersuccessful star. Behind the media hype, however, are battle scars that tell stories of survival. The defiance at the heart of the autobiographical narratives these stars produce significantly broadens the history of black women in popular culture and, more important, black women's writing itself.

In the 1980s, black female writers of fiction and poetry receive widespread scholarly attention from critics and scholars and from the lay readership as well. Research and scholarship by feminist critics during this black women writers' renaissance, such as *All the Women Are White, All the Blacks Are Men, But Some of Us Are Brave: Black Women's Studies* (1982) by Gloria T. Hull, Patricia Bell Scott, and Barbara Smith; *Reconstructing Womanhood: The Emergence of the Afro-American Novelist* (1987) by Hazel Carby; and *Self-Discovery and Authority in Afro-American Narrative* (1987) by Valerie Smith assist in making possible America's awareness of works by black women. Interestingly, numerous black female celebrity autobiographies explode onto the literary scene thereafter, including *Be My Baby: How I Survived Mascara, Miniskirts, and Madness, or My Life as a Fabulous Ronette* (1990) by Ronnie Specter; *Beyond Uhura Star Trek and Other Memories* (1994) by Nichelle Nichols; and *Ladies First: Revelations of a Strong Woman* (1999) by Queen Latifah. The black celebrity autobiography, however, receives little if any attention from academia. *Dancing on the White Page* recognizes the significance of black female celebrities writing autobiography to correct this omission.

Dancing on the White Page necessarily answers film critic Teshome Gabriel's call for a third cinema aesthetic. Although Gabriel primarily focuses on the liberating power of third world cinema, his discussion of the role of the critic inspires this project. Gabriel solicits from the film critic an awareness of the "relationship between the work, the society and the popular memory that binds them together" (62) in the study of black film actors. He explains that popular memory involves the act of excavating the past, extracting its political import, and disseminating its meaning to the masses. This act is antithetical to official Western history, and Gabriel contends official Western history "claims a 'centre' which continuously marginalises others" (53). Popular memory, however, initiates decentralization, leaving an open field to be filled in with personal histories, biographies, or autobiographies. Autobiography and biography augment our knowledge of black celebrities. *Dancing on the White Page* at times makes use of both autobiography and biography—auto/biography—to choreograph its inquiries into the lives of black female entertainers.

Parallel to the approach in this study, Gabriel's use of biography facilitates the interpretation of the performance of the dark-skinned Negro actor of the 1930s and 1940s, Mantan Moreland. Gabriel argues that too much attention has been paid to Moreland's cinematic routines of the eye-rolling "coon" and the "Negro clown supreme" with little or no regard for the actor's life as a black man in a segregated United States. "The animal that Hollywood tried to create," Gabriel says, "was simply a confirmation of their racism [and] a fulfillment of their racial fantasies" (62–63). The critic's curiosity about the Mantan Moreland behind the rolling eyes activates an interest in Moreland's life story since "[o]fficial film histories give us no clue beside the label they have attached to him" (62). Gabriel writes:

> Moreland was a young man . . . in Monroe, Louisiana, a state where white terror was rampant. When he was only seven years old, he had seen his shoeshine friend hung from a nearby post, his uncle's burnt body dragged down the street, and five black bodies hung dead. So at an early age his eyes rolled and his legs trembled, not because he thought one day Hollywood would discover him but because he lived in an atmosphere of terror. (62)

That his childhood tragedies inspire his onscreen performances indicates Moreland's ability to *transfer* his lived experiences to a character he plays. Transference occurs "through a continuing and overlapping series of substitutions from [his] own experiences and remembrances [and] through the use of imaginative extension of realities" (Hagen 34). Moreland's life story seeps into the actor's interpretation of his characters as Gabriel demonstrates by recalling this episode.

Similarly, the most popular knowledge of Hattie McDaniel and Ethel Waters, two other black celebrities of the early twentieth century is that of the mammy stereotype, but knowledge of their lives as black women humanizes them and illuminates their careers in film. Hattie McDaniel represents another sort of life among black celebrities of the twentieth century. Carlton Jackson, McDaniel's biographer, relates in *Hattie: The Life of Hattie McDaniel*, the Academy Award winner plays the saxophone and mainly tours with her father's Henry McDaniel Minstrel Show until 1916. Shortly thereafter, McDaniel tours with the Melody Hounds, a musical ensemble led by one of Denver's top black musicians, George Morrison. In the Melody Hounds, McDaniel hones her singing skills. A talented songwriter, McDaniel records many of her own songs on the Okeh and Paramount labels in Chicago. Her career in Hollywood playing maids, however, makes her a wealthy woman, and she lives in Hollywood splendor just as film stars would. McDaniel's contemporary, Ethel Waters, expresses her pride in playing the domestic in her films because playing that role, she writes in her autobiography *His Eye Is On The Sparrow* (1951), is a way to thank her grandmother, a domestic, and to pay respectful homage to those Negro women domestics who nursed families when other occupations are denied them.

Because of the distance between life and film roles (among other good reasons), Gabriel invites the film and popular culture critic to delve into the lives of black actors and actresses. This venture engenders a nuanced reading of the "relationship of works to the people" (62). The onus is on the critic to search for the intricacies of black celebrity experiences within their culture rather than to rely solely on an investment in the stereotypes that circulate about them. To ignore the culture or the life story, according to Arif Dirlik, is to "avoid questions concerning the ways in which we see the world; it is to remain imprisoned, therefore, in a cultural unconscious, controlled by conditioned way of seeing [. . .]" (395).

The women in *Dancing on the White Page* similarly parlay their life stories into their interpretations of character portrayals and onstage performances. Whoopi Goldberg's conversations with black women in Montgomery, Alabama, who work as domestics in the 1940s and 1950s, for example, free the actress to put aside her annoying discomfort over her choice to play nannies and maids. The attitude of several black actresses that the role of housekeeper is a degrading one engenders her uneasiness. She writes in her autobiography, *Book*:

> [. . .] I started talking with some of the black women [. . .] who worked as maids and nannies, who swallowed their pride and did what they had to do to raise their families and carry on. They sat me down and set me straight. "Look," one of them said, "you wouldn't have done it any differently. You just have a different sensibility[. . . .] When we were coming up, if you made any noise, they'd hang you. No questions asked. They'd come in the middle of the night, and they'd take your family, and they'd kill you." (111)

Goldberg concludes, "[t]hey kept the family together—theirs, and the upper-class white families they were working for. And they survived. So what the hell was wrong with playing them? Nothing. Nothing" (111–112). Goldberg's visit with the Montgomery women and subsequent conclusions about them basically enrich the actress's knowledge of the history of black female domestics. Goldberg's anecdote has three additional features. First, Goldberg gains respect for a "role" in which black women forcibly were cast due to the socioeconomic conditions of their times. Her admiration echoes Ethel Waters's respect for her own grandmother's plight. Second, Goldberg makes plain that these women "play" the part with dignity to protect their families. Finally, a sense of pride in the Montgomery women can be inferred. In *The Long Walk Home* (1990), for instance, Goldberg's respect and pride for the women are seen in her character portrayal of Odessa Cotter, a maid to a wealthy Southern white family, Miriam Thompson (Sissy Spacek) and Norman Thompson (Dwight Schultz). On the long walk home from work, Odessa and her coworker review a comment made by grandmother Thompson (Gleaves Azar) over Christmas dinner the domestics have prepared: "These niggers just want too much and they're not willing work for it!" Odessa tells her co-worker:

> But I tell ya, see, I sit up there and let her call me a "lazy nigger" and I walk; I walk till I got no legs left if I thought it was gonna give my children a better shot in the world. We work so hard [. . .] have some say what that woman said make you wonder if you gonna be sittin' in the back seat of heaven. [. . .]

Goldberg's delivery of her dialogue, along with every deadpan "yes, ma'am" and "yes, sir," conveys the resolve of the domestics with whom she has the interchange prior to her work in the movie.

Similarly, Motown's in-house choreographers and wardrobe mistresses Maxine Powell, Esther Edwards, and Andreena Johnson preen and primp the "rude [and] crude" unsophisticated young Supremes into ladies (Posner 115). Wilson recalls:

> "Young ladies always [. . .] " was [Maxine Powell's] stock opening phrase for [her] directions. Hats and gloves were mandatory attire for girls around Motown. [. . .] Mrs. Powell took her job seriously, and she would make us walk up and down the mirrored room while she critiqued our every move. I can remember feeling her eyes upon me as I walked around with books on my head. Were my shoulders straight? Was my posture good? Was my makeup—the little I wore then—feminine and flattering— not too brassy? Which fork to use, how to greet people, how to hold eating utensils, how to enter a room, how to find a chair, and how to sit gracefully were all part of the program. (Wilson 151).

Gerald Posner notes, "[s]ome rules were absolute: no closing your eyes when singing; no frowning; no finger snapping; and no spreading your legs or sticking out your buttocks. [. . .] The Supremes were [Mrs. Powell's] star pupils [. . .]" (115). The Supremes' performances and photo spreads of the group are distinct displays of Mrs. Powell's teachings. The young women follow the talent maven's counsel in fashion and public deportment that ultimately construct black ladyhood from the house of Motown. Their behavior and mannerisms, moreover, symbolize for a generation of young black teenagers *black American* ladyhood made available to them via television, concerts, and album and magazine covers in the 1960s.

Black celebrity auto/biography, then, accomplishes several things. First, the genres yield a more broad appreciation for the black actress' work and the society within which she works. This appreciation involves using Gabriel's theory of popular memory. Second, as Gabriel maintains, the genres liberate the black body from stereotype and generate the black actor's history. Auto/biography of black entertainers, moreover, bring forward *American* history. In Moreland's case, it is the history of the lynching of the Negro in the United States; Goldberg's excerpts highlight the history of black women in domestic service; Wilson's recollection of Powell's mentoring points out the networks that carry out black America's agenda to promote black ladyhood to America. Finally, black celebrity auto/biography in this project acknowledges the black mothers and matriarchs who form and shape a black womanhood contrary to that of the mammy/maid stereotype. This acknowledgement expands the dialogue on how stars are made, a credit so often given to Hollywood agents and publicists. Black celebrity autobiography research is one answer to Gabriel's invitation to film and visual culture critics to investigate celebrity auto/biography. These genres are literary tools that can be used to offer another literary space in the study of black women. In developing complex views of cultural history, Gabriel's analysis of black actors via biography motivates *Dancing on the White Page* to identify black celebrity autobiography as a valuable primary literary resource, rather than as a secondary one.

The secondary status of the black celebrity autobiographical narrative can be attributed to several factors. Generally suspected of being self-aggrandizing, purely entertaining, irrelevant, or inaccurate, the genre is vulnerable to dismissal. Black self-expression, however, always has been scrutinized intensely and interrogated for its verisimilitude since the slave asserted her right to literacy. Literary critic Selwyn Cudjoe maintains, "[f]rom its inception, the Afro-American autobiography has been subjected to the question of how authentic a statement it has been and whether or not the Afro-American had the ability or the capacity to make such a statement" (274). Early American literary critic William L. Andrews makes known one nineteenth-century antislavery leader's opinion of Negroes: "'simple-hearted and truthful' as fugitive bondmen from the South might appear to be, one 'must recollect that they are slaves—and that the slave, as a general thing, is a liar'" (90).

Phillis Wheatley's poems, concludes President Thomas Jefferson, "are below the dignity of criticism" (140). On October 8, 1772, her owner John Wheatley calls a tribunal of eminent Bostonians, including Massachusetts governor Thomas Hutchinson and the Reverend Samuel Mather, son of Cotton Mather, to subject the eighteen-year-old African poet to an oral examination. They are to determine through a series of questions to her whether Wheatley actually composed the collected poems while employed as a slave in the Wheatley household. Phillis Wheatley proves her poetry's authenticity, but Jefferson and other prominent white men's attitudes fester in the mind of some white Americans, who still question the intellectual capabilities of the Negro.

Despite vilification of the black intellect, black authors continually have expressed themselves on the white page. *Dancing on the White*

Page recognizes the black author's intermittant engagement with the written word through the study of the autobiographical texts black celebrities write. This recognition delivers black celebrity autobiography from scholarly exclusion. These texts, in addition, evaluate the systems of oppression that operate in the life of the entertainer. Critic George E. Kent states:

> [u]p through the early part of the twentieth century, black auto-biographies had usually found grounds for a leap of faith and optimism in the complex of ideas known as The American Dream. [. . .] Today the rhythms of the American Dream [. . .] run in parallel pattern with a more serious questioning of the Dream itself. (164)

The slave narratives of Olaudah Equiano, Mary Prince, Harriet Jacobs, and Frederick Douglass and later narratives by Zora Neale Hurston, Richard Wright, Malcolm X, and Maya Angelou persistently question the American Dream and its tenets of socioeconomic and political equality. The black celebrity autobiographers in *Dancing on the White Page* join the inquiry.

The black celebrity's use of autobiography is a means to assert the right to represent themselves and the group *(autos)* and to write themselves and the group into the annals of American history *(graphe)*. Their assertion complements the slave narrator's agenda. Literary critic Henry Louis Gates, Jr. argues that former slaves calculatingly design the slave narrative as an instrument to divest black culture of rampant mythical representations the dominant white culture espoused (Herskovits 1–2). Gates maintains:

> Each slave author, in writing about his or her personal life's experiences, simultaneously wrote on behalf of the millions of silent slaves still held captive throughout the South. Each author, then, knew that *all* black slaves would be judged—on their character, integrity, intelligence, manners and morals, and their claims to warrant emancipation—on this published evidence provided by one of their number. The slave authors therefore had to satisfy the dual expectations of shaping the random events of their lives into a meaningful and compelling pattern, while also making the narrative of their odyssey from slavery to freedom an emblem of every black person's potential for higher education and the desire to be free. (x)

The autobiographical "I" of the black woman celebrity connects with the collective black literary community by narrating her journey of harrowing familial persecution and communal expulsion, mean poverty, embarrassing insecurity, betrayal (from family and others), and the threat of violence in conjunction with racism and sexism. For example, telling of her relationships with white men in the film and nightclub industries, Dorothy Dandridge writes on behalf of all black women exploited by white men in power:

> My prime experience with white men, however—and I think it is typical of what most Negro women feel—is that I have been treated finally with the disrespect which has historically been accorded the women of color. [. . .] On the lower levels, in the South, the black woman was often the classic "kept woman" in a cabin. Today she might be in an apartment, or more likely visited from time to time, but in any case she is sexually used. (221)

This passage in Dandridge's autobiography *Everything and Nothing* eases an understanding of her on-screen performance as Aiché, the Dutch slave captain's mistress, in *Tamango* (1958). Dandridge transfers to her character all of her bitterness and rage not only over her own exploitation, but she also speaks for the abuse of black women since slavery through Aiché. In the film a disgusted though spirited Aiché rejects the "amorous" advances of the Dutch slave captain (Curd Jürgensen) aboard the slave ship, declaring "You! There's nothing about YOU that I like! I'm telling the truth to a white man for the first time in my life!" A familiarity with Dandridge's text sheds more light on her troubled relationships, and playing Aiché yields an opportunity for her to express feelings of resentment that otherwise would remain unheard. Dandridge's words, then, underscore black women's shared communal stories.

The lived experiences of black female celebrities are not in any sense comparable to those of enslaved black women during the American plantocracy. The black celebrity autobiographical narrative, however, coexists on the continuum of black written expression as it has been practiced throughout history by black women. Black celebrity autobiographers, nevertheless, must struggle to keep their place on that continuum. A film scholar once casually remarked to me, "People who write autobiographies, especially entertainers, outright lie in order to make themselves look good in the eyes of the public." Olaudah Equiano, the eighteenth-century ex-slave narrator, might agree because he believes "it

is difficult for those who publish their own memoirs to escape the impu-
tation of vanity" (11). For the celebrity, the threat of being accused of
constructing a story to feed the ego is accompanied by the dreadful
implication that the story of her experience as she says it was lived is not
accepted as definitive or authoritative. Considering the black female
celebrity's interpretation of her life experiences, it is not so much a question of *the* truth as it is an evaluation of *a* truth. What these black
women see, as well as experience, in the entertainment industry creates
histories that expose the complexity of black life as lived therein. Their
stories, feminist critic Joan Scott would posit:

> insist [. . .] that histories are written from fundamentally differ-
> ent—indeed irreconcilable—perspectives or standpoints, no one
> of which is complete or completely "true." [T]hese histories
> have provided evidence for a world of alternative values and
> practices whose existence gives the lie to hegemonic construc-
> tions of social worlds, whether these constructions vaunt the
> political superiority of white men [and/or] the coherence and
> unity of selves. [. . .] (24)

Lena Horne and Count Basie agree in their autobiographies, for
example, that they once met in New York. Horne claims Count Basie,
the legendary big band leader of the swing era, strongly encourages her
to leave New York, to go back to Hollywood, and to pursue a career in
films despite her dissatisfaction with the film industry. MGM instructs
its makeup department to apply burned cork to Horne's face, the usual
makeup actors in minstrel shows used, to counter any question of her
being a Negro. The test humiliates Horne so much that she is very reluc-
tant to return to Hollywood. Basie's counsel, according to Horne,
enables her to assess the significance of her presence at the major studio.
After spending time with the bandleader, she embraces the idea of and
seriously pursues a career in film in Los Angeles.

Count Basie, however, in his autobiography *Good Morning Blues:
The Autobiography of Count Basie* (1985), mentions Horne only as an
attendee at a party Basie also attends. Does Count Basie advise Horne at
all? Does Horne invent the encounter? If so, why? Why does Basie only
make a brief mention of Horne? Why does he leave out a crucial conversation with a well-respected Negro woman entertainer who was about
to open doors for Negro actors? As far as Horne is concerned, Basie
ignites a spark of self-confidence that inspires Horne to take charge of
the opportunity for racial uplift.

Whatever the circumstances, Horne's account of Basie's counsel is not significant for its "truth." More noteworthy is Horne's courage to expose her emotions about the magnitude of the Hollywood gamble. Her story highlights several major issues. First, it de-romanticizes the Hollywood star and her involvement in a film industry run by white male executives. Second, the Basie–Horne narrative reiterates the dilemmas Negro entertainers face—successful or otherwise. Third, by retelling the story of her meeting with Basie, Horne exposes herself as vulnerable and uncertain even in the midst of her exceptional success. Finally, the story reports on the slipshod treatment accorded to Negro entertainers and the racist ideologies that support this treatment; it marks out Scott's "lie [of] hegemonic constructions of social worlds," or how far short we fall of the ideal of equality in American society. Autobiographically, Horne's talk with Basie is as she remembers it, not as Basie may have. It is her experience—not Basie's. In Scott's words, Horne's experience is a "discursive production[. . .] of knowledge of the self, not reflections either of external or internal truth" (35–36). Horne interprets her meeting with Basie to make tolerable the memory of her Hollywood screen test. The autobiography is *Horne's* reality and *one* celebrity's experience.

The information about Horne's screen test is significant because it smashes the perception of stardom and its advantages the public believes black women enjoy in entertainment. The perceived advantage of stardom and fame these women eventually realize, on the whole, is thought to relieve them of any and all personal anxieties and life trials. The common perception of successful entertainers in general is that they are a group isolated or perhaps even protected from the toxic vortex of racism, sexism, and even more radically, violence. Film and visual culture critic Richard Dyer notes the star phenomenon carries with it the notion of "the most something-or-other in the world—the most beautiful, the most expensive, the most sexy" (*Stars* 43). What trials, then, could that star possibly have? Another opinion is autobiographies by women in the civil rights movement such as the late Coretta Scott King (*My Life with Martin Luther King, Jr.,* 1969) and Myrlie Evers (*Watch Me Fly: What I Learned on the Way to Becoming the Woman I Was Meant to Be,* 1999) are more meaningful literary representations of black women writing. Were black celebrities *really* in the trenches as Evers, King, and others? *Dancing on the White Page* brings into high relief the differences each woman makes in her own environment and on her own level. That aspect is the significance of these black women entertainers' story.

Behind their onscreen character portrayals, Horne, Dandridge, Kitt, Carroll, Wilson, and Goldberg wrestle with matters that correlate with those of the black community's. Each woman's autobiographical text illustrates that the quest for black self-determination, equality, and respect infiltrates every facet of black culture. Many black female celebrities become the symbol for racial uplift on their own volition or as granted to them from the black community. Their image, comportment, and sartorial style symbolize a respectable black womanhood. For decades black women in the United States labor to disengage themselves from the derogatory images that characterize black women as loose, lascivious, sexually promiscuous, and deviant beings (Gilman 76–92). These pejoratives justify early rapes of enslaved women, anthropological and medical studies abroad, and culturally negligent or abusive treatments of blacks in the post-Reconstruction Era. Certain contingents within the black celebrity community chose their roles carefully as did the women in *Dancing on the White Page*; but, not surprising, some members in the black community looked down on others who took roles they thought contrary to racial uplift. Certain roles such as the ingénue and the upstanding and law-abiding hero are regarded unequivocally as uplifting, whereas other roles are questioned, such as mammy. This stalwart stereotype is what troubles Spike Lee over George Clooney's reference to McDaniel.

The continuing challenge from the NAACP to Hollywood over this and other caricatures intensify during World War II. At this juncture the battle for equality by black women in film and visual culture escalates and continues over time. Lena Horne refuses to perform before segregated armed forces in the 1940s. Dorothy Dandridge practically sacrifices herself as she demands dramatic roles for black actresses in the 1940s and 1950s. In the 1960s, Eartha Kitt unwittingly sacrifices her career by speaking out for impoverished youth and against the Vietnam War at the White House; Diahann Carroll appeals for a different perspective on single black mothers and single black women. Mary Wilson fights for a cohesive black sisterhood. Whoopi Goldberg validates "locker room" discourses for black women.

These acts of resistance verify that the crusade for justice takes place on stage, on screen, and behind the lush velvet curtains, as well as in marches, against the fire hoses and police dogs, on buses and at lunch counters, and on the frontlines of war. These women push the boundaries of containment as they dance across genres of film, music, dance, theater, and autobiography. Their dance on the white page unveils them as women who confound the cultural dynamics of race as they operate within their entertainment networks and personal communities. Being a black female entertainer in times of racial and cultural crises is complicated—times that insist both on mobilization of and identification with the black race. The image the entertainment industry constructs makes a negotiation of race even more difficult because it has an economic investment in the product. It is the product that determines a profitable return on the industry's investment. We need, however, to connect the economic importance of black female celebrities with the human story. Black celebrity autobiography establishes a bridge on which the hired pen, the black female celebrity, and the audience can cross and together take part in the telling of her story. Listening to footsteps of each entertainer's life story teaches us that black celebrity autobiography is a way for the black female celebrity to inscribe and represent the "self" through the written word. It is a genre through which she can talk about herself apart from celebrity culture. Whether penned by herself or a ghost writer, black celebrity autobiographies are not only narratives about a single subject, but also are narratives about a collective of voices and shared experiences, a mark of solidarity with noncelebrity black women.

Dancing on the White Page shows that the constructed image of black women in entertainment as celebrity is often at odds with the private. Remember Phyllis Hyman? The image more often than not obfuscates the real person and, in turn, creates a silence. This study seeks to bring into the mainstream and, more important, to the academy the literary stories of black women in entertainment. It aims to give voice to those silences that generally go unheard or are disregarded in celebrity and academic cultures. The razzle-dazzle of celebrity culture always is lurking about to distract us from the dance on the white page black women in entertainment choreograph. We marvel at their performances, even going as far as to take from them without giving back. We can give back by listening to the footsteps of their dance because their stories correspond to what we already know of black women's experiences at different moments in U.S. history. We become acquainted with a wider community of black writers the silver screen, television, and the stage never could have offered. In addition, the very publication of black celebrity autobiography is each entertainer's plea to preserve her from the ash heap of popular cultural ephemera left behind. We *have* to care.

Remember Phyllis Hyman?

It is time to *listen* to the footsteps of the dance on the white page.

CHAPTER ONE

Lena Horne

The Symbol Must Stand for Something

It is a Friday night in 1973. My father cuts short his day of dry-cleaning pick-ups and deliveries. He walks through our door at exactly 7:30 P.M., brushes the dirt from his shoes, washes his hands, and saunters over to the recliner in the corner of the family room. He would eat later, not wanting to miss any portion of *Sanford and Son*, his favorite program. This one particular Friday night turns out to be a special surprise for him. Lena Horne is scheduled to make a guest appearance in "A Visit from Lena Horne." When she comes into view on the television screen, my father smiles, folds his hands across his paunch, and declares with much vigor, "Lena Horne . . . my my my my my!" My mother bolts from the kitchen—soapy dishrag in hand—and joins in. "Who hon? Uh, huh. Miss Horne! That woman is something *else*. Oh, you should have seen her back in the day!" Hearing the excited voices, I stop my sewing to watch this Lena Horne. A half hour later, I do not see what all the fuss is about.

This scenario illustrates the proverbial generation gap; but, more important, that particular *Sanford and Son* episode as well as Horne's performance as Glinda, the Good Witch in Sidney Lumet's *The Wiz* (1978) introduces Lena Horne to a new generation of young African Americans, who endured the enforced national incentive to integrate public high schools in the 1970s. The Gap's late 1990s' "Get into the Gap" Christmas television ad campaign introduces her to a hip ultracool urban audience. Actress-singer Wendi Joy Franklin's musical drama, *A Song For You . . . Lena*, and Leslie Uggams's musical *Stormy Weather: Imagining Lena Horne* (closed March 4, 2007 at the Prince Theater in

Philadelphia, Pennsylvania) (re)familiarizes the public with Horne's civil rights activism and entertainment career ("Lena Horne, Officially Retired" 58). During a retrospective of the late Ed Bradley, the *60 Minutes* and CBS news correspondent is asked to name and comment on his best profile. He declares, "[Lena Horne] was the first profile I did; and all of these years later I'd say it is the best profile I have ever done. . . . She had this song on [*The Lady and Her Music*] show *Bewitched, Bothered, and Bewildered*. And she talked about being a rich ripe juicy plum again . . ." ("First and Best").

My parents' spirited responses, however, later pique my interest in Horne. What is behind the fuss and the "Uh, huh"? Who is the woman behind the "my my my my my," and what is the "something else" to Lena Horne? I learn Horne is one of the most glamorized, memorable, and venerated entertainment icons of the twentieth century. Her refusal to entertain a segregated U.S. Army makes her a heroine in the eyes of World War II black troops; musicians in the 1930s and 1940s, including band leaders Noble Sissle and Count Basie, and jazz and blues singer Billie Holiday, hold her in high esteem as she captivates audiences in the prestigious New York Café Society nightclub; and Paul Robeson encourages her to understand more fully the history of the Negro in the United States and thereby strengthens her self-confidence. Her agreement with Walter White, the NAACP representative, that the time had come for a new Negro womanhood to be shown on screen in World War II America transforms Horne from the successful singer in New York café society into "something else." When she became MGM's first Negro star to sign a long-term contract, a cascade of "my my mys" and "uh, huhs" flow from the mouths of theatergoers.

In the words of song stylist Nancy Wilson during an *Online News-Hour* interview with PBS, "Lena had it all. . . . She had the walk, the talk, the look. She was able to be everything that anybody white or black would have wanted to be" ("Lena Horne Turns 80"). Eartha Kitt recalls, "I adore her. She does not know this, but when I was trying to figure out what I could do to be recognized, loved and wanted in showbusiness, I saw her in *Stormy Weather* with Katherine Dunham. I saw her on the screen, a high-class sophisticated lady . . . She gave me the feeling that I would be OK, that there was a place for me in show business" ("Lena Horne, Officially Retired" 58).

Horne's image—her hourglass figure, light skin, European facial features, and straight-textured hair—counters the image of Hattie McDaniel, the rotund, blue-black maid, the premier Negro star of the 1930s. Moreover, as the first Negro actress afforded on-screen glamour, she takes her place alongside the major white female stars, namely Ava Gardner, Lana Turner, Hedy Lamarr, and Veronica Lake.

She "had it all," and, as Kitt tells us, Horne's presence onscreen emboldens the spirit of Negro actresses. Walter White believes in her ability to become an uplifting symbol of the Negro race through the silver screen. Journalist Frank Nugent notes in 1945, Horne's "loyalty to her race [. . .] made her almost a symbol to the new generation of Negroes, many of whom [. . .] referred to her publicly as a feminine Paul Robeson" (54). This "symbol of racial uplift" bolsters the "something else" of Lena Horne. The symbol is a societal emblem a particular individual agrees to assume in the interest of the community. The community invests its hopes and dreams in an emblem-individual, hoping for sociopolitical change. In times of crisis, a symbol or hero(ine) arises out of the Negro community to undertake a perilous yet momentous journey to lead the masses out of oppression and into a fight for social justice. We have seen these symbols in the leadership of other women in the political arena, such as Anna Julia Cooper, Mary Church Terrell, and Harriet McLeod Bethune. When Horne signs a long-term contract with MGM, she becomes the symbolic figure to lead Negro womanhood from behind the apron of the cinematic mammy and into new roles.

Horne's autobiographies, *In Person* and *Lena,* reveal, however, that the contract with MGM activates several personal and professional concerns. First, the document launches Horne on a quest to deem herself worthy of the gift of being the first Negro woman to become a major contract player within the Hollywood studio system. Attendant to the question of "worthiness," Horne experiences an interior discomfort as she wrestles with the displacement of her on-screen Negro predecessor, Hattie McDaniel. Second, and finally, as a Negro performer, Horne works to discover a new meaning for "the star" and "the symbol." These components of popular culture have to signify more than mere spectacle for the enjoyment of the masses if she is to assume the role at MGM. Horne's quest, I will demonstrate, is not a simple search for acceptance from her colleagues; it is also a pursuit of an understanding of the symbol as it is mapped onto the body of the Negro actress in times of national trauma.

Historical Backdrop

Horne's texts can be read as parables of a singer who journeys to find ways to manage the position of being the first Negro woman star. They are also stories about a Negro woman who assumes the burden of representation for the Negro race during World War II. Horne's arrival on MGM's studio lot in 1942 paves the way for a new representation of Negro womanhood to supplant Hattie McDaniel's mammy figure. McDaniel's mammy role made her the first Negro in the history of film to win an Academy Award for Best Supporting Actress for her performance in Victor Fleming's *Gone with the Wind* (1939). Her Academy Award win is for playing a character that resonates with the American collective memory of the fictitious genteel South—rife with elaborate plantation vistas and "happy darkies." More tragic, after the release of D. W. Griffith's 1915 *Birth of a Nation*, the Negro community suffers from a cesspool of cinematic myths, stereotypes, and caricatures in general and the stereotype of the mammy figure, in particular, remains popular for approximately thirty years.

The mammy is one of the most enduring black stereotypes in film history. An idealized white notion of Negro women in slavery, the mammy figure functions as a tough but loving caretaker of her owners. Sociohistorian K. Sue Jewell points out that the perpetuation of this image, largely controlled by those with wealth and power in the print and visual media, "distorted images of African American women [. . . and made them] more pronounced and visible" to the American public (35). As film historian Donald Bogle observes, the mammy "is representative of the all-black woman, overweight, middle-aged, and so dark, so thoroughly black, that it is preposterous even to suggest that she be a sex object. Instead she was desexed" (*Toms, Coons* 14–15).

The popularity of the mammy figure as "all-black woman" is indicative of the Negro woman's place in American society at that time. Southern Negroes, skilled mainly in farming and agriculture, migrate to the industrial northern cities in the 1930s and 1940s. The employment they find generally is limited to domestic labor. As the mammy image in U.S. culture gains currency via literature and the media, racism feeds this limitation. The smiling, bandanna-clad Aunt Jemima on the pancake mix box stands firm on grocery store shelves.

The outbreak of World War II, however, prompts the NAACP to challenge Hollywood studios to present an alternative to the mammy tradition. The nation's engagement in a war across the seas to make the world safe for democracy calls into question its inequitable treatment of Negroes on the domestic front. Novelist Ralph Ellison writes in 1949 that because of World War II, "the United States' position as a leader in world affairs [was . . .] shaken by its treatment of Negroes. Thus the thinking of white Americans [was . . .] undergoing a process of change [. . .]" (277). The studios (in)voluntarily fall in line with this process of change. In the A&E documentary *Hollywood: An Empire of Their Own*, film historian and columnist Neal Gabler notes Hollywood has to scour for ways to manage the paradox of its portrayal of the Negro in film and the war effort. "A democratic state could not send minorities, immigrants and the poor to die for an America which excluded them," Gabler maintains.

The war leads to an unprecedented alliance between Washington, in particular the Office of War Information (OWI), and Hollywood. Aljean Harmetz, author-historian, affirms along with Gabler, an alliance between Washington and Hollywood facilitates the film studios' agenda to produce films with Negro actors fully integrated in plots and story lines. The industry uses the armed forces as the branch of government that could relay the message. Harmetz says, "[t]he American Army was not integrated except in Hollywood movies. And the Office of War Information was very eager to keep our enemies from making capital out of any sort of problems in America. So they didn't want movies that had any racial tensions of any sort" (*Hollywood: An Empire of Their Own*). The Hollywood moguls project racial harmony by producing films such as *Bataan* (dir. Tay Garnett, 1943), *Sahara* (dir. Zoltan Korda, 1943) *The Negro Soldier* (dir. Stuart Hiesler, 1944), and *Lifeboat* (dir. Alfred Hitchcock, 1944), wherein the Negro man is an integral part of the storyline. Meanwhile, outside of Hollywood, Negro women move out of the domestic space and into the industrialized work environment as laborers. The Negro woman in the industrialized workplace unfortunately is not as successful on screen, although *Carmen Jones* (dir. Otto Preminger, 1954) does present the Negro woman at work in a parachute factory. This film also highlights the conflict between the working Negro woman and the emerging Negro ingénue that Horne eventually will come to represent.

Discomfort and anxiety, nevertheless, attend Horne's representation within the Hollywood community Horne decides to enter. Horne's signature on the MGM contract causes a conflict within the old guard community of west coast Negro actors, many of whom consider the east coast upstart a menace to their economic "stability." This west coast/east coast rivalry results in a protest meeting. The west coast Negro actor elite assemble at McDaniel's home to discuss the impending shift in attitudes toward the roles they have made popular. Chief among the concerns is that if Horne (or Walter White's "guinea pig") and NAACP spokesperson Walter White antagonize the status quo and displace the so-called menial roles, the financial status of the actors cast in those roles will be threatened. For example, McDaniel earns $2,000 a week and Butterfly McQueen earns $600 by the time White arrives in Hollywood to rally for Horne (Cripps 47). Lincoln Theodore Monroe

Andrew Perry or "Stepin Fetchit," Bill "Bojangles" Robinson, and McDaniel live a high-style Hollywood life on the money garnered from their screen portrayals. Each of these actors works on contract, but not long-term contracts. The pre-Horne elite Negro actors' contracts are for terms of no more than six months with options that could be dropped at the whim of the studio. Others are bit players working for a few dollars a day, a box lunch, and bus fare (Cripps 48).

More important, the old guard resent the NAACP's snub of the already installed Fair Play Committee (FPC). Organized by the Negro Hollywood actors, the FPC campaigns for better parts for the Negro performers long before White arrives in Hollywood. White offends several veteran black actors, such as Clarence Muse (*Hearts in Dixie*, 1929), because of his failure to acknowledge the Screen Actors Guild. First on the FPC's agenda is to "lessen the screen images of blacks as a 'bunch of careless, illiterate porters, mammies, waiters, and sharecroppers'" (Jackson 102). White practically ignores the FPC and the Screen Actors Guild opting instead to consult directly with Hollywood producers. His gesture enrages Muse, who writes, "In laying his cards on the table here, Mr. White didn't see fit to address the Screen Actors Guild. [. . .] We feel that if an organization like the NAACP is sincere in its fight, they should work it out with the moving force of Hollywood, the actors, through their Guild" (Muse 20). Muse perceives, furthermore, that the NAACP's slight leaves no room for a discussion of their lives outside of the Hollywood regime. He realizes that the organization conflates the character and the player; it does not consider the actor as an individual, separate and apart from the roles played. Muse claims:

> [T]here is nothing wrong with a man being a porter in a picture speaking dialect if the character is noble. If he has ambitions. If he is a part of the plot and wins in the end of the play. If he is glorified, if the role is comedy, let it be clean and true to life. Bob Hope or Bob Burns, in their comedy moments, do not carry the slogan of race discrimination or an uplift of humanity. [. . .] Hattie McDaniel won the Academy Award because of her great artistry in portraying a character as written. Not Hattie McDaniel, but the part in the book, "Gone with the Wind." (Muse 20)

McDaniel maintains that if Mammy draws indignation from the NAACP and White, then the institution and its representative should find her a different role: "What do you want me to do? Play a glamour girl and sit on Clark Gable's knee? When you ask me not to play the parts, what have you got to offer in return?" (Jackson 100).

The anger, however, pivots on Horne's daring. This "bourgeois eastern upstart" has the nerve to question the contract, rather than to depend on the studio to guarantee her rights as an actress. "[E]very actor should have written into his contract all kinds of 'special protections,'" insists Horne (*Lena* 135). In *Motion Picture* magazine in 1944, Sidney Skolsky makes known that part of these special protections for which Horne asks is "the understanding that she would sing in pictures or play legitimate roles and not have to do 'illiterate comedy' or portray a cook, roles customarily assigned to colored performers" (82). This woman has the nerve to insinuate that the parts for which Negro actors have been cast to establish careers and attain financial stability are not good enough for her. To make matters worse, not only does the studio agree to listen to her, but a studio mogul also incorporates these "special protections" into a written document. Just who do White and Horne think they are? These issues anger the Negro old guard. "They were afraid of what they called 'my attitude,'" Horne recalls, "by which they meant the terms I had insisted upon in my contract. They feared the studios might think it was the beginning of a large scale campaign on the part of Negro actors to raise their status, or that I might be thought the beginning of a revolt against roles as menials" (*Lena* 136, 137).

Horne stands in the midst of this conflict—literally—and within the context of protest Horne begins her journey to find meaning for the symbol. As a first strategy Horne projects her voice into the chaos to dispel her fellow actors' suspicion and to gain their acceptance. During the protest meeting, she is "forced to get up and try to explain that [. . . she] was not trying to start a revolt or steal work from anyone and that the NAACP was not using [. . . her] for any ulterior purpose" (*Lena* 137). Horne's voice is the clarion call to the Negro old guard to understand the cultural implications of her contract; it is also the proverbial cry in the wilderness of one seeking to be anointed by her people for the journey to come. Audre Lorde instructs us to listen, "[W]here the words of women are crying to be heard, we must each recognize our responsibility to seek those words out, to read them and share them and examine them to the pertinence to our lives" (43). Only when this happens can the symbol fully assume the burden of representation.

The matriarch of cinematic Negro womanhood, McDaniel, answers Horne's call for support. Horne remembers:

[McDaniel] called me up and asked me to visit her. I went to her beautiful home and she explained how difficult it had been for Negroes in the movies, which helped give me some perspective on the whole situation. She [. . .] sympathized with my position and [. . .] thought it was the right one if I chose it. [. . .] Miss McDaniel's act of grace helped tide me over a very awkward and difficult moment. [. . .] (*Lena* 137–138)

Like Robeson before her, McDaniel represents what Joseph Campbell terms the "protective figure who provides the adventurer with amulets against the dragon forces [s]he is about to pass" (69). The act of grace, or Campbell's amulet, in effect symbolizes a passing of the scepter. By passing the scepter, McDaniel builds a bridge on which Horne, the ingénue, can travel. McDaniel's sharing of the history of Negro images in film, within her hearth and home, with this newly appointed symbol of Negro womanhood, conjoins the tradition of the mammy with that of the contemporary ingénue.

What does the linkage of these two symbols mean? In the African context, McDaniel acts as the community elder who encourages the new and vibrant youth in its endeavors. According to Malidoma Patrice Somé, the "very old honor youth as the source of collective physical stability and strength as recent arrivals" (124). The overarching significance of the response and the meeting, however, is the homage paid to film ancestry. To continue in the African context, Somé regards the ancestor as one whose way is that of tradition. She explains:

[t]radition is they way of the ancestors, the manner in which those who lived before once walked and talked, the knowledge and practices that allowed them to live long enough to bestow life upon others. [T]his is crucial to life, because to forget the way life used to be lived is to become endangered. [. . . T]o look to the old ways is to avoid death. (124)

In addition, McDaniel's move to initiate the meeting signifies her recognition of the need for Negro sisterhood in times of crisis. In the transmission of history from one Negro actor to another, both Horne and McDaniel acknowledge the imperative of tradition in the whirlwind of radical change.

The McDaniel–Horne association complements that of the Lena–Cora dyad and the Robeson–Horne relationship (discussed later herein). By speaking up and out to Negroes within a film industry that has marginalized their presence and by accepting McDaniel's invitation, Horne locates herself within the community of actors, rather than standing apart from them as does Walter White. Her move is important because in the NAACP's campaign these actors' character portrayals are judged an abomination to the Negro race.

Lena Horne's and Walter White's campaign to overturn mammy, however, is so complicated that it ostensibly forges a new color line in Hollywood, dividing the light-skinned entertainer and executive from the dark-skinned actors. Black film history illustrates that neither the entertainer nor the executive are alone in this creation. Horne joins other light-skinned Negro leading ladies of the silver screen and mulatoes cast in early race movies black and white independent filmmakers produce and direct. The "race movie" almost always features an exclusive Negro cast dramatizing stories targeted for the Negro audience. The filmmakers generally critique social issues such as the class and color caste system within the Negro community or model stories that mirror those by the Hollywood studios. Prolific independent black filmmaker Oscar Micheaux, black and white independent film companies such as the Lincoln Motion Picture Company, the Colored Players Film Corporation, and Million Dollar Productions, feature light-skinned actresses as leads in their motion pictures. Evelyn Preer, Micheaux's first leading lady, for example, stars as the educated philanthropist with a secret, Sylvia Landry, in the filmmaker's second silent film *Within Our Gates* (1920). In the silent feature *The Scar of Shame* (1927), Lucia Lynn Moses plays Louise Howard, a "tragic mullato" [sic] who commits suicide after her husband Alvin (Harry Henderson) refuses to come back to her after he discovers her low birth status. Lena Horne makes her movie and starring role debut in an all-black cast movie called *The Duke Is Tops* (dir. William Nolte) in 1938, produced by Toddy Pictures Company (founded by Ted Toddy) and Million Dollar Productions (founded by white producers Harry M. Popkin and Leo Popkin). Horne plays Ethel Andrews, a talented entertainer whom Duke Davis (Ralph Cooper, the "Dark Gable") vows to advance her career at any cost. This trajectory shows that Hollywood studios in the late 1920s and 1930s took cues from race, all-black cast movies or both when considering Negro women for lead actresses (Sampson *Blacks In Black and White*).

The major studios follow suit and choose the mulatto to star in films that address America's color consciousness as well as Negro culture and history. In 1929, MGM produces the first film with an all-black cast, *Hallelujah* (dir. King Vidor), and introduces America to a new light-skinned talent, Nina Mae McKinney. In 1934, Fredi Washington appears in Universal Pictures' movie about "passing" in the sentimental melodrama *Imitation of Life* (dir. John M. Stahl). Lena Horne and Dorothy Dandridge appear later in the 1940s and 1950s: Horne as seductress in

Vincent Minnelli's *Cabin in the Sky* and singer in Andrew L. Stone's *Stormy Weather* (1943); Dandridge as rebel seductress in Otto Preminger's *Carmen Jones* (1954).

The mulatto as ingénue or star popularized by all-black cast movies conceivably stimulates White's and Horne's Hollywood agenda. At first, the entertainer and the NAACP representative ignore the established Hollywood Negro actors. White especially negotiates only with the producers, studio heads, and the most popular white actors to rehabilitate the image of the Negro on the silver screen. Well-known (dark-skinned) Negro actors such as Hattie McDaniel, Clarence Muse, Mantan Moreland, and Butterfly McQueen receive the proverbial snub in the discussions. For example, White responds to the Sojourner Truth neighborhood and Woodward riots in 1942 and 1943 in Detroit, Michigan, by forming the Emergency Committee of the Entertainment Industry. Sponsored by CBS, the committee produces a program "through which well-known figures in the entertainment world could utilize their influence to create a countersentiment to mobism" (White 231). The roster includes luminaries such as Tallulah Bankhead, Duke Ellington, Lena Horne, Groucho Marx, Edward G. Robinson, and Orson Welles (White 232).

White also finds support from prominent Negroes in Los Angeles and the Negro press for his side-stepping of the old guard community of Negro actors. Interestingly, color consciousness and physical appearance factors energize the support. Walter White, blond and blue-eyed, is born into a deeply religious African-American family in Atlanta, Georgia, in 1893. White writes in his autobiography *A Man Called White*, that his parents are so light that they "guided themselves [. . .] along the course between the Scylla of white hostility and the Charybdis of some Negroes' resentment against us because we occupied a slightly more comfortable better-kept home and were less dark than they" (21). The recognition of his parents' strategies between the worlds of light and dark, imaginably informs his silence over a remark from a member of the Negro community. Kenneth Robert Janken, White's biographer, comments, "[White] accepted without comment the worst sort of pigment mongering by a prominent black Angeleno businessman, who told White not to meet with Muse, McDaniel, [Eddie "Rochester" Anderson,] and others" (271). Los Angeles businessman Norman O. Houston, secretary-treasurer of the Golden State Mutual Life Insurance Company, encourages White to dismiss the criticisms against him and Horne. In a special delivery letter dated September 16, 1943, Houston writes:

> Naturally, a person physically large (or small), dark, limited in background and appearance can not [sic] appear in parts

designed for ingénues, gigolos or dashing heroes; therefore, it is possible that a *sort of jealousy or inferiority complex* is associated with the whole matter, especially when we take into consideration your friendliness with Lena Horne—certainly not of the type mentioned above. (1, emphasis mine)

Houston suggests further the character and "personal prejudices" of these actors will compromise a formal meeting with them; rather, "a semi-social gathering, where refreshments were served" will massage the emotions of the hypersensitive actors as they party on food and drink. Houston's evaluation of dark-skinned African Americans—overweight or small—against that of Lena Horne's "type" undeniably delineates the aggressive color and class consciousness practiced among several in the Negro community. In Houston's estimation, moreover, dark physiognomy in the film industry "naturally" fails to transfer out of the mammy or tom or coon characterizations. The awareness of this disadvantage by the actor who meets the description, according to Houston, brings about a psychological disorder. Implicitly, the businessman welds the image stereotype to the actual actor rather than criticizes Hollywood's investment in portraying Negro actors in stereotypical parts.

Similarly, an editorial, "Hollywood and Walter White," in the *Chicago Defender*, a major Negro newspaper, claims the old guard Negro actors even fail to demonstrate the necessary competency to decide what is best for them because each "[has] been so used to playing menial parts that [she] can no longer conceive of getting respectable roles on the screen. The facts are that [they are] not capable of acting as judges of what is good and what is bad in Hollywood [. . .]" (14). Only White's collaboration with white producers and talent agents can position McDaniel and others to be cast in other roles because neither McDaniel nor Beavers has the intellectual wherewithal to change casting decisions of film producers:

Perhaps Hattie McDaniel and Louise Beavers would no longer cavort in servants' uniforms and Clarence Muse himself might not be called upon to put on a grass skirt and prance about as a jungle savage, ostensibly portraying an African. (14)

Horne's and White's résumé of similarities also add fuel to the fire. Both share upper-middle-class bourgeois backgrounds as well as similar physical characteristics of light complexions. Horne is born into an elite Negro family in the Bedford section of Brooklyn. She writes:

> [. . .] most of my successes were to be the result of being exhib-
> ited, as I was that first day [of my birth], as oddity of color—a
> Negro woman, and a Negro entertainer who didn't fit the pic-
> ture of personality and performing style the white majority used
> to expect. The world into which I was born, the one which
> exerted the strongest pull on my personality, was a small, tight
> world, [. . .] of the Negro middle class. [. . .] We were isolated
> from the mainstream of Negro life, seeing a relatively narrow
> group of people. (*Lena* 1–2)

Important to Horne's and White's Hollywood agenda are the bourgeois
attitudes both she and White bring with them, and these attitudes
encourage their isolation from the masses of the Negro population of
actors in Hollywood. That Horne and White conflate the celluloid image
with the actors themselves widens the gap even more between them and
the old guard.

Interestingl, however, is that although both Horne and White curry
class and intraracial dissension while carrying out their Hollywood
plans their paths eventually diverge. White continues lobbying Hollywood CEOs, but eventually learns "the immigrant Jewish cultural
agenda was to use prevalent white stereotypes of African Americans in
order to enter America's melting pot" (Janken 273). In addition,
Horne's autobiographies betray an admission that the arrangement she
and White make to introduce a Negro womanhood means casting off
the bourgeois isolation of which she is accustomed growing up in New
York. She cannot sidestep the old guard of Negro actors to accomplish
the task; understanding that the "symbol of racial uplift" involves the
interaction of the bourgeois ingénue with the "working-class" Negro
actors is imperative for her. Horne's texts lay bare an interrelationship
with those who have come before her, and she develops a shrewd perception of the insidious assignation of labels (that is, "star," "symbol,"
"the first Negro to") and its transitory nature. Thus, as she works with
her new colleagues in film, Horne transforms into my parents' "something else": an activist entertainer. As an activist entertainer, Horne
places herself in the thick of things, and thereby claims a grassroots
association with the people, not with the elite group of studio heads for
whom she has agreed to labor.

Horne's migration to New York City after her screen test also is an
important aspect of her journey. In New York, Horne meets Count
Basie, the big swing bandleader. She confides her discomfort in Hollywood and her yearning to be with her people. She writes:

[. . .] I told [Count] Basie that I wasn't going back to Hollywood. I can't go back. I'm lonely; I can't see my own people. I
don't want to be a movie star. [. . .] I was especially surprised at
the seriousness of the advice he gave me when I said I didn't
want to go back.

"You've got to go back," he said. "Nobody's ever had this
chance before."

"But I don't want it," I sniffled. [. . .] Basie wasn't buying.
"No you've got to go back," he said. "They've never had
anyone like you. [. . .] They never have been given the chance to
see a Negro woman as a woman. You've got to give them that
chance." He made me believe it would somehow help all of us
(*Lena* 142–143).

Exactly what kind of "Negro woman" does Count Basie mean they
(white audiences) have not seen? Judging from the history of Negro
women in film prior to Horne, Hollywood, especially MGM, is quite
familiar with Horne's type through fair-skinned leading ladies Nina Mae
McKinney, who plays Chick in King Vidor's production of *Hallelujah!*
(1929) and Fredi Washington, who plays Peola in John M. Stahl's production *Imitation of Life* (1934). For example, Irving Thalberg, MGM's
powerful producer, and director King Vidor considered McKinney "one
of the greatest discoveries of the age," and Thalberg "predicted a glori-
ous future" for her. Bogle maintains, "[t]he *New York Post*'s Richard
Watts, Jr. called her 'assuredly one of the most beautiful women of our
time'" (*Toms, Coons* 33). McKinney so enchants the studio, MGM signs
her to a five-year contract. According to Bogle, McKinney establishes
the tradition of the treasured mulatto in Hollywood: light-skinned beautiful Negro women who are given a chance at leading roles because they
meet the white ideal. The emerald-eyed Washington "emerges as one of
Black America's most exciting dramatic actresses" and "[f]or a spell it
looked as if Hollywood had a serious young black actress it would have
to reckon with" (Bogle, *Brown Sugar* 79).

Like Horne, these actresses work in the theater and the nightclub
circuits prior to work in film; and, like Horne's stint as a chorus dancer
in Harlem's famed Cotton Club, McKinney dances in the chorus of a
Harlem show, *Blackbirds of 1928*. McKinney's and Washington's film
careers, however, hit dead ends, while Horne's only stalls. In the late
1950s, an assistant cameraman finds McKinney working as a maid in
New York. Fredi Washington fairs better, but Hollywood stereotyping
eventually lead her to abandon a career in film and embrace the role of a

civil rights activist and founder of the Negro Actors Guild of America in 1937, whose goal "was to eliminate stereotyping of roles [. . .] for blacks" ("Fredi Washington"). With these similarities, what unique quality does Basie believe Horne can bring to Hollywood?

Horne appears in Hollywood with a very impressive résumé and entourage, including a solid upper-middle-class bourgeois Brooklyn, New York family. Lena Horne is born on June 30, 1917. She starts her career as a dancer in Harlem's famous Cotton Club at age sixteen. Of that time, she observes, "[. . .] for the employees, [The Cotton Club] was an exploitative system on several levels. The club got great talent for very cheap, because there were so few places for great Negro performers. [W]e were underpaid and overworked in the most miserable conditions" (*Lena* 47, 48). Her interpretation of Harlem's nightclub scene is perceptive, and her perceptions are honed at a young age by her wise but stoic grandmother, Cora Calhoun Horne. Calhoun Horne is a significant force in the singer's belief that she can act as the Negro symbol for racial uplift.

Horne's childhood exposures to racial injustice via participation in Negro institutions prepare her to endure and speak out against racism upon her entry in the entertainment industry. Her grandmother is an active member of the NAACP and the Urban League in the early 1900s. Horne accompanies her grandmother to many of the meetings, where she sits quietly memorizing the discussions. Horne writes:

[F]or of her many good works, it was, naturally, the NAACP, along with the Urban League, that ranked highest in [my grand-mother's] interest. [. . .] I have vivid memories of accompanying her to the meetings. [. . .] I was always the only child there, sitting quietly, listening because I knew I would be questioned later about what I had heard. [. . .] I was learning to "speak up like a little adult" in order to earn one brisk sign of approval from Grandmother. (*Lena* 10–11)

Observing these activities, repeating the deliberations therein, and "speaking up like a little adult" plant firm roots in Horne's consciousness. I have shown how her grandmother's training of Lena bears fruit in her dealings with the west coast league of Negro actors.

Horne's association as a young entertainer with the internationally renowned singer Paul Robeson is also important in her choice to stand as a symbol for racial uplift. Anxious over her decision to pursue a career in entertainment rather than the formal education her grandmother favored, Robeson helps Horne understand that her resolve to pursue a career in entertainment does not show disregard for her grand-mother's teachings. Robeson assures her that even though Calhoun Horne takes a different approach to education, Horne's work comple-ments the very principles on which the matriarch stood. In her 1950 autobiography, *In Person*, Horne recalls Robeson's affirmation during a backstage visit at New York's Café Society nightclub. Robeson reminds the young entertainer:

> [Cora] was fighting for opportunity just as you are fighting for opportunity. If she could see you now, she'd be mighty proud of you. [. . .] She'd be proud of you because you both have the same drive for the same principles. [. . .] Aren't you always studying and rehearsing to improve yourself and do a better job? (*In Person* 186–187)

Robeson's words of encouragement facilitate Horne's reclamation of her self-respect, which is lost in the quagmire of racial injustice; Robeson affirms that he, too, "carried the same denial, the same rejection all our people suffer" (Horne, *In Person* 188).

The best information Robeson grants Horne, however, leads her to a deeper understanding of the plight of the Negro in the United States. In a 1947 interview with *Ebony* magazine, "Meet the Real Lena Horne," Horne confesses:

> I hated my own people because I saw them pushed around and taking it. [. . .] But one night Paul Robeson came into Café Soci-ety [. . .] and that night changed my whole way of thinking. [. . .] I got some idea of the greatness of our people. I learned why they were being pushed around and how big people we Negroes can be if we learn how to see things clearly and fight. (10)

Robeson's mentorship in the backroom of New York's Café Society nightclub equips Horne with the vision and the ability to rightly judge appearances in an entertainment world.

Finally, the after-hour bull sessions held backstage at Café Society expose Horne to liberal whites who hold an abiding respect for Negroes in America: "[T]hey [. . .] knew what life was like for us [. . .] and how we react[ed] to what [. . . was] done to us. [. . .] These white people were doing something to help us overcome the unfair conditions of our lives" (Horne, *In Person* 194). There are conversations with and stories about Negro artists and musicians—such as the West Indian classical pianist

Hazel Scott, blues singer Billie Holiday, and actor Canada Lee—who protest discrimination in the United States. These sessions put Horne in close contact with whites and Negroes familiar with the Harlem Renaissance literati, including Langston Hughes, Arna Bontemps, Richard Wright, W. E. B. Du Bois (to whom Horne refers as Dr. Du Bois), James Weldon Johnson, and Countee Cullen. The café society congregation of lawyers, newspapermen, writers, engineers, architects, doctors, and other professional people expands Horne's grandmother's wisdom and pedagogical approach as she hones her craft as an entertainer.

The congeries of occasions makes Horne "grateful for the deep respect [. . . she] was learning to have for [. . . her] own people" (Horne, *In Person* 193). While she has had to recite the tenets of the Urban League and the NAACP to her grandmother, the bull sessions afford her a front row seat to observe the system of beliefs in practice. Furthermore, in these discussions Horne most likely becomes familiar with Dr. Du Bois's theory of racial uplift as outlined in his February 23, 1893, journal entry: "I am willing to sacrifice. . . . I therefore . . . work for the rise of the Negro people, taking for granted that their best development means the best development of the world" (Carby 9). For Horne, racial uplift means bringing up a new cinematic image for Negro women. The privilege of being the first Negro woman to be offered a long-term contract, glamour, and stardom at MGM is not enough for the bourgeois Lena Horne: she has an entire community of Negro women to liberate from the trammels of stereotypes on celluloid. Horne writes, "[m]y chief interest was in protecting my opportunity to sing" and to "set my own terms in the movies and also be successful [so that] others might be able to follow" (Horne, *Lena* 137). Here, Horne aligns herself with Du Bois's theory of sacrifice. She refuses to buy into what film historian Richard Dyer calls "that hype and the hard sell [that] do characterize the media" because she senses its "manipulation, insincerity, inauthenticity" (*Heavenly Bodies* 16), and instability from the start.

The support of the NAACP and its representative Walter White; an established reputation in New York's Café Society nightclub; the respect of her peers, both Negro and white, including Noble Sissle and Charlie Barnett; and, most important, the sociopolitical and racial issues of World War II America are other salient features of Horne's life. As Horne's onetime mentor and friend in New York, Basie knows Lena Horne is the most privileged, coddled, protected, and respected Negro female entertainer in the business at that particular time. Herein resides the difference between Horne and her predecessors and contemporaries. These elements, in particular the aspect of a protected Negro woman, constitute the "Negro woman as woman" Basie perceives.

As for McKinney, in his article "Black Garbo," Stephen Bourne informs us that off screen, McKinney's life is filled with strife and contention. He writes:

> During the filming of *Sanders* [*of the River*], her love affair with Paul Robeson came to an abrupt end when his wife, the ever-protective Eslanda, found them out. At the same time, Nina's "star temperament" made her so unpopular in show business circles that she began to lose work. . . . Her replacement, Elizabeth Welch, later recalled: "Nina thought that being a star meant that you must be temperamental and nasty. Admittedly she was very young and immature, clearly unable to cope with fame, but she made herself unpopular, and ruined her career." By this time, Nina had become addicted to drugs. [. . .] (112–13)

Bourne speculates further, "although very little is known about Nina's affairs with women, she is rumored to have had a 'liaison' with the white Hollywood star Clara Bow." Bourne continues:

> Though not acknowledged at the time, many women like Nina found themselves drawn into relationships with women. Maude Russell, one of Nina's contemporaries, explains: "Many of us had been abused by producers, directors, leading men. In those days men didn't care about pleasing a girl. Girls needed tenderness, so we had girl friendships, and some of us became lovers, but we had to be discreet because lesbians weren't accepted in show business." (112–13)

Moreover, we find no indication that any field representative from the NAACP serves as agent for either McKinney or Washington, even though the organization has been fighting for changes in film images since 1915.

Basie understands the full implication of her contract and of the potential for her presence in the film industry. As a son of a domestic who witnesses his mother "take in washing [. . .] which meant that she did all of the washing and ironing of all the clothes and household linen for several well-to-do families around town," Basie promises his mother that once he becomes successful and financially secure, she never would have to work as a domestic again (xi). The bandleader, therefore, regards Horne's contract as an occasion to add another dimension to Negro womanhood, just as he anticipates the chance to lift his mother out of the role of the domestic. In other words, Negro womanhood has another side. Herein is the "symbol" in Horne. Horne enters Hollywood as a would-be movie star and actress, a well-accomplished singer, and a political activist. These constituents make for a more holistic Negro woman rather than one frozen in an image of beauty, fair skin, and domestic servitude.

Basie's directive has another element. Horne's return to Hollywood means a distribution of the gift that is Horne. If Horne rests in the familiar comforts of New York, the gift is in danger of stagnating. Horne's gifts—her "look," her upper-middle-class pedigree, and the subsequent seven-year contract—are not only about Lena Horne. These gifts also will confront the nation's long-held beliefs about the Negro woman as the nation stands at the threshold of change. Basie's edict for Horne to go back is a request for her to understand the seriousness of the business at hand. In Basie's mind, Horne must appraise the gift in the grand scheme of things, even if doing so means relinquishing the comforts of home.

Gift theory hinges on the concept that circulating the gift means ensuring a perpetual living space, rather than one that is motionless. Dinesh Khosla and Patricia Williams agree, "in the circularity of gift, the wealth of a community never loses its momentum. It passes from one hand to another; it does not gather in isolated pools" (621). This is not to say that Horne should act as sacrificial lamb to her own personal detriment. On the contrary, if the bearer of the gift passes it on, this means, according to Khosla and Williams, a personal sustenance as well. Distributing the gift "enchance[s] the self in relation to others, not alone. They continue, "[t]he spirit of the gift brings forth the self as part of a whole relationship: it brings forth the individual self, the group self, [and] the emotional self" (622, 623).

The assessment that Horne offers after hearing Basie's charges makes evident the singer's coming to terms with Khosla and Williams's theory of the gift. By listening to Basie and analyzing his words, Horne finds meaning for the symbol. She explains:

> [W]hatever his understanding of my possible symbolic value, [Basie] had also been able to see *me* within the symbol. [. . .] He was the first person who I thought had some objectivity about me, to imply that I was worthy of this favor. [. . .] [T]his was the kind of favor you prove yourself worthy of only after it is given. That is, the way you use it is the important thing, not the question whether you really deserved it in the first place. [. . .] I returned with the sense that I belonged somewhere. [. . .] (Horne, *Lena* 144–145)

Basie's belief in her abilities enables a self-appreciation and a better understanding of the meaning of the symbol, how it should work, and its relationship to her as a person. Through her history with Cora Calhoun Horne, Paul Robeson, café society, the west coast Negro community of actors, Hattie McDaniel, and Count Basie, Horne unearths an inner ability to make the symbol stand for something in the presence of movie mogul, Louis B. Mayer.

From New York to Los Angeles; from Basie to Louis B. Mayer

On one level, however, Horne's arrival indeed problematizes the tradition of the mammy. On another level, Horne complicates the very contract that ushers in the possibility for a new representation of Negro womanhood. Horne biographers James Haskins and Kathleen Benson agree that during her initial appointment with MGM, Horne "was a bit overwhelmed by the reception[,] suspicious of the excitement she had generated[, and] didn't want to get caught up in the excitement . . ." (67). Horne is familiar with the demeaning roles Negroes play in films: "[The Negro actors] were mainly extras and it was not difficult to strip down to a loincloth and run around Tarzan's jungle or put on a bandanna and play one of the slaves in *Gone with the Wind*" [Horne, *Lena* 138]. Her keen insights prepare her to hold a clear view of the studio system—unlike her predecessor McDaniel and her contemporaries Lana Turner, Marilyn Monroe, and Dorothy Dandridge. Horne's texts lay bare a shrewd perception of the insidious nature of the labels (that is, "star," "symbol," "the first Negro to") from the onset, rather than as a regret in hindsight. This shrewdness protects her from the baleful emotional, physical, and mental pitfalls her film-star colleagues—black and white, predecessors and contemporaries—experienced.

Hattie McDaniel, for example, identifies with the mammy figure for years. Her biographer, Carlton Jackson, notes McDaniel embraces the mammy so much that she even signed one correspondence "Mammy, Hattie McDaniel." McDaniel champions the role by going on national tour as Mammy after the popularity of the film *Gone with the Wind*. But in the end, with the changing times, McDaniel grows quite depressed. Jackson writes, "[Hattie] told friends that 'I don't belong on this earth. I always feel out of place—like a visitor.' During Hattie's 'time of troubles' in the late forties getting movie parts, she became so despondent that she attempted suicide" (144, 146). After nursing an entire nation through her character, "Mammy" dies of breast cancer in 1954.

Lana Turner, an MGM established star, laments that the sexy "flesh impact" image that director Mervyn LeRoy "fix[ed] in the viewers' mind" clung to her for the rest of her career: "I was the sexual promise, the object of desire. [. . .] the movie star in diamonds, swathed in white mink" (Turner 9). Marilyn Monroe's biographer, Donald Spoto, relates that even though Monroe managed to create an enormously popular sex symbol for the studio and the public, "she [had become] trapped by an image with whose manufacture she had wholeheartedly co-opted since her modeling. Close relationships had meant mostly sexual relationships" (187). As in her private life, her on-screen characters position her to be "taken advantage of or humiliated" (Dyer, *Heavenly Bodies* 46). In 1962, Monroe dies of an apparent drug overdose without having been released from her sex-symbol status. She was thirty-six.

Dorothy Dandridge, who is the first Negro actress to be nominated for an Academy Award for Best Actress (*Carmen Jones*), realizes that the acquisition of stardom does not guarantee equitable treatment from studio heads. Nor does it secure respectability from white men in the business—a thing she craves throughout her career. Dandridge writes of her angst, "I was too light to satisfy Negroes, not light enough to secure the screen work, the roles, the marriage status available to a white woman" (165).

Importantly, the dissatisfaction that white stars such as Turner and Monroe articulate and their conflicts with the studio systems bring to focus a desire to expand their careers and express themselves as something other than cinematic sexpots. Their autobiographies do not reveal any need in them to create different roles to uplift neither the white race, nor white womanhood. Moreover, none of them is an experiment in U.S. race relations. Turner and Monroe, especially, enjoy the full benefits of stardom despite their grievances against the studio. In fact, Monroe's image made her the most popular American icon in the history of entertainment. McDaniel, Dandridge, and Horne struggle against society's refusal to see them as American women, however, and a society that opts, instead, to relegate them to an on-screen role as household servant or sex goddess.

The Paradox of Beauty

Horne has agreed to uplift the race: "Walter [White] felt, and I agreed with him, that since I had no history in the movies and therefore had not been typecast as anything so far, it would be essential for me to try to establish a different kind of image for Negro women" (Horne, *Lena* 134). Horne's narratives uncover an oppressive tolerance, which comes to the fore during precontract deliberations and within the formal contract, as well. Likewise, the texts reveal a skeptical chanteuse who refuses to accept the written document without question, "Neither [my father nor I] believed in the damn thing," said Horne (*Lena* 135). The following section examines how Horne manipulates her contract negotiations not only to debunk the historical constructions of Negro womanhood, but also to ensure a fluid and multiple interpretation of the "different kind of image for Negro women" she wishes to establish.

At the advice of a fellow musician, Horne learns to place beauty in its context:

> You know, for a long time this "beauty thing" was a hang-up. . . . And I was taught very early by a black man, Tiny Bradshaw, not to get any conceit about beauty because, he told me, . . . there were thousands of other black women who looked as good as I did and better who didn't get the chance. And when I went to California [. . . my beauty] kept me from being in any of the molds they were allowing Negro people to be in. ("Lena Horne Joins . . ." 132)

Horne realizes through Tiny Bradshaw that relying solely on glamour is futile and, worse, dangerous. The "beautiful" Negro actress must choose how beauty can be used once it enters the public arena. What will it stand for in the public's view? As critic bell hooks states, "the issue of [. . .] representation is not just a question of critiquing the *status quo*. It is about transforming the image, creating alternatives, asking ourselves questions about what types of images subvert, pose critical alternatives, and transform our worldviews and move us away from dualistic thinking about good and bad" (*Black Looks* 4). Horne is aware that to embrace glamour, stardom, and beauty fully without introspection could install another tradition. Herein is the subversion. Horne believes that remaining fixed in beauty, sex symbolism, and stardom is just as dangerous as sustaining the mammy figure as do Hattie McDaniel and Louise Beavers.

In the early stages of the war, the president of Warner Brothers Studios, Jack Warner, loves to point out that the chemical ingredient in film also is used to make smokeless gunpowder (A&E 1998). Warner's statement points to the threat inherent in celluloid: The actress cloaked in an image contained therein is always already in personal peril, and subject to explosion or implosion.

In her actions, Horne abstains from judging Hollywood good or bad; but she understands that beauty is the weapon needed to break the stereotypical molds into which Negro women are being poured. According to hostess and socialite Elsa Maxwell, glamour was "the most powerful of all social weapons" (*Bitter Fruit* 336). Horne's consent to the contract signifies a conscientious move to create the alternatives for which hooks calls and her awareness that beauty is one of the tools that can create them. This discernment speaks for Horne's tenacity, skill, and forethought. Beauty must not be trusted to sustain a career, but an entertainer can, in conscious awareness of its power, use it as a tool for positive change. Horne's decision to leave her firmly established New York supper-club career for that of a film ingénue is an example of this awareness.

The Casting Call: Mayer's "Cryptic-Sounding Phone Call"

The weight of her choice plays out in the story of her audition at MGM. Horne's account of her MGM audition critiques the casting process and shows her contempt for studio chief Louis B. Mayer and, by extension, white patriarchy. She writes, "[we], the Hollywood crowd nervously await[ed] to see whether the *great man*, L. B. Mayer, would *deign* to see us." And then, "in a little while there came a *cryptic-sounding* phone call" (Horne, *Lena* 133; my emphasis). The final moment makes plain Horne's detachment from a funny consociation:

> [Mayer] seemed very genial and fatherly to me. I sang to him and I remember him just sitting there, beaming at me through his round glasses. After I had done a couple of songs he disappeared into some *inner sanctum* and reappeared with Marion Davies on his arm. She was just visiting, but I had to sing for her too. It was kind of funny. But not funny, too. By this time everyone was all charged up, excited by some possibility that I could not see. (Horne, *Lena* 133; my emphasis)

Horne punctuates the description of the waiting room with words of sarcasm: "great man," "deign," "cryptic," "inner sanctum." In her sarcasm Horne reacts to a complex set of dynamics: family, ownership, and property. Veteran white actors remember the studio system and its contract determine an actor's position within the studio colony. "Everyone was owned" is the first rule for running a Hollywood studio lot (*Studio System*), and the document that makes an actor part of a lot's domain was the seven-year contract. Film historian Ronald Davis writes:

An actor whose test was approved was signed to a seven-year contract with options, starting at a salary between $75 and $250 a week, depending on experience. "With options" meant that the studio could drop the newcomer at the end of each six-month interval of the contract period, or raise the actor to the next salary level. Usually the casting director decided who received contracts and who didn't, although the studio mogul had final approval. (83)

"When you're under contract, it's a family feeling; you have a family to go to if you have a problem," maintained late actor DeForest Kelley, most famous for his role as Dr. Leonard McCoy on *Star Trek*. "[T]here is someone you can go to that has your interest at heart." Charlton Heston has a darker view, "the studios would loan their actors back and forth; but that was just like trading in grain futures. The actors were, as I understand it, largely properties then and treated as such [. . .]." The late actor Jack Lemmon remembers, "there were straight seven-year contracts and you were owned body and soul" (*Studio System*).

How would Horne fit into this particular family? As a Negro actress, this notion, indeed, has a "funny" or peculiar potential. By bringing white actress Marion Davies to the table, Mayer constructs a potential family, but Mayer and Davies here act as master and mistress. For Horne to create a productive distance in the beginning indicates a fear that she could indeed become a part of this family and thereby inherit Kelley's "family feeling" with its risk of ownership. Horne's membership in this family could be very troubling. Horne writes, however, she sings "to" Mayer rather than "for" him. She maintains a distance, and her word choice further unveils a criticism of her audition and of the studio chief.

In one way, Horne's audition in the presence of Mayer and actress Marion Davies hearkens to the spectacle made of African women on the auction block during the plantation era in the United States. Horne chooses her words very carefully about being discovered for the movies: "[. . . my agent had set out to *sell me* to Hollywood" (*In Person* 201; my emphasis). Saidiya Hartman examines the dehumanizing conditions slave women endure under the gaze of the master planters at slave auctions. Recapitulating one slave woman's experience, she writes, "Ethel Dougherty stated that at slave sales women were forced to stand half-naked for hours while crowds of rough-drinking men bargained for them, examining their teeth, heads, hands, et cetera, at frequent intervals to test their endurance" (38). Although the studio audition is not as degrading as the slave auction, Horne's audition, nevertheless, is a minor echo as the studio examines and bargains for her labor. Frank Nugent explains in 1945, "Lena had sung for two hours in [Freed's] office, [and] for two more in Louis B. Mayer's" (52).

Horne laments the farcical nature of her screen test. "My first screen test, which came after the signing of the contract, was a farce. [. . .] They kept smearing dark make-up [*sic*] on me. In the end it was a disaster" (*Lena* 136). Although potential actors and actresses are commonly subjected to a barrage of critical comments about their physical bodies and their looks, applying burnt cork (cork heated until charred then applied to the face) to white actresses for a screen test was not the norm. Horne remembers:

> [. . .] the man in the make-up department started by using burnt-cork on my face. The moment I saw him reach for that stick, I objected. I was afraid he was going to make me look like a minstrel, I said, and I refused to look that way. [T]he white-jacketed young fellow, [said] "I'm not going to make you look like a minstrel." And he explained that he had been given instructions to make me up so the audiences wouldn't mistake me for a white girl. All he was going to do with that stick of burnt cork was see if they could darken me. (*In Person* 211–212)

According to Davis, at that time contract actors and actresses undergo a silent photographic test and a sound test. The talent then read a short scene from a screenplay or a drama script. The photographic tests are in black and white because color is so expensive. Screen tests take place either in New York or on a California studio set. Department heads, studio executives, and producers view the test either with or without the actors present. In Horne's screen test, the studio attempts to maintain the absolute division between Negro and white, which is why the studio wants to apply the cork makeup. Dyer notes that Horne's light skin is significant, yet troublesome, because:

> As a very light-skinned black woman, [. . . Horne] was unplaceable except as the ultimate temptress in an all-black musical, *Cabin in the Sky* where the guarantee of her beauty resid[ed] in the very fact of being so light. Otherwise she could not really be given a role in a film featuring whites, because her very lightness might make her an object of desire, thus confusing the racial hierarchy of desirability. (*Heavenly Bodies* 44)

Horne proves Dyer's analysis as she recalls a remark made by a club owner at an audition,

> Just for luck, I started the song I'd auditioned for Noble Sissle. "I'm in the Mood for Love . . . / Simply because you're near me. . . ." I didn't get much further than that. Because by the time I had finished the second line, I could hear them talking. "No sir," the manager was saying, "She's not for us. Look at those lips. Look at that nose. Nobody will ever believe she's a Negro. Why, she looks like a sun-tanned white girl!" (*In Person* 147)

In the audition with Mayer, Horne stands in the studio office before Mayer—one of the most influential moguls in the film industry—and he is silent. What is funny, or peculiar, about Mayer's silence is its sinister nature. If Mayer issues a formal verbal assessment and approval of the singer (or to decide to sign her up), then he legitimates Horne as a woman and actress, not a Negro woman or actress. The studio chief must therefore retreat to the inner sanctum, which contains the chalice of white womanhood (in this case, Marion Davies).

In his analysis of the meaning behind Marilyn Monroe's image, Richard Dyer makes known, "[t]he white woman is not only the most prized possession of white patriarchy, she is also a part of the symbolism of sexuality itself" (*Heavenly Bodies* 44). Paradoxically, with Davies on his arm, Mayer has permission to look on Horne, the Negro woman before him. In this funny way, Horne's very lightness and her ambiguous look threaten to make her an object of desire. If Mayer acts as his own agent, he upsets "the hierarchy of desirability" (*Heavenly Bodies* 44). This reality poses a danger because it threatens to create a continuum of womanhood with Horne on it, and there cannot be such a continuum with a Negro woman.

The Davies–Mayer mise-en-scène, for certain, points out Horne's anxiety—an uneasiness Horne has to negotiate. While DeForest Kelley speaks of inheriting a family in the studio colony, Horne discerns that this family depends on racial hierarchy. Mayer's beam manifests in Davies's appearance or white womanhood, and Heston's and Lemmon's statements that the contract automatically regards those within it as property of the studio are possibilities Horne cannot see. For the painful paradoxes involved in a Negro woman's being owned by the potential family of the master and mistress is indeed a cryptic-sounding call. Therefore the audition compels Horne to contemplate the actual contract she is to sign. This is a noteworthy contemplation, especially at

MGM, whose movie mogul, Louis B. Mayer, considers the *women* he signs on as *Daddy's little girls*. Mayer uses the long-term contract to demand total subservience to him and to exact absolute control over every aspect of each *girl's* life. Joan Crawford, Greta Garbo, and Judy Garland are just a few of the *girls* Daddy controls in his studio, and each of them fits the following criteria film historians Peter H. Brown and Pamela Ann Brown reveal:

> Louis B. Mayer needed a stable of girls [. . .] [he could] dress, [. . .] pamper [. . .] and then hand them the opiate of fame and power, they would be his family—Daddy's little girls. [. . .] They had to be low enough on the social ladder, or hungry enough or so lacking in identity that MGM in general, and Mayer in particular, would become their salvation. They weren't hard to find—these girls who would drink from Mayer's goblet of temptation. (6)

Horne enters Mayer's world as a woman whose talents have been tempered in the prestigious world of New York café society. What is more, as previously demonstrated, the Negro family and its community of institutions shape, mold and polish Horne. Horne, therefore, matches none of Mayer's criteria. This mismatch makes for a tenuous relationship between Horne and the studio. First, Mayer hasn't a blueprint to manage an entertainer such as Horne. Second, and more meaningful, Horne's training equips her with the interior fortitude to tenaciously defy the movie mogul's sovereignty. Enter the black patriarch, Teddy Horne.

I and My Father Are One: Lena, Teddy Horne, and Louis B. Mayer

Horne's audition narrative illustrates the actress's reluctance to accept wholeheartedly the studio system or to believe in its patriarchal curators. Horne writes, "I *suppose* I was excited [about being in the movies] [. . .] but I could not seriously believe anything would come of it. [. . .] [M]y hopes were not exactly high" (*Lena* 131–132). And the moment Horne realizes that MGM might hire her, she distrusts the process: "[. . .] I had no illusions," remembers Horne, "I'd been in the theatre long enough to have learned that there wasn't a single Negro who could earn a living in the motion picture industry" (*In Person* 201). She continues:

> I decided I needed someone I could absolutely trust to talk this over with, someone who had no interest in the business except

my interest. [I]n my dealings with the [. . . Gumm and Shurr Office] I carried with me my habitual distrust of white men. Now when it began to look as if M-G-M were serious about hiring me I called [. . . my father] and said, "I'm alone and don't trust any of these people. Come to me." He quickly agreed. His basic mistrust of white men is so deep he was able to be very cool with the studio people. Flattery and empty promises get you absolutely nowhere with my father. (*Lena* 133–134)

Lena Horne is no fool, and neither is Mr. Horne. Horne practically dismisses the hype behind stardom and glamour. The Hornes' basic mistrust of the powerful white patriarchs means any time a Negro is offered an opportunity by those who hold power, that opportunity has to be interrogated to the fullest, especially when the issue of race enters the picture. The elements of entertainment—stardom and glamour—do not mean the same for Horne as they do for, say, Lana Turner or Marilyn Monroe. True, the studios invest much effort to develop movie roles or star vehicles to accommodate the new talent; the actress is ensured dramatic roles and romantic leads. Horne and her father, however, know the history of Negro women in film, in general, and the empty promises made by the dominant powers to the Negro over time. Horne's telephone call to her father aligns Horne with the Negro family and community—an alignment that crosses the grain in the movie colony, wherein agents and managers are the primary caretakers of film talent and the studio mogul is *the* patriarch of the studio lot.

To grasp the overarching meaning of Mr. Horne's presence at the negotiating table fully, however, we must look at his personal history. Teddy Horne grew up in a New York black upper-middle-class family— one of the first prominent families of Brooklyn—but he prefers the life of the streets to education. At age seven, he skips school to take odd jobs to earn his own money. He is a veritable rascal, and his mother, Cora Calhoun Horne, has to help truant officers take him from various jobs back to school. Through it all, Teddy Horne is a man acutely aware of America's stance toward the Negro and the power of money as well. Horne writes of her father, "Despite his knowledge of the power of money and the independence it bought, he found holding down a regular job, with hours to keep and bosses to heed, became a drag. Also, he hated working for 'the man'" (*Lena* 6). Teddy Horne, then, begins a successful "career" in the gambling spots in Harlem, "the only place a Negro man could make quick money without holding the usual sort of job" (*Lena* 6). So, at an early age Teddy Horne assuages his hunger for independence to appease his character and temperament. As a major player on the gambling scene, Mr. Horne is well groomed in the art of deal making and backroom-barroom politics; plus, by the time Horne asks him to speak for her to Mayer, Teddy Horne is a wealthy self-made man. Teddy Horne owes no man anything. Mayer may be a major force in the movie industry, but Teddy Horne could not give a damn. Teddy Horne's attitude is what Lena Horne has to demonstrate to Mayer.

Horne's call to her father has a greater significance, however. While Mayer turns the gaze on Horne through Davies, Horne returns the gaze through Mr. Horne. This strategy enables Horne's father to legitimate her as daughter, as part of her own father's household; she cannot enter Mayer's harem of women desperate for fame. Additionally, Mr. Horne speaks up for his daughter, man-to-man to Mayer: "I don't want my daughter to work, I want to take care of her myself," Mr. Horne begins. "Now many people are telling her how wonderful it is to be a movie star. But the only colored stars I've seen so far have been waiting on some white star in the picture. I can pay for someone to wait on my daughter if she wants that" (Horne, *Lena* 135). This is a powerful stance. Through her father, Lena put Mayer on notice that he will have to answer to a Negro patriarch if her career is mishandled. Mayer listens, but here is the dig: Mr. Horne makes known, in Mayer's own guest seat, that Negroes are watching movies. Not only are they spectators, but they also are critical thinkers cognizant of their on-screen portrayals. Specifically, Negro men are aware Hollywood casts Negro actresses as mere helpmates to white stars. Mr. Horne repudiates the Hollywood system, but he antagonizes Mayer's entire strategy for building his Hollywood family. If Horne is daddy's little girl, she is Teddy Horne's.

Horne's negotiations of MGM's contract delimit the power of the document. Her consultation with Teddy Horne, simultaneously, displaces Mayer and Davies as parent or master and mistress. Contract theory, according to attorney and culture studies critic Patricia J. Williams, imagines a document that limits the actions and the rights of the individuals therein. Williams observes:

> one of the things that has always impressed me about the law of contract is a certain deadening power it exercises by reducing parties to the passive. It constrains the lively involvement of its signatories by positioning enforcement in such a way that parties find themselves in a passive relationship to a document. [. . .] Contract law reduces life to fairytale. The four corners become parent. (224)

I agree with Williams and I assert Horne exploits the constraints of the contract to her own benefit. Rather than using the master's tools to dismantle his house, Horne uses the contract as a tool for speaking out in the news media about the inequities of the Hollywood system. Not only does she speak out during her tenure at MGM, she continues her critique of Hollywood well after. In other words, Horne recognizes the power of the studio system, and rather than fight the system, she turns it into her own venture for her equality and for other Negro actresses as well.

For example, in an interview with Barry Ulanov in 1947, Horne reiterates that at this particular time in U.S. history, the field is plowed for Hollywood. It is ready for planting: "The time is ripe now for scope in the handling of Negro artists." She rebukes MGM for not giving her movie roles that would boost her career in film: "I guess it isn't telling any secrets to admit that M-G-M kept me in drydock for a long time because I wouldn't play a gambler's floozy in *St. Louis Woman* on Broadway" ("Meet the Real Lena Horne" 14). Although the studio continues to pay her weekly salary, studio development of pictures are few and far between, if at all. So Horne is indeed dry docked, but in body only. She uses the forum of the one-on-one interview to discuss racism in Hollywood and how it precludes the studio from seeing her as other than a singer: "I'm *in* Hollywood but not *of* Hollywood because I'm a Negro. I'd like to do a good serious role in a mixed cast movie instead of being confined to café singer parts" ("Meet" 14). In an interview with Darr Smith in 1949, Horne states that if Hollywood treats the Negro as an actor, rather than as a Negro actor, then the industry itself would grow. Of Horne, Smith writes, "She thinks if she or any other Negro could play in a picture without being identified at once in the script as a Negro, but play it simply as a human being, the motion picture medium would advance immeasurably as an art form" (23). In 1968, Horne relates to *Ebony* magazine she detests the mapping of white actress Hedy Lamarr onto her persona: "What they did was name me in all of their releases the sepia Hedy Lamarr. Now that in itself is an affront. I wouldn't have minded if they'd said [. . . Hedy Lamarr] is a white Lena Horne. That never happened" ("Lena Horne Joins" 134).

Her comments in 1951 to Erskine Johnson, however, are the most telling. In an interview for the *Daily News* (Los Angeles), Johnson asks Horne if she will make another movie for Hollywood. Horne replies, "Doggone it, they keep bringing me stories about South Sea island damsels or poor girls who kill themselves over the love of white men. Or they come to me and say, 'have you a story in mind?' Why should I have a story in mind? They're producing the picture" (19). What is interesting about these remarks is that Horne indicts the studio's presumption that her light skin could pass for other ethnicities and that her own Negro race is unacceptable. Hollywood is more comfortable with its own racist notions of the Negro, preferring the wild and untamed "jungle" and the primitive "jungle bunnies" therein. Correspondingly, Hollywood feels comfortable resting in mammy's bosom. According to Jewell:

> Mammy's large bosom has been described as a haven or safe comfortable place for men to lay their heads. Verta Mae likens mammy's large bosom to that of popular symbols of woman-hood, such as Jayne Mansfield or the Gibson Girl. [. . .] The conspicuousness of mammy's teeth can be attributed to several factors. First during slavery, Europeans and Americans were impressed by the soundness of slaves' teeth. The continuous dis-playing of teeth, in a grin or smile, suggests satisfaction and con-tentment, which was important to the owners. (41)

Horne's physical features are antithetical to those of the mammy character, and the cork makeup does not help fashion her into the Negro MGM thinks she should look like. MGM encourages her, then, to pass for Latina when she arrives. Horne points out she is a Negro and the studio will not de-race her. Horne's subsequent resistance to offer story ideas is her way of casting responsibility back onto the shoulders of those liable for the perpetuation of insidious representations of the Negro in the first place. Furthermore, Horne's insistence on legitimate roles and stories at the onset of her career is the signal to the studio of Horne's interests. Her comments suggest that Hollywood, in 1951, still cannot think of the Negro woman as anything other than a mammy or a subjugated, helpless, and suicidal girl.

By exposing her inequitable treatment in her autobiography and during interviews, Horne shines more light on Hollywood's beliefs about Negro women still holding firm during World War II. In 1942, Horne embarks on a relentless search for respite from the emotional and psy-chological anxieties that accompany her to MGM's studio. The contract is not an end in itself: the document is an important weapon in the con-tinuing campaign for another screen image of the Negro woman and for fair financial treatment of Negroes in Hollywood. Political activist and culture critic Angela Davis will agree:

[. . .] we must climb in such a way as to guarantee that all of our sisters, regardless of social class, and indeed all of our brothers, climb with us. This must be the essential dynamic of our quest for power—a principle that must not only determine our struggles as Afro-American women, but also govern all authentic struggles of dispossessed people. (*Women Culture Politics* 5)

Although Horne's signature causes a major upheaval within the old guard community of Negro actors, her eventual *association* with that Negro community—climbing up through it, wading through it, and affirming it—enables her to find meaning behind the symbol and the star.

Horne turns to the community of Negro actors, musicians, and Negro patriarchy to construct her own family in entertainment. This strategy rejects wholeheartedly Mayer's family along with his harem, and she fully assumes the weight of the contract's attendant sociohistorical and cultural implications. On a larger scale, the entertainer's actions stand up for the shackled African woman on the auction block, whose chattel status affords her no negotiation rights much less parentage; the African women whose voices are silenced between the auctioneer and the master planters; and those African women whose bodies are on display, prodded and probed to determine fitness for labor.

My investigations of Horne's autobiographies *In Person* (1950) and *Lena* (1965), furthermore, untie the common thread of the American Dream: You can be anything in America as long as you are industrious, diligent, and persevere to reach your set goals. Horne's autobiographies indeed testify to her commitment to the precept of the American Dream and to her resultant momentous achievements and triumphs in entertainment. Her pursuit at MGM, however, activates the Negro actress's resistance to Hollywood white patriarchy. Horne makes the symbol stand for the family of Negro Hollywood actors, and each victory she realizes consequently affords black actresses a legitimate space in the predominantly white arena of Hollywood filmmaking.

CHAPTER TWO

Dorothy Dandridge

The Dance of the Black
Female Child Entertainer

Dorothy Dandridge's autobiographical dance, *Everything and Nothing: The Dorothy Dandridge Tragedy* (1970) incorporates a movement that, at heart, is unique. Black female childhood trauma, choreographed along with the overzealous will to perform in the amphitheater of entertainment, distinguishes Dorothy's dance from that of the other women examined herein. Her text turns our attention to a time in her life when she, like many black children growing up in the United States, has no rights and no spokesperson to safeguard her from daily treachery. Dorothy's autobiographical dance of childhood trauma is of paramount importance in light of the recent successful attempts in the 1990s to excavate her from the back shelf of Hollywood history: Her biographer, Donald Bogle, covers the life of the actress in *Dorothy Dandridge: A Biography* (1997); HBO greenlights Academy Award winner Halle Berry's project *Introducing Dorothy Dandridge* (1999) and exhumes the star; with Berry's Golden Globe win for the HBO feature, Berry makes the 1950s screen goddess a household name. These literary and filmic recuperations (re)introduce Dorothy's life and her image to a generation that has all but forgotten her and to a new generation that finds pleasure in her discovery.

We indeed find pleasure in looking at Dorothy Dandridge, the voluptuous, sensuous, alluring, and talented celebrity trailblazer for black women. Dorothy's tale of suffering in her early years, nevertheless, submits an imperative to the public: Each of us will be aware of the child sacrifice that invokes in the audience the awe as well as the desire to gaze on and to revel in the star's accomplishments. Film critic Richard Dyer asserts, "[s]tars are obviously a case of appearance—all we know of them is what we see and hear before us" (*Heavenly Bodies* 2). As (inter)national star and cover girl of the 1950s, Dorothy Dandridge and the fearsome teams managing her career dare not disturb the star's astonishing appearance. But in the 1960s, Dorothy Dandridge amazingly seizes the potential value of the dance on the white page and releases the sobering story of Little Dottie, the child who pays a huge price for the public to have her celebrated image in the first place. Via this narrative we *see* and *remember* the little black girl forfeited for the sake of our own voyeuristic enjoyment. Little Dottie, abused child, the star declares, accompanies every illustrious image of her. If we do not listen to Little Dottie's footsteps on the white page, then, Dorothy Dandridge, for all of her celebrity glory, remains a counterfeit image.

Everything and Nothing joins an ensemble cast of black female writers and autobiographers who query across literary periods the peculiar status of the black child in the United States. This focus on the black child and childhood distress can be traced to slave narratives wherein narrators, including Sojourner Truth (*The Narrative of Sojourner* 1850) and Harriet Jacobs (*Incidents in the Life of a Slave Girl* 1861), give testimony as children who live within the oppressive slave regime. These small voices, according to slave historian Wilma King, largely are ignored, "because they, more than other enslaved persons, were 'silent and invisible'" (xvii).

The slave narrative is not the only literary period that chronicles the plight of the black child in the United States. On reflection, Harlem Renaissance novelist Jesse Redmon Fauset analyzes the observations made by a light skinned child of parents who play the game of passing in *Plum Bun: A Novel without a Moral* (1929); Pulitzer Prize winner Gwendolyn Brooks looks into the effects of color consciousness on her dark-skinned poetic protagonist Maud Martha; and Ann Petry mines the influence of poverty on Bub, a child of eight, living in tenement housing in Harlem in her novel *The Street* (1944). In the 1970s, novelists Toni Morrison and Maya Angelou expand the discourses of black childhood. While they probe the intersections of poverty and racism and their effects on black children, Morrison and Angelou profile child abuse and trauma along the axis. They appraise how these intersections impact young black girls in the midwest and the South in *The Bluest Eye* (Morrison, 1970) and *I Know Why the Caged Bird Sings* (Angelou, 1970).

Dandridge's childhood story continues their tradition in the genre of celebrity autobiography. *Everything and Nothing* generates interest in black children coming of age in the entertainment business, and validates King's assertion that "[c]hildren's history has come of age, and there is now greater interest in the black child than ever before" (xvii). Dorothy's autobiography, a 1970 posthumous publication, finds an easy place in this chorus line of writing and takes a solid position next to Morrison and Angelou.

Everything and Nothing rescues Little Dottie, a young black star, from oblivion. Today, much attention is paid to the troubled childhood of stars such as Drew Barrymore, Tatum O'Neal, Dana Plato, Todd Bridges, Gary Coleman, Macaulay Culkin, and the former "King of Pop" Michael Jackson. Parents of child celebrities, such as Jaid Barrymore, Joe Jackson, and Willie and Sue Coleman now receive widespread currency in the discussion of childhood abuse, a careless disregard for the well-being of their children, or both. These stories, however, are about famous people who are white and male or female or black and male. Dorothy's rescue of Little Dottie surveys the life of a black *female* child whose childhood is abbreviated by her success. *Everything and Nothing*, if anything, moves Negro womanhood and *motherhood* forward as she confers on us Little Dottie's legacy of a working black girl's sacrifice to the entertainment world. While the Dandridges acquire wealth and fame, Dorothy's autobiography shows us that the insatiable drive for success at such an early age is at great cost to her emotional and psychological health. Lurking behind the star's beauty and well-designed look are the bruises Little Dottie endures both physically and emotionally for Dorothy to become Dorothy Dandridge, the star. When we listen to Little Dottie's footsteps on the white page, then, we not only appreciate a little black girl's fear and dread, but we also are moved to applaud her resilience because she ushers Dorothy Dandridge into stardom. As a result, Dandridge's literary dance is really her finest performance and, as a celebrity autobiography, her dance is a powerful addition to the dance of the footsteps by black children on the stage of African-American storytelling.

Dorothy pinpoints the *everything*, the *nothing*, and her subsequent tragedy in her childhood. "Dorothy Dandridge: The Dance of the black Female Child Entertainer" stumbles across a lumbering one-step dance routine of childhood trauma Dorothy weathers in the arena of entertainment. Dandridge's narrative acknowledges that even though Hollywood had its penchant for satisfying U.S. society's cultural norms and mapping onto the black female actress's body its desires and stereotypes on celluloid, the industry only shoulders a modicum of culpability in her tragedy. Dorothy Dandridge, then, arrives on Hollywood's doorstep *already* defective.

Dorothy Dandridge's narrative of childhood trauma is an exceptionally significant text in light of the responses black women made when they heard she was writing her life story in the 1960s. Dorothy discloses at the end of her storytelling:

> One Sunday late in 1964, as I prepared to do this book and held the contract in my hands, I telephoned some friends to break the news. Much to my astonishment they said, "What, an autobiography? Who are you to do an autobiography? What have you accomplished? If you tell your story, you'll set Negro womanhood back a hundred years. You make a damned poor image of a Negro woman. You will do us no good. Nothing in your career has any meaning for the Group." (Dandridge 226)

These reactions are puzzling in light of the star's social and film achievements. Dandridge's nomination for an Academy Award for Best Actress; her marriage to Harold Nicholas, a member of one of Hollywood's most popular and talented black tap dance teams; and her intimate relationships with an entourage of powerful white men, such as actors Peter Lawford and Curt Jürgens and film director Otto Preminger, fully integrate the black woman into the center of the white entertainment industry. Even as early as 1942, guests at her wedding with Harold Nicholas include Oscar-winner Hattie McDaniel, jazz singer Etta Jones, Hollywood choreographer Nick Castle (*Rookies on Parade,* 1941), and other luminaries. The Dandridge/Nicholas union propels her entry into the best of white Hollywood's society as Geri Branton, Dandridge's sister-in-law and best friend, tells Donald Bogle:

> Every once in a while, people like Tyrone Power and of course, Carole Landis and Rita Hayworth and a few daring Whites would mingle with us. [. . .] A lot of White movie stars would come to the Plantation Club. George Raft was a frequent visitor there. Betty Grable and Lana Turner [. . .] too. (Bogle, *Dorothy Dandridge* 115)

Not only does Dandridge cross racial lines in a segregated Los Angeles, Dandridge's stunning beauty, vulnerability, and mixed heritage later facilitate romantic liaisons with Lawford, Preminger, and Jürgens, and these romances fortify her place within an exclusive Hollywood club of white playboys, influential directors, and actors once reserved for white actresses. The Oscar nomination for Best Actress in 1954, however, clinches Dorothy Dandridge's reconfiguration of the black female celebrity. Her inclusion in the lineup of Hollywood white actress darlings such as Grace Kelley, Judy Garland, Audrey Hepburn, and Jane

Wyman brings the black female celebrity full circle in the dance of entertainment at a time when segregation still has a stronghold throughout
the United States.

In spite of her screen goddess distinction and popularity in the
realms of Hollywood culture and celebrity, Dorothy's friends deem her
story to be one unworthy to be told. Where is the "no good" in
Dorothy's story? The dance of black accomplishment certainly is there;
why is it seen as meaningless? The answers are in her childhood narrative. Detailing the salacious details of life as an adult—after all, one can
blame the movie industry—is one thing, but Dandridge's detailed
accounts of childhood trauma in her autobiography put under the
microscope highly revered black institutions. Talking about hidden
secrets of the black mother and church—the pillars of black culture and
society leading and guiding black youth, particularly in the 1960s when
the civil rights movement is at its peak is blasphemous. Perhaps this context explains why Dandridge's autobiography is published in 1970, five
years after her death in 1965.

Trouble in the House of Dandridge: My Father and Mother Fight

Dorothy discloses that, according to her mother, "Cyril [Dandridge] was
no provider" (16); her mother tells her he had no backbone and was
"tied to his mother's apron strings." Cyril and Ruby live with Cyril's
mother, and the daughter-in-law is subject to her mother-in-law's whims
and wishes. Although Cyril gainfully is employed, Ruby claims in her
"Answer and Cross-Petition" to Cyril's "Petition for Divorce and Custody of Children," "[Cyril] failed to provide her with a home; that she
was compelled to live with relatives; . . . that for a considerable period of
time [Cyril] contributed nothing toward her support nor that of their
children" (*Dandridge v. Dandridge*). Ruby yearns for a living environment antithetical to the African American tradition of the extended
family. She, instead, prefers a familial situation that would allow her,
Cyril, and children to bond as a nuclear family—one exclusive of the
mother-in-law.

Trouble soon comes into the Dandridge camp. Like most black
women in the 1920s, Ruby caters to her husband and does the house-
keeping. According to Donald Bogle, this life threatens to stifle Ruby,
who has a hearty enthusiasm for adventure. Cyril Dandridge agrees with
and practices these principles of patriarchal rule in the family by which
the wife subordinates herself to the husband's will. If he determines, for
example, that his family shall reside with his mother, then so be it. As the

primary breadwinner, Cyril expects his wife to take care of the home. Ruby, however, eventually rebels against these rules and "ignored the acceptable social codes of the day" (Bogle, *Dorothy Dandridge* 10).

The conflict between mother-in-law and daughter-in-law only makes the situation worse. Florence Dandridge, Cyril's mother, insists that her daughter-in-law abide by her rules. Ruby complains to her friends, "[s]he couldn't rearrange one thing in the house without fear of a sharp rebuke from Florence[; she] had become a nonperson without any say . . ." (Bogle, *Dorothy Dandridge* 7).

Ruby finally "escapes" the marriage pregnant with Dorothy. Soon, with the one-year-old Vivian and newborn Dorothy in tow, Ruby does what she believes Cyril should have done: find the family their own home. Reflecting his rebellion, in amended and supplemental petition to his divorce suit, Cyril accuses his wife of abandonment. The document reads:

> Plaintiff says that he has always borne himself as a devoted husband to Defendant ever since said marriage. [. . .] that the said defendant without any just cause of legal excuse, abandoned Plaintiff in July, 1921, and remained away from him and their home for six weeks against Plaintiff's objection. [. . .] Defendant likewise abandoned Plaintiff in July, 1922, and has remained away from him ever since. [. . .] He charges Defendant therefore, with willful absence for over three years. (*Dandridge v. Dandridge*)

When she uproots herself from the Dandridge household, Ruby severs her husband from any and all ties of fatherhood, she denies him access to his children under all circumstances, and she prohibits him from having any contact with them, even though Cyril desperately wants to be a part of their lives. According to Bogle, after Dorothy's birth, Ruby marshals the strength of will—even in the turbulent 1920s—to close the door on that chapter of her life:

> [She] wanted nothing more to do with [. . . Cyril]. If it were possible, she would have erased him completely from her memory. For many years, she managed to erase him from the memory of her daughters, who as children never saw their father, and for years would never know some of the more complicated reasons why their mother had left him. The girls were raised believing Cyril had no interest in them. And for some years, Ruby even told them that he was dead. Later she admitted he was still

living but claimed he had deserted them. (Bogle, *Dorothy Dandridge* 9)

The survival of the family now becomes Ruby's responsibility, and she faces it with all of her strength. The transition from wife to single mother tests her mettle, and she realizes she can carry on alone. The successful passage, however, transmutes her dream of becoming an entertainer into an unbridled lust for a career in show business at the expense of her children. Her departure from patriarchal tradition (marriage, domestic life) jeopardizes the well-being of her daughters in other ways as well. Ruby takes away the possibility for Dorothy to be known as a grandchild and to know a grandmother. In Dorothy's autobiography, she refers to her grandmother as a "mother-in-law." Ruby's far-reaching steps indeed demonstrate incredible resolve, but Dorothy writes revealingly of her mother's desperate move to oust Cyril Dandridge and replace him with another woman, Eloise Mathews, also known as Mrs. Geneva Williams. Ruby, apparently, has another hunger to feed that ties directly to her personal need for artistic expression. Dorothy writes, "A *proxy parent* came into the picture. This *substitute father*—that is what it *turned out* to be [. . .]" (18; my emphasis). The phrases "proxy parent" and "substitute father" imply a relationship beyond that of mere friendship between the two women. Not only does Ruby Dandridge sidestep social convention by leaving her marriage, Dorothy tells us quite shrewdly her "progressive" black mother flouts the *heterosexual* norm, which explains "the more complicated reasons" for Ruby's departure from Cyril and his family. Dorothy's mother is a lesbian at a time when being so definitely was avant-guarde in the black community. It is not so much that the Dandridge/Williams pact is wrong—on the contrary—it bespeaks a kind of feminist independence. This independence is bolstered by the vibrant 1920's era of the flapper whereby some women exploit a new sexual freedom. Ruby's decisions suggest this era's appeal to and influence on her. The interaction between the two women, however, quite possibly opens the way for confusion in two girls whose community of the 1920s and 1930s may not reflect what they have at home. Fortunately, that the girls are entertainers shields the family from all-out scrutiny from the community. Dorothy clearly knows her mother and Mrs. Williams are lovers. Bogle explains:

[b]y the late 1930s, Dorothy and Vivian no doubt fully understood the nature of Ruby's and Neva's relationship. Neither sister used the word lesbian to describe that relationship. They would grapple with fully accepting it for years to come. . . . As

Ruby became better known as an actress, so, too, did the stories of her sexual proclivities. Dorothy McConnell, who as a little girl had played with Dorothy in Cleveland, said that upon later moving to Los Angeles in 1957, she heard stories all over town that Ruby was a lesbian. . . . (Bogle, *Dorothy Dandridge: A Biography* 50, 107)

To express her sexuality, Ruby tears down the heterosexual familial model and inserts an impressive matriarchal one that later evolves into one of the most formidable star-making machines to rival Hollywood's.

Ruby's revolt, however, eradicates Dorothy's father and leaves Dorothy little choice but to form negative opinions of him. This is accomplished by a clever scheme that consists of an "attack" on Christmas Eve; it is a scheme that conflates the black father with the venerable (white) patriarch for all children—Santa Claus. Ruby commands her daughters to wait upstairs in anticipation of jolly old St. Nick; but in reality, Cyril Dandridge is scheduled to appear with gifts for the children. "Santa" arrives, but bears "gifts" of violence and fear. Dorothy remembers:

In a little while, we heard Santa arrive. Instantly there was a rising of voices. We couldn't hear what was said, although we listened hard. Santa was fighting with Mother. Bitter, hard arguing. I grew afraid of Santa Claus. I said to Vivian, "I hate Santa Claus." Vivian and I began to cry. We cried because it was fearful and violent below. [. . .] Finally we heard the door slam. [. . .] Mother peeked into our quarters and told us to come out. "Stop crying," she said. "Your father is gone. In the morning you'll find nice things on the tree." (17)

Little Dottie, then, comes to associate her father with fear and violence, the mystery of Christmas and Santa Claus, and gifts after the storm. Santa/Cyril fights with mother, on a night when mother has filled the house with holiday excitement and decorations. In little Dottie's mind, Santa Claus's arrival shatters the atmosphere of merriment Ruby meticulously creates for her and her sister. More important, in Dorothy's eyes, Santa Claus/Cyril threatens her mother's safety.

The Christmas Eve scene is significant for another reason. Dorothy's story infers that Mrs. Dandridge stages and manipulates the entire ruckus for her and her children's benefit. It is part of Ruby's strategy to create an invisible audience of daughters pressed to discern the truth of the scene only through the voices. In effect, Ruby plants the idea firmly in her daughters' minds that their father, and by extension all males including Santa Claus, bring nothing but conflict and hurt. Santa Claus/Cyril has to be eliminated from the family's lives. That Ruby tells the children to come out from the upstairs attic after the argument indicates that she knows her children are listening. The scene's denouement, moreover, crowns Ruby the victor. The children recognize her as the conqueror who rescues them from the "malefic bearer of gifts." Ruby keeps the hearth and home safe from the intruder ("Your father is gone"), and saves the family's boon of Christmas gifts in the process ("you'll find nice things on the tree"). This Christmas event purges the last vestige of her one possible guardian-protector—her father—from Dottie's life. In essence, Dorothy connects the Christmas Eve debacle to the final disintegration of her innocence and childhood and the installation of her mother's lover. This occurs when she is between age three and six.

Because the mother abnegates the father, Dottie assumes the companionate role to the parent, occupying the father's space, until Mrs. Williams arrives at least, and attempts to keep the family intact. Dottie seeks this role because Cyril's absence causes her to be hyperpossessive of her mother:

> I had a jealous regard for my mother. I wouldn't let men sit beside her in church. [. . .] I did this over and over again, not allowing men to be near my Mother; [. . .] I could tell when a chastising was due from her for this offense. I said to Vivian, "I'm in for it now." Mother berated me for my possessiveness. I had no father, knew no father. It had something to do with that. (21)

This passage informs us of Dottie's desire to fill the gap her father left and to obstruct any other man in his pursuit of it. She further notes her mother's dissatisfaction with the girl's struggles against potential suitors. Ruby does not understand the effects the separation from her father has on Dottie. Furthermore, by berating her, Ruby betrays her unavailability as a nurturer and counselor "over and over again." Dottie is seen as an unnecessarily possessive child, when what she requires is her mother's assurance that she holds a central emotional presence in her life.

Ruby's extrication of Cyril from Dottie's life no doubt motivates the child to cling to her mother. This relentless campaign on the mother's part establishes an anxiety-ridden father-daughter meeting when Dorothy is fourteen. Cyril fights for custody and visitation rights through the court system, until finally on June 6, 1933, when Dorothy is eleven years old, Cyril files a final petition for divorce, "pray[ing] that he be divorced from said defendant, [Ruby Dandridge]" (*Dandridge v. Dandridge*). Cyril meets Dorothy for the first time since the Santa incident when she is a successful performer in an ensemble called the Dandridge Sisters (Dorothy, Vivian, and Etta Jones)—ten years after the Christmas Eve fiasco. The distance from childhood to that point makes for an extremely awkward meeting between father and daughter. Dorothy believes her father contacts her only because of the popularity of the "Wonder Kids." Both parties are stunned on first contact. Cyril's "slight and meek" manner surprises Dorothy because she expects "a man with a big chest, a diamond clip on his tie—a dramatized and outsized version of a man" (49–50). She immediately identifies the similarities between them, however: "I knew who he was as he walked up to us, for I recognized in his facial features a similarity to my own" (50). Her father's first words to her at the meeting in her apartment, however, distress her:

> "Stand up, Dorothy."
> I stood.
> "Turn around, daughter."
> I turned, like a model.
> "Turn around again."
> I turned again, like a mannequin on wheels.
> "You're very pretty."
> I wanted to disappear. It didn't matter to me whether I ever saw him again. (50–51)

When Cyril gazes Dorothy, his very first request is for her to perform before him. He notes her appearance before he asks about her health, happiness, or emotional well-being. Her father solicits from her what the audience and her mother demand every night: to display herself and act before them. More jarring is Dorothy's use of nouns peculiar to the fashion industry, "model" and "mannequin." Her father's gaze looks past her, his human breathing daughter, toward a perceived, made-up, manufactured spectacle, first to be looked at and then approved. By using the term "mannequin," Dorothy's text suggests she feels her father regards her as a "life-size full or partial representation of the human body or a dummy" (*Merriam-Webster*). At first, she is Dorothy, the person; as she turns, she becomes daughter-model-mannequin-pretty thing. These "model turns" dehumanize Dorothy amidst forced smiles and in the presence of her sister Vivian and Mrs. Williams. Cyril's gesture represents the absence of a real relationship and illustrates the success of Ruby's efforts to keep father and daughters apart during the girls' formative years. Trying to find some entry into her life, Cyril starts with the daughter put before him, but after the meeting, Dorothy desperately wants to disappear because her father's gaze makes her feel somehow dehumanized and molested. The schism Ruby made between father and daughters has taken hold, and with a vengeance.

In her text, however, Dorothy (re)members the severed part of herself in reclaiming the shards of her paternal inheritance. To begin with, she keeps her father's name, Dandridge. Dorothy Jean Dandridge is the legitimate daughter of Cyril Dandridge. She has a father. Second, even though she cites the "melting pot" characteristics of her maternal grandmother, Dorothy attributes the majority of her racial hybridity to her father. She writes, "much of my mixture descends from the father I never knew as a child. [. . .] [H]e was the son of a white British gentleman and an African woman [. . .]" (15–16). Although her father treats her like a mannequin, and her mother and lover have made her into one, Dorothy makes herself into a person by accepting her father as a part of her heritage.

Bereft of a father figure, despite her later claim of his paternal legacy, Dottie observes her mother's courage and strength of will during the hard economic times of the Great Depression. What will become the Dandridge/Williams team, however, proves to be a razor-sharp, double-edged sword. On one side, Mrs. Williams's early tutelage instills in Dottie a stern discipline and hard-core work ethic; in the future, this earns the actress a lucrative career in film and café society, the biggest payoff of which came in 1954, when Dandridge receives an Academy Award nomination for Best Actress for her portrayal of Carmen Jones in the film of the same name. At the awards ceremony March 30, 1955, Dandridge projects a composite of charm and poise; she is a tremendous beauty projecting (upper) middle class mobility nationwide. Her look, Dandridge maintains, complements the "melting pot characteristics" in the United States (Dandridge 15). The Dandridge/Williams team's mercenary undertaking manufactures one of Hollywood's first African-American sex goddesses, leading ladies, and Oscar nominees.

On the other edge of the sword, the Dandridge/Williams dyad turns Dorothy into a virtual human commodity, and this team is preoccupied with youth, money, titles, and, of course, stardom. Dorothy marries Harold Nicholas, for instance, largely because of his potential to amass wealth. She explains:

> The Nicholas brothers were moving up in the entertainment world. Harold had talent and money and a career before him [. . .] you'll thrill as hard if a guy shows he can pay the rent.

[. . .] My mind was made up when the Nicholas Brothers
secured a contract with Twentieth Century Fox in Hollywood."
(Dandridge 59)

The Dandridge/Williams partnership molds Dorothy Dandridge into
a veritable product of the entertainment trade, practically devoid of an
interior life. Excessively primed and groomed since age three, Dottie and
Vivi transform from child prodigies to products of the entertainment
industry. In the process, Ruby and her lover fail to equip Dorothy with
the internal grounding necessary for survival in a business focused exclusively on the external. Hard work puts food on the table—has to—and
maintains an affluent lifestyle with unimaginable material luxuries. In
what ways, however, does the sacrifice of an interior life make material
gain worthwhile? The childhood trauma she experiences (discussed
shortly) affects every one of Dorothy's relationships, and before her
death she squanders her energy on many men who treat her badly. As I
argue here, Ruby's lack of intervention on behalf of her daughter results
in Dandridge's lack of self-worth as well as an inability to make sound
financial decisions and healthy choices in relationships with men.

The actress enters Hollywood a burnished sex goddess with blinders
on, fixated solely on the American Dream. Her exotic beauty supposedly
transcends race and makes certain she will achieve status as an *American*
movie star just as Walter White had hoped Lena Horne's extraordinary
beauty would. The first line of Dandridge's autobiography reads:

"Exotically beautiful saloon singer of the Western World," the
critics called me. They never went in for the understatement.
". . . One of the great beauties of our time, a sex symbol to magazine editors the world over, and Hollywood's first authentic
love goddess of color." I had been pursued and courted by leading Caucasian film people, North Americans, South Americans,
and Europeans. (1)

The world crowns her an international star by the 1950s. Even
though in the end Dandridge implies that the experiment of using the
light-skinned Negro woman as the symbol of a new Negro womanhood
fails, the more pointed message is that every effort made by Ruby and
her lover to mold Dandridge into a star and a product works. The exclusive concentration on celebrity and success, and economic prosperity,
however, renders Dandridge defenseless in a culture "in search of beautiful flesh" (Dandridge 22). As well, her autobiography makes clear that

behind the glamour lay a damaged child whose story would not be known until she found the courage to tell it.

Ruby Dandridge and her lover, Geneva Williams (or Auntie Ma-ma), choreograph each step for the young Dorothy and the church stages her first performances. From the time she is three years old, Mrs. Dandridge, Mrs. Williams, and the black church subject Dottie to hefty doses of greed through child labor exploitation: she is subjected to physical and sexual abuse, emotional deprivation, and maternal abandonment. To keep the dance going, her mother cuts Dorothy's father out of her life, and the child star grows up not knowing a father's love. Dorothy even likens her start on the stage to the religious sphere, christening it an "abnormally early baptism in show business" (20). These misdeeds occur in the domestic sphere in gothic proportions, replete with "unusual" marital arrangements, sinister adult behaviors, and corrupt domestic business practices, which Dorothy Dandridge—the toddler, the teenager, the adult/star—must hold secret for her daily survival. The plan of action Ruby adopts—a poor single black mother living in the midwest—to bypass the degrading occupation of domestic in the households of whites and to cross the border of poverty into economic security and middle class status may distract us from a close inspection of her daughter's childhood trauma, but it is important that we make one.

"The Dance of the Black Female Child Entertainer" answers Dorothy's entreaty for an investigation into her "crying childhood" (18), the root of her adult life tragedy. Indeed, the tragedy of Dorothy Dandridge is set in motion in the sphere that should protect her, the home. Her mother's staggering poverty and the psychologically crippling occupation of domestic servitude incite a grievous dance of incidents. The parties involved mean no harm—not, anyway, in the strictest sense—and each has relatively good intentions, but the damage inflicted on Dorothy as a child will be lifelong.

The Poem Recited in the Kitchen:
The Making of Little Dottie, Child Star

Something happens for this commanding matriarchal dance to take place for Dottie. The story begins in the kitchen in Cleveland, Ohio. Ruby Dandridge—single mother of two, singer, dancer, and acrobat—groans over another night's performance scheduled at a church social to recite Paul Laurence Dunbar's "In the Morning." The poem "had been a favorite piece" of her mother's (Dandridge 12). That Dorothy reveals

"In the Morning" as her mother's best-liked poem forecasts parental discord and a contempt with which her mother holds for her father that would play itself out for the rest of Dorothy's life. Dorothy summarizes Dunbar's rhymes as "a ballad about a man named Elias who sleeps all the time, and his wife couldn't get him awake in time to do any work" (12). Fatigue sets in from one more day of work. Seeing her mother's weariness, three-year-old Dottie offers to go in her stead. Ecstatic and relieved, Ruby agrees. Dottie's desire to relieve her mother of her weariness indicates how eager she always will be to please her. As Dottie recites the poem in the home space of nourishment—the "center of the kitchen"—Ruby immediately places a price tag on the performance—"a great big fifty cents" (Dandridge 13). "I'll make you a promise," says Mrs. Dandridge, grabbing her baby daughter up in her arms. "If you go out there and do [Dunbar] for me, and you don't cry, when you get home I'll give you a great big fifty cents" (Dandridge 13).

The mother's tactic, however, formulates a dubious equation no matter the intent, for her promise of payment correlates with the tradition of blacks in entertainment dancing for white people's money. From her mother's knee, Dottie learns that performance generates money and also produces the motherly regard and attention she is seeking inside the home rather than outside in the impersonal space of the theater. Dottie commits to memory the skits and poems she watches her mother dramatize as she accompanies her to every performance. She has paid attention to detail, ". . . engrossed in Ruby's every move, mood, gesture, vocal inflection, and change of expression" (Bogle, *Dorothy Dandridge* 14). The stage and its demand for rehearsal time, nevertheless, separate an already physically overtaxed mother from her child, and leave the domestic sphere open only for expressions of enervation. Dottie, then, strictly speaking is spectator/daughter to her mother and, therefore, consumer of all Ruby makes available to her outside of the home. Three-year-old Dottie's innocent bid that night in the kitchen signifies a child's longing to be nearer a mother whose presence is truncated by the dispiriting socioeconomic conditions of the 1920s. Struggling for money, she tells us, is a "childhood hassle" that "left a scar of anxiety upon [me]" (36).

That the appreciation Dottie receives for "taking care of mother" eventually situates her as the secondary wage earner for the Dandridge household means financial relief for the family. The need to dance up and over their lower socioeconomic status of domestic servitude yields the coveted middle-class status and ladyhood of the mother's aspirations. After Dottie excels in her recitation of the poem, Mrs. Dandridge conceives of a way out of domestic servitude for her daughter: "You ain't going to work in 'Mister Charley's kitchen' like me. I don't want you to go into service. You['re] not going to be a scullery maid. We're going to fix it so you['ll] be something else than that" (Dandridge 14).

The sphere of "Mr. Charley's kitchen" places the Negro woman at the beck and call of white employers and their family members, often resulting in victimization. Harriet Jacobs's slave narrative, *Incidents in the Life of a Slave Girl* (1861), recounts the strategies the slave, Linda Brent, must use to thwart the sexual advances of Dr. Flint as she serves as a domestic in his household. She must avoid the extreme jealousy of Mrs. Flint as well. Brent manages to avoid Dr. Flint's overtures on several occasions, but he terrifies her at every turn. Brent says, "I hitherto succeeded in eluding my master, though a razor was often held to my throat to force me to change this line of policy" (36).

A further example of the sometimes humiliating treatment of Negro servants is dramatized in the film *The Divine Secrets of the Ya-Ya Sisterhood* (dir. Callie Khouri, 2002). In one scene, a white mother allows her adolescent son to berate their black maid at breakfast. The maid, Willetta, has accompanied the Ya-Ya sisters—Necie, Viviane, and Teensy—on a trip to Atlanta to see the premiere of *Gone with the Wind* (dir. Victor Fleming, 1939), itself a racist film. The morning of the opening, Willetta enters the dining room to serve her wards hot chocolate, while the mother, Aunt Louise, and the children discuss the possibility of Margaret Mitchell's appearing at the premiere. When Willetta enters, James, Jr., interrupts the conversation. "Who told you you could walk your black ass into our dining room? You got ears nigga? Get on outta here!" he shouts. The camera focuses on Aunt Louise, but there is no reprimand from this authority figure. The medium close-up shot on Aunt Louise's silence points out the liberties white adults have allowed children to take with grown-up black domestic servants.

Domestic servitude makes Mrs. Dandridge and her daughters vulnerable to the threat of similar humiliating occurrences in "Mr. Charley's kitchen," but her motivation for shielding her daughters from that threat has less to do with protection of them and more to do with an absolute thirst to augment the household's income. Mrs. Dandridge believes "two adorable entertaining children could make far more money than [. . . she] ever could being a cook or maid" (Bogle, *Dorothy Dandridge* 25). Her interventions include "drill[ing] [the girls] in memorizing poetry, explaining how to punch or emphasize important lines, how to smile and laugh at certain moments, how to pull for emotion in others. She taught them to sing, dance, and perform acrobatics—*just as her father had done with her*" (Bogle, *Dorothy Dandridge* 15; my emphasis). Ruby's attention to performance minutiae continues her father's legacy of artistic development. By immersing her daughters in the quotidian regimen of drama, Ruby links herself, as well as her daughters, to a broader black history and tradition of turning to grueling work schedules in entertainment. The mother's dance, nevertheless, evolves into a ferocious quest for economic relief from poverty and welfare in that the children cease to be daughters and become exclusively child commodities sold on the celebrity meat market.

The "fix-it" person who makes this all possible is another black woman, when Mrs. Dandridge accepts wholeheartedly into the Dandridge home a preacher's wife, Mrs. Geneva Williams. Her presence is another intervention Mrs. Dandridge makes to prevent her daughters from a life of domestic servitude. Employment as a domestic uses the skills of cooking, cleaning, and sewing; it is the occupation awaiting the majority of young Negro women once they enter the labor force. Negro girls are hard-pressed to find occupations using any other skills. Although Ruby Dandridge's father offers his children the luxuries of music lessons and religion, "[s]till [they] didn't help [. . . Ruby] much in the early years, for like most Negro girls, she was in Mister Charley's kitchen where she was scrubbing and cooking . . ." (Dandridge 15). The mother hands over her daughters to Mrs. Williams to pursue aggressively her own career in entertainment. A perfect arrangement develops: Mrs. Dandridge anoints Mrs. Williams the primary caretaker of the home, chaperone of the children, and, more important, manager and talent coach for the girls. Mrs. Dandridge assumes responsibility as the principal breadwinner for the family working as a domestic by day and an entertainer by night. Mrs. Dandridge and Mrs. Williams enlist another partner, the black church, which provides the venue for the Dandridge family to hone the group's techniques in singing, dancing, and acting. The institution plays a major part in their careers as it propels the group to financial stability and fame.

The Wonder Kids and the Black Church

The black church has built a solid reputation as the master cultivator of young black talent who later mature into some of the top entertainers in show business. Mount Moriah Baptist Church in Atlanta, Georgia, for example, polishes the elegant skills of Gladys Knight before the Pips join her. Knight develops self-assurance and self-esteem as a singer while a member of the church choir. Knight recalls:

It was a very secure feeling to worship as a family [at Mount Moriah]. I believe our shared religious background and the principles that were instilled in us in those early years helped to nurture us through childhood and then guided us in relative safety into our adult years. [. . .] My first solo recital at Mount Moriah was but one of the many showcases that parents provided for their children in order to build their self-esteem. (26)

Aretha Franklin also sharpens her vocal talents in her father's church in Detroit, Michigan's New Bethel Baptist. She writes:

When I was nine or ten, I sang my first solo in church. [. . .] Big mama was right there in her favorite seat, nodding her approval and encouraging me with all the power and passion of her faith. [. . .] The church gave me comfort. Like my father, the church always gave me a special kind of love. (13, 22)

For Dottie, however, the black church delivers an "ecclesiastical weariness which no child should have . . ." (Dandridge 29). This "ecclesiastical weariness" differentiates Dorothy's church performance narrative from Aretha's and Gladys' narratives. The Franklins and the Knights delight in Aretha and Gladys as child prodigies whose talents can uplift the race. In the church, Aretha and Gladys gather comfort, encouragement, and love from the community. The black community, the church, and the family protect these young black girls from being exploited as children in entertainment. Class is the major factor affecting these black female entertainers: Aretha and Gladys grow up in solid middle-class families, and their class status leaves room for a concentration on nourishment of seeds of self-worth and confidence within them. Poverty coupled with the welfare system assault the Dandridge family daily, and that Mrs. Dandridge takes advantage of every available means of labor to supplement the family's income is not surprising.

The Great Depression causes an obsession over bills, and although Ruby boldly faces the consequences of leaving her husband, Dorothy relates, "my mother worked, worried, faced fears of the landlord, and carried the burden of food-getting because she had the complete economic responsibility" (Dandridge 19). Barely six years old, Dottie witnesses her mother's daily efforts to find work in depression era Cleveland, Ohio. She watches as her mother asks for food from the welfare office and fights with welfare workers in her own home. Dorothy recollects, "For a time [. . . mother] was on WPA [Works Progress Administration money] with the Hall Johnson Choir earning about

ninety-two dollars a month, and I recall the bitter visits of welfare workers who came to see whether Mother deserved the ninety-two dollars"
(Dandridge 36). The management of the "business" of government assis-
tance—an outside source of conflict—infects the family, and Ruby and
her lover look to Dottie and Vivi to subsidize the household income. The
way out of economic hardship comes through the girls dancing in the
community halls of the black church.

The minister's wife refines the talents of Dottie and Vivi to the
extent that the Dandridge Sisters become the hottest national Negro girl
group by the mid-1930s. The children earn a place in Negro entertainment after paying their dues performing on the church circuit, billed as
the Wonder Kids. As the Wonder Kids, Dottie and Vivi are a dynamic
duo of pure entertainment, skilled in role-playing, singing, acrobatics,
and tap dancing. The Dandridge/Williams alliance shape-shifts into a
star-making operation, producing a profitable Negro girl group to entertain through the 1940s. Mrs. Williams quickly assesses and concentrates
on the girls' talents. So popular are the Wonder Kids that "in every
town, on arriving, [Dottie and Vivi] always saw posters on the church
lawns of the coming of the Wonder Kids. First, Second, and Third Baptist Churches" (Dandridge 27).

Dorothy's careful documentation of the scripts of the "swift little
entertainments" her mother prepares for her daughters to perform publicizes more of the "ecclesiastical weariness" she experiences (Dandridge
14). Some of the skits Ruby composes for her children have adult
themes, such as insurance scams. At least one skit Dorothy describes the
Wonder Kids performing has highly charged sexual overtones:

> I did a parody of Al Jolson's "Sonny Boy" [. . .] Offstage I
> was handed a candy bar called Chocolate Bunny Boy, and then I
> went on:
> Climb into my mouth, Bunny Boy,
> You were meant for me, Bunny Boy . . .
> I went down on my knees, as Al did, to that chocolate bar. I
> emoted and salivated over it. Halfway through the song, the
> crowd was always in a gale of amusement. At last I received my
> reward—I gobbled the candy, going at it greedily as a little boy
> might, while the audience applauded. (Dandridge 27)

In this section of her autobiography, Dorothy exposes the black church's
underside of insatiable appetite for bawdy entertainment. According to
her, secular entertainment and religion seemingly go hand-in-hand:
"Night after night I stared into a sea of dark faces. . . . We gave a per-

formance for adults one evening, and the next night we entertained the kids" (Dandridge 26). The institution not only saves souls; it also enjoys a particular sort of risqué performance. The simulation of oral sex prepared by her mother is pornographic, and Dottie's performance stirs up the congregation's emotions to a tempestuous high and brings the group to an explosive climax of applause—night after night. Her mother "knew how to exploit [. . . the] smallness and vitality" of the Wonder Kids (Dandridge 24).

Cross-dressing allows these routines to be played as "harmless" sketches. Mrs. Dandridge and Mrs. Williams outfit Dottie and Vivi as "two urchin boys, with caps on [their] heads, knee pants, [their] pockets bulging with string and clothespins" (Dandridge 24). These costumes signify traditional gender roles in which little boys are urchins in the street running scams for pocket change; little boys usually go on fishing trips; as little girls, Dottie and Vivi participating in activities traditionally assigned to boys will cause the audience discomfort. Picture Dottie performing as a girl in the chocolate bunny boy skit, for instance. Dressed as energetic little boys, the Wonder Kids placate concerns the church crowd might have about exploiting the girls' sexuality. The child actresses are too cute and too sweet dressed as boys and provide pure family entertainment!

In spite of the inappropriate nature of the skit for a child, Dottie comes to like it because performing in such an adult way gives her a sense of control she lacks in her off-stage life. She holds the church assembly in the palm of her hands as she determines when to eat that chocolate bunny boy. She also gains a sense of power and learns how her own body brings the multitudes to a climax. Dorothy derives sensual pleasure as well, because her chocolate gratification, combined with the response from the crowd, relieves her anxiety over conditions at home with a sense of welcome from strangers, acceptance of her as an appealing kid, and bodily pleasure.

Another aspect of the Wonder Kids' routine involves selling autographed photographs of themselves and interacting with members of the audience backstage:

> We stood backstage while people filed by, shook hands, and asked us silly questions: Do you like dancing better than singing? How long have you and your sister been doing this? Do you miss going to school? "I don't know," I answered, "I've never been to school." Everything was pointed toward taking in money. There is an education in that, if nothing else. (Dandridge 28)

Dorothy's sharing with church members the fact that she does not go to school is a cry for help and a signal for someone to recognize the sisters' exploitation. Clearly, the heavy emphasis on making money overshadows basic child care issues, such as literacy and health. For all of her stage work, Dottie comprehends very early that money and performance settle in the same hand. This description of scenes backstage perhaps is the saddest facet of all in Dorothy's early professional life because she uncovers the crowd's awareness that two young girls are responsible for fulfilling their appetite for entertainment at the expense of their education. These church patrons, however, ignore the sacrifice Vivi and Dottie make to entertain them. Even though Auntie Ma-ma homeschools Dottie and Vivi, the "grinding, blurry, abnormal childhood" the children endure clearly affect their ability to concentrate on their studies (Dandridge 31). She remembers, "As I was admitted into the fourth grade, my education couldn't have been too much neglected. But I didn't know how to read" (Dandridge 35).

There's an Ogre in the House: Where's Momma?

Mrs. Dandridge's strategies conform to the tenets of the American work ethic, especially the "pull yourself up by your bootstraps" credo. Specifically, this mother's imaginative construction of a black family during the 1930s concurs with feminist and social critic Angela Davis's assertion, ". . . Black people, both during and after the slave era, have been compelled to build, creatively and often improvisationally, a family life consistent with the dictates of survival" (*Women Culture Politics* 75). The merciless imposition of the American work ethic on herself and her children, however, transforms Mrs. Dandridge into an indifferent and irresponsible stage mother. Dorothy experiences physical abuse from Mrs. Williams because Ruby's absences allow her to take unrestrained liberties with the girls. As I describe later, Dorothy makes known the violence Mrs. Williams shells out at will.

Dorothy describes Williams as "a proxy parent," "substitute father," "ogre," and, more eerily, "near-sinister creature," for whom she "developed a permanent fear and hate" (Dandridge 18). Her description indicts Mrs. Williams as a malevolent functionary who riddles the child's life with unwarranted suffering and pain. Her portrayal also makes clear the intimacy between her mother and "the creature" to whom she has entrusted the children. The "cruel and incessant discipline" she receives at the hands of Mrs. Williams leads Dorothy to describe these years as her "crying childhood" (18, 19). Describing Mrs. Williams as an "ogre" and "near-sinister creature" conjures up baleful images from a child's nightmare or a horror film. In Dottie's living space, the dance of the bogey-woman informs her daily reality as that nightmare figure comes out from under the bed living and breathing, walking around the house with an insatiable appetite to menace her innocent victims. Dorothy writes:

> This woman who, from the first, became an ogre to me, stayed with us until we grew up and until I could break away from her. Now you don't do that, you do this, slap, bang, wallop, do what I tell you, be good, that's bad, bang, wallop. I had a crying childhood. This mistreatment could occur because my mother was always at work and didn't know what was going on, and when I told her, it seemed not to register, nor to alter the whippings in any way. [. . .] (18–19)

Here Dorothy exposes the onomatopocia of her childhood brutality. She is a virtual hostage in her own home with an authority figure raging war therein. bell hooks would observe, in her "family" Dorothy is "the true victim [. . .] of intimate terrorism in that [she has] no collective voice and no rights. [She] remain[s] the property of parenting adults to do with as they will." hooks continues:

> There is nothing that creates more confusion about love in the minds and hearts of children than unkind and/or cruel punishment meted out by the grownups they have been taught they should love and respect. [. . .] [T]housands of children in our culture are verbally and physically abused, starved, tortured, and murdered. They are the true victims of intimate terrorism in that they have no collective voice and no rights. They remain the property of parenting adults to do with as they will. (*All About Love* 17–18, 19)

Dandridge's rendition of her caretaker's violent behavior reveals her mother's refusal to run interference for her child, which had to produce a sense of supreme vulnerability and feelings of betrayal. The ruthless condition of poverty coupled with the strong desire to be lifted out of it blind Ruby to the uninterrupted terror meted out on Dottie at home. In this way, Dorothy's childhood dance complicates the more popular notions of black motherhood and the black family as protective forces in a culture of racism. Certainly Dorothy feels cared for in some sense, and she does have a strong mother. Mrs. Dandridge's temerity and spirited independence carry the family through many economic hardships and, despite the poverty, she turns the house into a home. Dorothy remembers, "[w]e had poorer food. [. . .] The dinner table had cheap meat—chitlin's, pig's knuckles, everything from the pig—and grits and potatoes; *but mother baked bread that was good*" (Dandridge 33; my emphasis). Ruby's deeply flawed maternal dance step, nevertheless, subverts the pristine model of black motherhood—even black sisterhood—celebrated in black culture. Dorothy argues that, for her, the prototype of the loving and protective black mother widely heralded in the black community does not exist. Nor is there present, for that matter, the benevolent black female elder.

Dorothy must find her own way out of this cruel situation because Ruby is unavailable. Until she is able to do so, survival means taking the abuse, even expecting it. Auntie Ma-ma's "whacking away" at Dorothy's backside is, conceivably, her method of instilling in the young entertainer obedience and discipline in the arts, but Dorothy's dance begs a closer inspection of Mrs. Williams's barbarous acts. Mrs. Williams practices extreme caution so that her beatings do not draw attention, and this strategic behavior is our cue to see it as abuse. Mrs. Williams knows exactly what she is doing, and she calculates where to place each of her strokes. That Mrs. Williams takes care to "punish" Dorothy on her backside rather than on her face, arms, and legs means the battering is hidden. Marks from the beatings neither will alarm the public, nor will they impair the visual image Dorothy presents to it. That Dottie's bruised flesh remains hidden means there is no verification of it. Secrecy and silence, then, become Dorothy's lone recourses.

Auntie Ma-ma releases an inherent meanness, and practices it on a whim. Dorothy concedes, in spite of this, "[i]t's conceivable that I received some kind of training or teaching from her which was helpful in show business," and that "[s]he cultivated our talents. She considers she is helping to make something of us" (Dandridge 19). As a step-mother-father-anointed chaperone, Mrs. Williams installs a "strict, highly structured, repetitive regime of rehearsals—for hours daily—in dancing, singing, and acrobatics [with] unending drills and rehearsals" that went well into the night (Bogle, *Dorothy Dandridge* 17). Dorothy quickly asserts of these rehearsal periods, "in nothing did she endear herself to me," and "I am unable to look back upon her overseership of me for a period of fifteen years with any gratitude. . . . She had ability behind her stern nature, and she slammed it into me" (Dandridge 19). This particular statement and others throughout Dorothy's narrative of childhood abuse are significant for her assessment of the physical pain she suffers under Auntie Ma-ma. Her analysis, in addition, points the reader to the more significant aspect of her abuse. Dorothy's phrase "slammed it into me," connects Mrs. Williams to an aggressive assault on Dottie's *interior* emotional life, which can have more brutal effects than the physical.

Dorothy reminds us that Dottie's household is lacking its protective nurturing function, and runs counter to bell hooks' assertion that since slavery, the black family has provided a space for self-affirmation of its members:

> [Home space] was about the construction of a safe place where black people could affirm one another and by so doing heal many of the wounds inflicted by racist domination. [. . .] We could not learn to love or respect ourselves in the culture of white supremacy, on the outside; it was there on the inside, in that "homeplace," most often created and kept by black women, that we had the opportunity to grow and develop, to nurture our spirits. (*Yearning* 42)

Dandridge's narrative, however, demystifies and interrogates the institutions of the black home, motherhood, and womanhood much in the same way as Morrison does through her character Pecola in *The Bluest Eye.* Tyranny runs rampant in Dottie's home, so much so that it mirrors in some ways the terror of abused slaves the plantation overseer debased. Much has been written about black women's resistance to white supremacy, violence, dominance, and oppression. Dorothy's narrative, however, documents her battle against these elements in her own home as a child. Dorothy has to install defenses against a black woman who administers slaps, wallops, and bangs, and somehow excuse a black mother who fails to safeguard her from them. Like Morrison's Pecola, Dottie has no secure space, and she is indeed a captive abused body. Dorothy's memories of these incidents provide the most potent passages of the text.

Mrs. Williams sets to drive out Dorothy's will with "that hair brush, sometimes the bristle side, sometimes the flat" (Dandridge 19). She intends to drill into her, through the flesh, a strict adherence to performance to ensure economic prosperity. Dorothy carefully observes another reason why Mrs. Dandridge so readily accepts Mrs. Williams:

> I can understand how my mother, with her rearing which prized education, could take to Eloise. This woman had been a music teacher at Fisk University. She was a good singer and had been

musician and singer in churches with her minister husband. [. . .] The woman was qualified to teach us. (18)

Dorothy here identifies another culprit in her tragedy: the black community's preoccupation with titles and prestige, a most important one because each contributes to racial uplift. Fisk University is one of the premier historically black universities in the nation at the time of Mrs. Williams's arrival. Founded in 1865 by abolitionists and named after its major financial contributor, General Clinton B. Fisk, assistant commissioner of the Freedmen's Bureau for Tennessee and Kentucky, Fisk University graduated scores of top black artists and scholars. The most prominent Fisk alumnus is W. E. B. Du Bois, who is "a major black leader and a force to be reckoned with on the national scene" (Richardson 175). In 1931 the university's prominence rises to a point where Edwin R. Embree, president of the Rosenwald Fund, considers it "the finest black college in the land" (Richardson 137).

Mrs. Williams enters the lives of the Dandridges certified to teach and train the daughters without Ruby questioning her. Dorothy concludes, "My mother must have badly needed Eloise Matthews" (19). A closer look at Mrs. Williams's claim uncovers a more intriguing fact: Fisk University Special Collections Librarian Beth Howse reveals that the library has no record of a Mrs. Geneva Williams or Eloise Matthews being employed in any capacity nor enrolled as a student at Fisk. Howse states:

> I have searched high and low [in the] Fisk catalogs from the early 1900's to the 1930's for Geneva Williams/Eloise Matthews but did not see the names listed anywhere. [. . .] I have checked the university catalogs for both Eloise Matthews and Geneva Williams but have been unable to find their names among the list of students during the 1920's–1930's. (e-mail)

This revelation points to Mrs. Williams/Matthews knowing that the reputation of Fisk University gives her credibility. Her "employment" as a member of the music faculty at Fisk consecrates her as the quintessential teacher. Ruby should be honored to have her in the house as her presence brings with it all of Fisk's status.

By association, then, the Dandridge household gains a certain distinction of its own, but its merit becomes more tainted when research uncovers no record of Mrs. Matthews. What she brings is a spurious lie that having taught music in Fisk's hallowed halls and enjoyed a modicum of success "singing in churches with her minister husband" legitimates Mrs. Williams's place in the Dandridge house. These aspects of Mrs. Williams's "qualifications" quell any malicious gossip their cohabitation might raise—both of them being without husbands. It looks good to the community that this well-qualified black woman—a God-fearing woman of the church, even—lives with Ruby to help out with the children, especially after the experience she had with her spineless husband.

Dorothy's narrative, however, raises issues surrounding the black community's adulation of those who receive a formal education from prestigious black institutions. The "rearing" of Dottie in a small way implicates the black community's preoccupation with education as the paramount prize. The community's acceptance of Mrs. Williams implies titles and degrees could qualify a person to do virtually anything and releases the perpetrator from any fear of reprisal. More important, Mrs. Dandridge fails to heed her daughter's cry for help partially because of Mrs. Williams's background and associations.

In 1939 Dottie turns into a sixteen-year-old Dorothy, and the teenager suffers continued severe whippings at the hands of Auntie Mama. She writes:

> She beat me till I cried, and then she beat me because I cried. Eventually it got so that I just guarded my face while she hit me, and I never let out a sound. I don't know when I stopped showing my pain, but I began to simply absorb that punishment, to grit my teeth, to give her a hateful look afterward, and then to walk off. (Dandridge 53)

Dorothy characterizes this stage of her youth as one of silent absorption of abuse. Dorothy's "crying childhood" melds into a painfully silent adolescence as she absorbs the pain inflicted on her. Dorothy's silence "is a sign of the effectiveness of the pedagogical principles applied" (A. Miller 7), and Auntie Ma-ma is so effective that she has enough freedom to commit another crime against Dorothy, one from which she never would recover.

What Have I Done?

Auntie Ma-ma takes egregious advantage of her place in Dorothy's life and wields an inordinate amount of power over Mrs. Dandridge's children. Not only has she been given full responsibility for developing

Dorothy's talent, but she also commandeers authority over her body. In this atmosphere, Mrs. Williams can transform into a nefarious being sucking the very life out of her charge. Dorothy later describes her as "the incubus of Auntie Ma-ma" (Dandridge 77). By far the most traumatic incident in Dorothy's younger life occurs in her sixteenth year. Auntie Ma-ma rapes Dorothy while the Dandridge Sisters are on tour in Europe, and Mrs. Dandridge has stayed behind in Los Angeles to audition for work. Dorothy writes, "[. . .] she put her fingers inside [. . .] once more [she] fingered me in spite of my resistance" (55). Dorothy believes the friendship the sisters form with an unmarried pregnant British teenager, Eldrith Hogan, instigates the offense. Auntie Ma-ma inquires, "Have you done what Eldrith did?" (Dandridge 54). Dorothy continues:

> "What have I done?"
> "I don't know. That's what I want to find out." She looked squat and forceful. Her face looked ugly.
> "Get on the bed as I say!"
> I rose and walked toward the bed, sat on the edge. [. . .]
> "Lay back." She pushed me. My head fell on the pillow. Of a sudden, she raised my dress and yanked down my panties.
> "I'm not going to hurt you." Her voice changed. "I simply want to find out something I have to know. I'm responsible for you." (Dandridge 54–55)

Auntie Ma-ma's suspicion about Dorothy's virginity could easily have been solved by an examination by a doctor. Why is taking on this role necessary for her? These shocking actions—clinical and cold in their import and delivery—illustrate the total isolation within which Dorothy lives. More terrible, the language typifies that used by a rapist ordering the victim to "go along" until the act is over.

An insidious undercurrent runs through this childhood narrative. At this time, Dorothy develops the courage to voice her anger over the constant travel and work to which she is subject under the watchful gaze of Auntie Ma-ma. What is more, Dorothy has blossomed into an extremely attractive sixteen-year-old young woman who catches the eye of male admirers. When the Dandridge Sisters open at the Palladium in London, "a line of would-be suitors lay in wait" for Dorothy afterward (Bogle, *Dorothy Dandridge* 68). But Auntie Ma-ma continues to spank Dorothy's backside at least three times a week. When Dorothy and Vivian befriend an outsider (Eldrith), Auntie Ma-ma becomes alarmed, and violates Dorothy not Vivian, even though Dorothy is a virgin.

What does this string of assaultive acts signify? On the one hand, Auntie Ma-ma's "product" seriously is compromised when "it" associates itself with a young teenage pregnant girl. Dorothy's body is the means by which Auntie Ma-ma and Mrs. Dandridge maintain economic and financial stability. The Dandridge Sisters are national and international hot commodities. Part of Auntie Ma-ma's duty as stage mother and guardian is to ensure that her manufactured product remain in excellent condition. Auntie Ma-ma's sexual violation, however, insinuates something else. This is Dorothy's first sexual encounter. Why does Auntie Ma-ma check Dorothy's virginity and not Vivian's? Dorothy and Vivian are sisters as well as best friends weathering the wrath of Auntie Ma-ma—although Dorothy to a greater extent—and Dorothy's association with Eldrith automatically implicates Vivian. Could it be, then, that Auntie Ma-ma has an attraction for Dorothy? If that is the case, if Dorothy experiences any type of sexual experience, would Auntie Ma-ma perpetrate the deflowering and thus possess her? An affirmative answer makes obvious Mrs. Williams' transformation into a fiendish entity siphoning the life force out of the teenager and corroborates Dorothy's naming her "the incubus of Auntie Ma-ma" (Dandridge 77). Or is it that Dorothy's talents and beauty far outweigh those of her sister Vivian's, and Auntie Ma-ma perceives who the real money-maker is in the group? One other possibility is that Dorothy's jealous regard for her mother poses a threat to Auntie Ma-ma's relationship with Mrs. Dandridge. Dorothy is in the way, and the guardian has to break the bond between mother and daughter just as Mrs. Dandridge did with Cyril. Auntie Ma-ma forces Dorothy to search constantly for reasons why she is subjected to her abuse. This incessant self-examination keeps Dorothy somewhat distracted from her mother and preoccupied with pleasing Auntie Ma-ma, though to no avail.

The fingering episode, on the other hand, compels Dorothy to confront her abuser, and precipitates a dramatic physical rebellion. Ironically, the cinema provides her the means to initiate the reclamation of her life: "I leaped off the bed," Dorothy remembers, "and clenching my fists as I had seen men do it on Hollywood sets, I hit her on the chin. Then I lit into her, storming upon her with blows harder than any she had ever given me with the bristle side of her brushes. I was in a rage" (Dandridge 56). The implication of this scene points to a huge power play that includes every possible aspect of Dorothy's being, much like grown-up Miss Celie's actions in the *The Color Purple* by Alice Walker when she points a carving knife at her abusive husband. Dorothy's "rebellion" typifies the "kiddie divorce" or the legal recourse contemporary child/teenage actors of the 1980s use to emancipate themselves from years of parental malfeasance operating on several levels, including fiscal mismanagement ("Kid Star Parents").

Although Dorothy does fight back against her abuser, the years she endured it destroy her ability to experience sexual intimacy later in life. Dorothy writes of her honeymoon:

> My feet were glued to the [bathroom] tile. I couldn't make the turn to the bedroom door; then I couldn't turn the knob. [. . .] I had a fear that something terrible was going to happen. [. . .] I suffered through it. I tried not to show it, but everything in my background contributed to making me feel that this normal event was a violation. (Dandridge 60–61)

The effects of the maltreatment intrude into her marriage bed, and the honeymoon night with her husband, Harold Nicholas is a disaster.

Interestingly, a concurrent dance movement is performed, along with Dorothy's childhood narrative when she unearths these two Negro women entrepreneurs who devise a formidable alliance that matches any Hollywood studio in its making of a star. The Dandridge/Williams team turns out to be a collaboration that works in a white male–dominated business famous for manufacturing stars such as Marilyn Monroe, Ava Gardner, and Lana Turner. That Dorothy looks fixedly on her mother's stage performances as a child conditions her to aspire to the same herself. By accompanying her mother to social events and church halls and to local theatricals, Dorothy, a young black girl, absorbs the image portrayed and later emulates what she saw: a black female-mother entertainer. Mrs. Dandridge unconsciously passes down a celebrity legacy to her black daughters—not Hollywood. Ironically, she subverts the modus operandi of that white power structure with its ruthless determination to circulate a score of stereotypes people have of Negro women and girls in the U.S. labor force.

Despite every accomplishment, Dorothy's story of her childhood years bears out the history of her commodification long before Hollywood ever touches her. The autobiography refutes a prevailing critical narrative about Dandridge. As film critic Marguerite H. Rippy asserts:

> Dandridge was destroyed *first by a media obsession* with reproducing the commodification of white femininity on a black body and second by the cultural desire to sample black exoticism without having to confront the national history of exploitation and violence that accompanied that body. (179; my emphasis)

Dorothy admonishes the reader that such is the preoccupation with her exotic beauty, her representations of black femininity, her tenure in Hollywood, and her Oscar nomination (for example, "The first Negro to . . .")—the everything—that the real perpetrators of her tragedy are unnoticed by the public, yet are at the heart of who she is. Dorothy's childhood narrative entreats film historians and the public to investigate those people and institutions that do not keep her safe, and that held little or no regard for her emotional and physical well-being as a work-ing child actor in the 1920s and 1930s. Dorothy also reveals that her commodification in the home gave permission for others to treat Dottie and her sister as objects of the adult gaze, and an object has no rights; it is a thing. Child advocate Paul Petersen confirms, "parents of a working child are entitled to its custody, income and services. Children [in enter-tainment] are no different than a cow or a car . . ." (*VH1 News*). *Every-thing and Nothing*, overall, demands foremost a demystification of the three major black institutions: motherhood, the home, and the church. These institutions are credited with administering unconditional (tough) love, support, character building, self esteem, and soul salvation to black people in general and most specifically, a sanctuary for black children. Strangely enough, Dorothy Dandridge accuses this triad of creating the tragedy she associates with her life—the *nothing*.

CHAPTER THREE

Eartha Kitt

The Dance of the
Autobiographical Defense

> *I been 'buked and I been scorned*
> *Yes, I been 'buked and I been scorned children*
> *I been 'buked and I been scorned*
> *I been talked 'bout sho's you born*
> —Negro Spiritual

I remember in the late 1990s watching the banter between the host of a now-canceled talk show and his guest. She was part of the cast for a popular sitcom featuring an ensemble of single black women navigating through life in a northeastern cosmopolitan city. The host asks his guest to name the most difficult actress with whom she has worked. The guest calls out Eartha Kitt, who made a guest appearance on her show. According to the actress, Kitt brought her entourage to rehearsals. She spoke a foreign language—French, she thought—and no one understood a word she said. Her presence proved an interminable challenge for the cast and crew. I'm listening to the insipid chitchat, witnessing the laughter between the host and the guest, and think through squinted eyes, "They're talking about this woman."

There is more. Talk about Kitt moves from the talk show to the sitcom. On the "After the Fall" episode from *The Steve Harvey Show* (1996–2002), Harvey's friend and television producer Byron Clark (Wayne Wilderson) visits Booker T. Washington High School to film a documentary on Harvey (the music, art, and drama teacher) and, of course, students and administrators overact for the film crew. Principal Regina Greer (Wendy Racquel Robinson) especially tests Clark's patience as she insists on being photographed on her "good" side. Clark, exasperated, declares, "Oh, she's worse than Eartha Kitt!"

To be "talked about" means that two or more people (regardless of gender) gather in your name to rehearse some wrong you did or to divulge gossip about you. The "gathering," at its very worst, betrays confidences, slanders reputations, and scandalizes names. It usually convenes at a bridge party, over the telephone, on the front porch on a cool Sunday afternoon, or in the church parking lot—and on national television. Hushed tones activate the conversations: *I'm not supposed to tell . . . you did not hear it from me, . . .* or *quiet as it's kept. . . .*" Information cuts through the proverbial communal grapevine, and after the "talk about" session, the participants look the defamed straight in the eye, and with a Cheshire cat smile declare, "How nice it is to see you today!" This practice of "talk" fosters a deceit within the community; what makes the practice more vile, however, is that you are not invited, as Kitt has not been on that talk show or *Harvey*, to defend yourself; the "gathering" closes the gate to your side of the story because it has an investment in keeping sacred its own estimations about you. This closure seals off any other interpretation of storytelling about you than its own. It is a mean-spirited exclusionary dance.

This chapter invites Eartha Kitt to the "gathering." It locates then deliberates on Kitt's rhetorical interference to the sensational talk about her. Kitt is a celebrity autobiographer making the most of the dance of autobiography to "take up for herself" against the bully of defamation. In the process, the entertainer's dance on the white page at various intervals preserves a place for her at the gathering and subverts the exclusionary act as well as the speculation of the gossips. Participation in the whirlpool of rumor does not displace rumors being spread; rather, the objective is to recuperate excluded discourses and thereby add vibrancy, color, and vitality to them. Kitt's side of the stories ensures this recuperation and these additions as well.

Eartha (Mae) Kitt's dance on the white page produces a chaîné or a series of connected autobiographical movements: *Thursday's Child* (1956), *Alone with Me* (1976), *I'm Still Here: Confessions of a Sex Kitten* (1989), and *Rejuvenate! (It's Never Too Late)* (2001). This chaîné charts her growth as a black woman in the United States over certain moments in history, and Kitt choreographs, more pointedly, an unremitting series of autobiographical defenses. Literary critic James Craig Holte concludes, "in a defense a writer makes an effort to clear [her] character or to defend an action or belief" (28–29). In the formal or academic sense, Kitt's autobiographical corpus characterizes the defense. Her literary style and tone, however, also typify the vernacular of the playground: "Girl, you'd better 'take up' for yourself; ain't nobody else gonna do it." In all of her memoirs, Kitt takes up for herself in three significant periods in her life. Starting where the talk all began seems appropriate. Her birth as Eartha Mae within a segregated destitute rural Southern town activates talk about her and results in her being ostracized in the 1920s and 1930s. Eartha Kitt takes up for Eartha Mae and defends her right as a black child in a most remarkable way to belong to the black community despite attacks against her physiognomy.

Kitt's second defense centers around the tenuous relationship she has as a teenager with the famous dance choreographer Katherine Dunham during her tenure as a dancer in Dunham's troupe in the 1950s. Finally, Kitt defends her right to dance as an activist when in adulthood she takes up for the nation's poor and mothers whose sons are soldiers serving in the Vietnam War at a White House luncheon in 1968. Each of Eartha Kitt's chaînés illustrates her husbandry of a robust interior life that later advances her into an emotionally stalwart person and entertainer as well unlike Dorothy Dandridge. Maternal abandonment and poverty practically damage Dandridge; but Eartha Kitt draws inner strength from these two life phases.

The entertainer's textual defenses are crucial because each one reiterates it takes black women to choreograph the steps necessary to take up for themselves and for each other. Taking up for one's self means assuming responsibility to protect the self after being talked about when no one else comes to your defense. One literally stands alone amidst a barrage of attacks. When a black woman takes up for herself, she generates such interior strength that she is able to choreograph a dance of protection for other black women and for the black community at large. She can stand in their stead or in the idiom of popular culture, she can "have their backs."

To grasp the full import of Kitt's autobiographical accounts, we must first briefly overview what has been said about her. The talk about Kitt begins long before that talk show banter and before Harvey is born. Eartha Kitt's history of being talked about is launched in a variety of venues soon after she steps off the stage from her smoldering critically acclaimed debut performance in the Broadway musical review *New Faces of 1952* (prod. Leonard Sillman). The black and white media both talk of "indecorous" behavior. Her interpretive delivery of songs at a Los Angeles banquet causes Los Angeles politicos to denounce her performance. *Time* magazine reports in 1953, "Next day, some of Los Angeles' councilmen were shocked. Says one attendee: 'It was low-level entertainment, repugnant to all decent citizens.' Eartha's songs, according to Mayor Norris Poulson, were 'filthy, risqué and off-color'"

("People" 48). Brooks Atkinson of the *New York Times* declares, "Eartha Kitt not only looks incendiary . . . she can make a song burst into flame" ("Salty Eartha" 61). Atkinson's quote in one way applauds Kitt, yet the language portrays her as a dangerous woman.

Talk about Kitt dances within *Ebony* magazine, the premier of black entertainment and news media. In the article, "Why Negroes Don't Like Eartha Kitt," a columnist writes:

> [. . .] where the suddenly-successful Eartha Kitt was concerned, many Negroes [. . .] had found her to their disliking—often rude and thoroughly disagreeable . . . that the newborn singing star is uppity and snubbing her race. [H]er aloofness has become a subject of much talk. [. . .] [T]oo many Negroes have happened to catch her "between acts" when her shrewish character is at its ill-mannered best. [. . .] Eartha doesn't seem inclined to do too much about it. (29, 32, 37)

According to Kitt, the Central Intelligence Agency (CIA) establishes a dossier on her, wherein an informant states, "Subject was a very confused woman and because of her lack of emotional stability could not handle success. . . . The informant also commented on Subject's unfavorable moral reputation in regard to men other than those of her own race" (Kitt, *Alone* 262).

Summarily, Kitt is not only talked about, but also is viewed with contempt and disrespect. All of this talk about her, from the past to the present, seems to validate the talk show gossip and Clarke's assessment of the entertainer. Kitt's voice is too weird; the multiplicity of (foreign) tongues in which she speaks aggravates people and her fan base, and makes them uncomfortable to be around her. Ultimately, she is cast about, talked about, rebuked, and scorned in the black and white communities. Kitt, of course, must have done something to prompt this kind of talk about her; no one would go to such lengths to defame her if she did not antagonize the circumstances herself.

In the area between taking up and talking back, Eartha Kitt's star ascends on the bipolarized world of the 1950s wherein television injects streams of white ladyhood via sitcoms in America's living rooms such as *Father Knows Best* (1954–1960) and *Leave It to Beaver* (1957–1963). In the meantime, Negro women adhere to strict rules of ladyhood to divest themselves of negative historical appropriations. Dorothy Dandridge and Lena Horne definitely are the sex symbols, but no one can accuse these ladies of "indecorous behavior" in their heyday. Kitt's risqué moves relegate her to the genre of the burlesque if not the striptease, consequently sending tremors throughout the black and white communities. Thus, the talk begins about Eartha Kitt.

Kitt indeed provokes many of these responses, but this provocation immediately follows Kitt's taking up for herself. Kitt takes up for herself—in varying ways—with those in power, whether they are family members, people responsible for her livelihood, or the President and First Lady of the United States. As she makes public in her autobiographies, Eartha Kitt takes up for herself by challenging fixed boundaries threatening her personal and artistic growth. Or she talks back to hold people responsible for the agendas in which they invite her to take part. Kitt, therefore, becomes the annoying guest who does not conform to the prescribed norms of behavior (politeness and approachability) of the 1950s and 1960s, even if her taking up endangers her artistic and economic livelihood. The ultimate taking up occurs through Kitt's dance on the white page (four times), and her literary dances not only record a defense against diatribes leveled against her; but conjointly, her written words mitigate the weight of defamatory stories circulating about her in her absence.

In Kitt's first defense, she takes up for Eartha Mae in the retelling of her birth story and, in the process, demands the black community examine its class and racial hierarchies. She joins Toni Morrison in her critique of the intraracial dynamics in the black family. An examination of her texts brings to bare the practice of verbal, sexual, and physical abuse within the black community, just as Morrison does in *The Bluest Eye* (1970), *Sula* (1974) and *Paradise* (1998). Kitt's autobiographies identify slavery as the culprit and, through her, we learn of the cultural continuities playing out among members of the black community. Each of Kitt's texts highlights the necessity of naming the cause behind such practices, the exigency of searching for ways to break the cycle, and the obligation of each community member to begin a process of healing, to begin the process of love. Equipped with knowledge of national history, members of communities can take up for themselves by demanding socioeconomic parity.

Eartha Mae Kitt believes the progression out of an unhealthy community begins with an assessment of one's interior life. Consider 1974. It is a momentous year for Eartha Kitt, the consummate and enigmatic entertainer. The night is wonderful, one filled with laughter and gestures of congratulations to Eartha Kitt from patrons at Carnegie Hall. Eartha Kitt. Entertainer extraordinaire! The year 1974 closes the door on the entertainer's "professional exile" from the United States resulting from the 1968 White House controversy (later discussed herein; Kitt, *Alone* 1). As Kitt walks through the crowded corridor between the lines of fans and theatergoers, a voice calls out of the crowd, "Eartha Mae, do you remember me?" (2). Grace, Eartha Kitt's stepsister from whom she had neither seen nor heard since her tumultuous times in rural South Carolina, comes from out of the shadows. Kitt, hysterical, screams, "Why, after all these years, are you trying to find me now? Where were you when I really *wanted* someone?" (3). A friend and a policeman escort her out "crying and screaming, '[w]here were they when I wanted and needed them? What do they want from me *now*?" (3). This "family reunion" brings back to Kitt memories of specific harrowing experiences, as well as a "person" Eartha Kitt, the entertainer, has managed to shroud with a blanket of protection: Eartha Mae, Eartha Kitt's other self—the "ugly, unloved, [and] unworthy" child (4). Eartha explains:

> The adult I have molded is Eartha Kitt: self-reliant, afraid of nothing, even defiant. . . . She is so very far removed from the basic nature of Eartha Mae that I can—and do—think of her in the third person. She's *she*, not me. She's a name on a marquee. I'm curiously detached from her and yet suspended within her and totally dependent upon her for my survival. She has some of my better qualities, as a loving mother and as a friend to those who accept Eartha Mae, but I have none of hers. And until that evening at Carnegie Hall, no one ever got to Eartha Mae through Eartha Kitt. Never.
>
> Eartha Mae psychs [*sic*] herself up to become Eartha Kitt for public appearances; she wears an impenetrable mental armor. [. . .] But the woman who called herself my step-sister [*sic*] asked Eartha Kitt if she remembered Eartha Mae, and [. . .] I was thrown into being both personalities at one time, and there was a tremendous conflict as to *who* I was. (4)

Kitt clearly delineates the distance between the selves through the use of the first (Eartha Mae) and third (Eartha Kitt) persons. Through the first person "I," Eartha Kitt retreats to Eartha Mae. Eartha Mae, in turn, joins the reading audience in an attempt to think through with them the meaning behind Eartha Kitt, the entertainer and the persona. Kitt and Mae have disparate natures: one is independent and sure of herself, and the other is dependent and afraid. Eartha Kitt shields Eartha Mae from harm. She protects and nourishes Eartha Mae, all the while maintaining an "impenetrable mental armor" to ward off any violation of the psyche from the past, her paying audience, or the media.

Although Eartha Mae and Eartha Kitt share the qualities of friendship and love, nevertheless the confrontation with her stepsister adds violence to the arrangement between the personas. First, in the public domain Eartha Kitt exclusively claims, the confrontation calls Eartha Mae out of her hiding place. Prior to that the two enjoy a comfortable distance, and Eartha Kitt and Eartha Mae have an understanding of the role each has to play. The "I" and the "she" smash into one another despite all of the Dunbarian masking—in this case the dazzling costume of the stage replete with theatrical makeup and wigs. Eartha Mae is to stay suspended while Eartha Kitt performs onstage; she appears only in some cases, "to those who accept[ed] Eartha Mae," off stage. The uncomfortable encounter forces the "I" and the "she" to collide, and Eartha Kitt "went to pieces" (*Alone* 4). Eartha Mae Kitt embarks on a quest for identity in diverse communities to reassemble Eartha Mae and place her back in Eartha Kitt's protective and "impenetrable mental armor."

Eartha Mae Kitt is born on a plantation in North, South Carolina, in 1927. There begins her introduction to intraracial prejudice. The birth of the "yella gal" inaugurates the contentious relationship between Kitt's mother, Anna Mae, and Anna Mae's uncle. Kitt's exclusion is a result of her mother's decision to "run-off" with a light-skinned man of whom the community does not approve. Kitt has limited knowledge of her mother's relationship with her father, but learns the reaction of disapproval from Anna Mae's uncle stems from her mother's having left the community without its blessing. As a result of Eartha Mae's light coloring, mother and children are cast out into the forest to search for food and shelter. Kitt remembers that time as a "long, long period" of travel: "I don't know where we had come from or where we were going, only that the road was the longest road I had ever seen. [. . .] Most of the time we lived in the forest," Kitt writes, "or at least slept there covered with pine straw" (*I'm Still Here* 1). Kitt's birth arouses a righteous indignation in others, and it places her outside of the institution of family with no sense of place except with that of nature.

Eartha Mae remembers her mother's pleas for food and shelter after the family arrives on the community's doorstep: "Moma [*sic*] asked for shelter and food, pleading softly with the woman. I could hear her saying, 'Just for tonight . . . my children are hungry and tired . . .'" (*I'm Still Here* 2). Food is nourishment and sustenance, both physically and communally. To sup at the community's table symbolizes kinship and a connectedness to something greater than you; and it means participating in the maintenance of a culture's soul. "The sharing of food," asserts Deborah Lupton, "is a vital part of kinship and friendship networks in all societies." Lupton continues, "[t]o the extent to which an individual is invited to share food with another individual is a sign of how close a friend or relative that person is deemed to be" (37). To be denied food denotes a cultural aspersion or even the threat of death. The sight of Eartha Mae, the yella gal, hardens the hearts of her mother's relatives and deprives her of nourishment. These descriptions, remarkably, allude to the Nativity, a popular, revered, and potent traditional story in all of its sentimental currency. There literally is no room at the inn for poor Anna Mae and family. Her babies are wrapped in the swaddling of pine straw. Curious to Kitt's "nativity narrative" is the absence of a report of an actual taking up for herself. The very act of reporting these incidents through a dance of allusion on the white page, however, compels the reader to "take up for" Eartha Mae. This literary device is Kitt's genius. The reader has to join Kitt and stand up for Eartha Mae and her right to the very basic needs of a black child—food, shelter, and family—just as the nation annually feels the "poor Christ child" deserves shelter more fitting than that of a stable and a manger lined with straw.

The first notice of the little "yella gal" Eartha Mae incites a mean-spiritedness in her mother's uncle. Before he slams the door in Anna Mae's face, he yells, "that yalla man you went off with was no good to anyone. Nobody liked him but you. No one asked you to have a child by him" (*Thursday's Child* 10). The uncle accuses Anna Mae of holding the community responsible for her and her children's condition. Her affair with a "yalla man" or a man who is very light-skinned, moreover, signifies Anna Mae's audacity to defy her uncle's patriarchal voice; but her "disobedience" taints his house. It is one thing for her to choose a relationship with a man who can pass for white; it is another for her to "flaunt" the consequence of the union—a product that does not reflect the uncle's household. Anna Mae returns to the community not as a heroine, but as an embarrassment, bearing illegitimacy and single black motherhood. In this single parent family, "yella" skin ostracizes them from the communal fold. Kitt's skin is a veritable curse, and causes the community to scorn and rebuke her, and eventually renders her a poverty-stricken motherless child.

Eartha Mae's status obstructs the possibility for the formation of a new family for her, and Anna Mae's new suitor ignores Eartha Mae. Kitt writes:

> He played with my sister in between the times he was smooching with my mother. I sat and watched the coochie-cooching he'd give my sister, the rocking of her on his knee, the baby talk that passed between them. Mama would smile at the both of them and I would stare into the fire, wondering why he

did not coochie-coo with me. [. . .] There was no me, as far as he was concerned. (*Thursday's Child* 13)

Her skin makes her invisible; her exclusion makes her self-conscious of her own difference. Anna Mae does nothing to stop the treatment, although Eartha Mae witnesses her mother on her knees pleading with her new suitor to take her children. He replies, "No, I don't want that yella gal. She would cause trouble with my children. [. . .] I'll take Pearl, not Eartha Mae." Eartha Mae concludes, "I was in the way, a problem to [Momma]. No one wanted us because of me, the yella gal." After a careful perusal of her baby sister, Eartha Mae surmises, "If I was the same colour as Pearl, Moma would not be having so much trouble" (*I'm Still Here* 6). Eartha Mae's fears materialize when Anna Mae runs off with the man and leaves both girls behind. The children will only see their mother sporadically.

If Eartha Mae's light skin sidelines her incorporation into the family, it also marks her as an easy target for physical and sexual abuse. After their mother abandons them, Eartha Mae and Pearl are left in the care of relatives, the Sterns. The Sterns have two teenagers, Gracie and Willie, who make "fun" with Eartha in the absence of the adults. As "punishment" for smoking tobacco, Willie orders Eartha Mae to strip naked as his sister, Gracie, watches with glee:

"Eartha Mae, come here, let me see what you look like. Pick up your rags," he said, "More!" As the private parts of my tiny body became exposed [. . . Gracie and Willie] started laughing: "Damn, you're yella all over, ain't cha? Turn around," Willie suddenly said. As my body turned, the switch came across my backside with a sting that would make the devil cringe. I gritted my teeth. [. . .] Willie swished the switch in the air a few times, allowing the blood stains imprinted on it to dry before finally tossing it onto the woodpile. I stood there, head bowed to the ground, holding my crocker [*sic*] sack dress up around my waist. [. . .] I could see their shadows move away from my area. I picked up my wound-healer, the broom, and continued sweeping my hurt under the rose bushes. (*I'm Still Here* 10)

Willie's call for Eartha Mae to reveal herself to him and Gracie uncovers their knowledge of the talk about Eartha Mae's skin. More insidious, because the Sterns's regard for Eartha Mae has been passed on to their grandchildren, Willie and Gracie learn the art of intraracial discrimination at an early age. Only after Willie surveys her body and names it—"you yella all over"—does he begin his punishment of her. Willie wants proof of what he has heard about this new addition to the family.

Gracie's practice of "sexual intercourse" on Eartha Mae is another incident Eartha Mae endures alone. Kitt writes:

> Gracie softly called me into the house. "Lie down on the floor," she said, "on your back." Gracie kneeled beside me. She gently rolled my crocker [sic] sack dress to my waist. She had something in her hand. It looked at first like a piece of stick but it was this cloth-like stick. [. . .] I couldn't understand what she was going to do as she placed her body over mine trying to move this cloth-like stick between her private parts and mine. Cringing, I closed my eyes. [. . .] (*I'm Still Here* 11)

Gracie never pulls this stunt again and the two children never mention the incident. Gracie and Willie threaten Kitt with more harm if she tattles on them, thus forming a shroud of secrecy among the children. The Gracie and Willie stories affirm the malignant alliance between the children in the Stern household that is fed by Eartha Mae's light skin. Pearl does not suffer the same maltreatment, and the sibling, seeing who holds the power, eventually turns against Eartha Mae.

That Kitt picks up a broom is significant; she calls it her "wound healer." This gesture not only symbolizes a cleansing, but the sweep also represents Kitt's effort to cut off Willie's spite and nastiness from infecting her *self*. The broom is a symbol of nature; it is a household implement used to brush away dirt from unwanted places. On a psychic level, the broom is the "object made of plant matter [. . .] a wise woman [uses] to keep her psychic environ uncluttered" (Estés 96). As Kitt uses nature to purify herself of the dirt that Grace and Willie heap on her, she begins to build the internal strength that steels her against future challenges.

Generational Inheritance—Kitt Talks Back on the White Page

Anna Mae's uncle directs his anger to her because she consorts with someone whom he imagines is of no use to the community (he was "no good to anyone," "nobody liked him"). This is not as much because Anna Mae has had a child out of wedlock, but that she has one without the community's blessing as well as with someone whom this patriarch feels diminishes its members. Hunger and homelessness, therefore, are paybacks Anna Mae receives for expressing her own self. Anna Mae's flagrant show of independence (or lack of respect) incites the community to curse the product of her self-expression, Eartha Mae.

Kitt's birth narrative draws up two points. First, Kitt informs us of an ominous postslavery color hierarchy breeding abandonment, molestation, and abuse. These elements plague the black community and further influence the ways in which members interact with one another. Anna Mae's constant pleas are more than a solicitation for bread and shelter; metaphorically, she asks the community to break the vicious cycle of exclusion based on a color hierarchy that undermines attempts for humane social interaction. Second, in defying the edicts of her community and acting as her own agent and, further, in skirting the ideal of black motherhood, Anna Mae sets a precedent for Eartha Mae's own audacious behavior in the future. In other words, Anna Mae unwittingly bequeaths to Eartha Mae (Kitt) an attitude that later would roil societal expectations.

Kitt's childhood narrative charges slavery's legacies as the major influences on the behaviors Eartha Mae's relatives act out. The metaphor of the auction block plays out in Willie's punishment. Open and defenseless against the shenanigans of unsupervised children, the "cousins" parade Eartha Mae before them like an African woman put up for sale in a public square. Kitt's language—"the private parts," "exposed," "I stood," "head bowed to the ground"—illustrates a captive whose body is inflicted with pain, just as was an enslaved woman's body. Kitt's tone, imbued with the language of the slavocracy, not only exposes Eartha Mae, but it also indicts her community for continuing the slavocracy's legacies.

Willie's treatment of Eartha Mae demonstrates a cultural continuity from enslavement, and Kitt stresses the importance of remembering history as well as understanding the inheritance of slavery. In *I'm Still Here* she notes, "we [. . .] were dragged here in the bottom of slave ships. And we have had a very hard time with hunger, poverty, and even being accepted as Americans. [. . .] And the blacks are standing still, for every time they make a move to become a partner they are back up against a wall of poverty and neglect" (170–71). According to Kitt, the way the legacy of slavery places our communities in a practical chokehold and the way this chokehold virtually squeezes out of its members the tendency to practice love are important to remember. An unbridled mean-spiritedness denies love and threatens an out-of-doors existence.

Kitt alludes to slavery through a cotton trope, thereby exposing the shadow of slavery hovering over the community. Kitt describes the virtual passageway through which the outcasts have to travel on their way to find shelter: the baleful eyes of cotton follow them. Kitt recounts, "cotton followed us each step of the way and I imagined the bogeyman peering from the long rows of stalked fields. Their bulbs seemed to get bigger and bigger as the night came on stronger. I wished Moma [*sic*] could find us a place for us to sleep before the bogeyman got us" (*I'm Stilll Here* 1). The bogeyman with a thousand bulging eyes that inhabits the cotton fields calls out the ghost of the slave regime, and the vestiges of this regime infect Kitt's southern community with the cultural and psychic diseases of poverty, disenfranchisement, and meanness. Its eyes grow to great proportion under the cover of night; therefore, it is stealthy and creeps such that it cuts off an awareness of its treacherous current.

Even Thomas Jefferson, in his *Notes on the State of Virginia*, anticipates slavery's harmful effects on future generations of master planters. In the chapter aptly named "Manners," Jefferson contemplates:

> There must doubtless be an unhappy influence on the manners of our people produced by the existence of slavery among us. The whole commerce between master and slave is a perpetual exercise of the most boisterous passions, the most unremitting despotism on the one part, and degrading submissions on the other. Our children see this, and learn to imitate it; for man is an imitative animal. (162)

Jefferson is concerned about the effects on the master, Mary Prince, a West Indian enslaved woman, however, observes the predilection of the sons of master planters to be treacherous. She says, "I must say something more about this cruel son of a cruel father,—He had no heart—no fear of God; he had been brought up by a bad father in a bad path, and *he delighted to follow in the same steps*" (200, my emphasis). Both Jefferson and Prince attest to the deleterious residuals of slavery. The consequences wound *all* members of society and, as Kitt avers, have noxious results. Kitt unearths the outcomes of slavery in the long rows of cotton, and she keeps watch of its legacies through the written word. Her acknowledgment illustrates that the grim reaper of slavery imprisons the very community into which her family tries to (re)enter.

For Kitt community building and care of it require its members to contend with the past. The primary concern for meaningful black progress is to examine "the profound sense of psychological depression, personal worthlessness, and social despair" (West 13). This course of action assists the black culture in (re)building a healthy environment for decent treatment of its members. Without it, cruelty threatens to grow to megaproportions.

From Eartha Mae to Eartha Kitt:
Migration South to North, Rural to Urban

After Anna Mae's death, Anna Mae's sister sends for Eartha—about six or seven years old—to come to New York and live with her. Eartha Mae's migration to the urban center of the North is a welcome relief from the travails endured in the rural South. The move, however, carries forward the abuse by another relative. At first, Aunt Mamie attends to Eartha Mae such that the young child develops an insatiable appetite for knowledge. Aunt Mamie feeds and treats her well. She arranges for Eartha Mae to learn piano and participate in the church choir, recitals, and in school plays. Eartha Mae develops self-assurance, and her diligence in school advances her from junior high to high school early. She auditions for and is accepted into Metropolitan High School, now the New York School for Performing Arts.

Eartha Mae feels the "amens and hallelujahs [. . .] [the] shouting and jumping up and down [. . .] and the spirit of the love of God permeate the church." After she leads the children's choir through song, though, her aunt refuses her any encouragement or approval. Later, Aunt Mamie neglects her, and Eartha Mae's clothes "became shabbier and shabbier." She later learns her clothes come from welfare relief, and her apparel stigmatizes her as poor (*Alone* 55–56). Kitt remembers that Aunt Mamie "was always yelling at [. . . her], frequently slapping [. . . her], and occasionally beating [her . . .] and so it went constantly" (*Alone* 72). When there is no food in the house, Eartha Mae invites herself to the homes of others to eat.

Because of her impoverished condition, Eartha Mae develops an acute self-consciousness, especially about her looks at a time when identity is most crucial—the teenage years: "I began thinking of myself as a tortured child; then I began to think that I really was a good-for-nothing. I withdrew more and more into myself" (*Alone* 74). Here in her interior, however, Eartha Mae begins to assert her herself: she takes a job as a sales clerk and as a seamstress. Thus, she culls a minim of independence from her aunt and relief from the condition of poverty. The Cuban and Puerto Rican communities give Eartha Mae another space of relief from her condition, and her coloring gives her access as member. Eartha Mae acquires friends by passing, in a sense, as a Cuban or Puerto Rican:

[. . .] I hadn't the faintest idea of what they were saying , so I reacted accordingly: They would chatter and smile. I'd smile. They would chatter and laugh. I'd laugh along with them. They would chatter and frown. I'd shake my head in sympathy and frown fiercely. I became immensely popular with them; I'm sure they had never found a kindred spirit like me, one who shared their *every* view. (*Alone* 61)

Eartha Mae's fascination with and personal drive to be with people who spoke a "strange language" (61) earns her passport into new and energetic communities holding no regard for her economic condition or the color of her skin. They introduce her not only to the Latin rhythms played on "tin cans, garbage-can lids, boxes, and bells", but these boys and girls, who gather on the city's stoops and in the streets, also draw out of her a love for dance. "They were a wonderful gang, and I loved every one of them. A couple would get up and dance in the middle of the street while I watched, my body moving in imitation of theirs. The rhythm would carry me away. It was wonderful," she writes (61). Eartha Mae's imitation and observations construct for her home a place of root-edness and a safe space in which she can move her body without the threat of abuse. We see no arrogance here, just a willingness to learn and to associate with others.

The fresh and vibrant island cultures are respites for Eartha Mae's body from the taunts and abuses inflicted on it, and she pursues the culture in the Cuban dance halls on Friday, Saturday, and Sunday nights:

The dances were wild, frenzied, and furious. I learned them quickly; I learned a lot in those dance halls. I learned that boys thought me attractive and, when they saw that I had natural dancing ability, they were willing to teach me their dance steps as well as their language. (*Alone* 62)

If foreign languages and dance bestow on Eartha Mae acceptance among foreign peers, the positive gaze of the opposite sex within that group nurtures in her a confidence in her own looks. The powerfully wild and frenzied fury of the dance and dance hall literally divests Eartha Mae of the name "yella gal." Eartha Mae deliberately breaks Aunt Mamie's curfew and "gladly [. . . took] the beating for the extra two hours of dancing" (62). Dancing "set the spirit free, [. . .] it was also a celebration of life and of the soul" (63). Dance delivers healing and a release from domestic troubles. More important, rhythm empowers Eartha Mae to resist containment. For Eartha Mae, dance means freedom.

Aunt Mamie, however, reacts to Eartha Mae's employment and "Saturday night fever" with disgust:

"Get out of this house and don't come back! You're a *tramp*, a no good. You stay out all hours of the night. Nobody knows where you are. One day you'll turn up pregnant, and then who'll take care of you? *Me!* I don't want anything like that in *my* house! Go on back to the street where you belong!" And she slammed the door in my face. (*Alone* 75)

Again, Eartha Mae is called names: "tramp" and "no good." Aunt Mamie exercises the same cultural continuities Anna Mae's family has when she forms a relationship with someone against the wishes of the community. Eartha Mae is put out for the same reason: she antagonizes her aunt by flaunting the rules. Eartha Mae breaks curfew not only to nourish her love for Cuban dances, but also to take up for Eartha Mae and nurture her desire and claim her right to belong to this community.

Aunt Mamie's overarching preoccupation, however, centers on the biological function of Eartha Mae's body. The guardian essentially forecasts a grim future for the teenager: pregnancy, illegitimacy, and economic stress. Aunt Mamie has cause for alarm. Negro teenaged girls could be expelled from school for becoming pregnant, and worst, their reputations sullied. Males are exempted from responsibility; after all, (Negro) men have futures to nourish. As time passes, the very mention of the mother's name would inevitably bring back a discussion of the time *she* got *herself* pregnant. More hurtful, these young women literally are shunned, hidden away, or kicked out of the home. Pregnancy automatically turns a teenager into a grown-up black woman. Underage "grown-up" black women, then, lose the "privilege" of education and gain the responsibility of paying rent and utility bills. Likewise, the child bears the permanent label of "illegitimate." It is the moment inchoate wherein the slave child follows the condition of the slave mother. Aunt Mamie reduces Eartha Mae's dance to a vulgar biological level. The dance with boys produces babies, not joy and celebration. Some of these same socio-cultural values are dramatized in the television production *Life is Not a Fairytale: The Fantasia Barrino Story* (2006), the life story of *American Idol* Fantasia Barrino. When the community learns of sixteen-year-old Barrino's pregnancy, many members judge her a bad example for other young women. Barrino, however, uses her situation to vitalize her dream for success as she performs on national television as an *American Idol* contestant. In the end, Barrino finds acceptance from American viewers who vote her their American Idol for 2004. Eartha Mae, too, finds approval—through observation of the urban culture, communication with it through its foreign language, and participation in it through dance. Kitt's dance within the Cuban and Puerto Rican communities cultivates the seeds of internal strength and serves as a fortress against her Aunt Mamie, preventing her aunt's taunts from taking root.

Kitt, in the next phase of her growth, meets with the Katherine Dunham Dance Troupe when she wins a scholarship at age fifteen. Kitt earns $10 a week and, during that time, she changes her name from Eartha Mae to Kitty and Kitten. Her association with Dunham offers her the chance to carry forward her knowledge of the urban streets and its dances and to join another family. Kitt writes:

> [. . .] we were to imitate [the leader]. I watched every arm, foot, head, and body movement. [. . .] I went down the floor, imitating what I had seen as closely as I could. [. . .] I moved my pelvis freely and worked my feet furiously. I wiggled and twitched, bounced, and exhausted myself. (*Thursday's Child* 72)

She inherits from the "rehearsals" with the urban teenagers in Brooklyn prior to that—watching and imitating the movement and rhythm of their bodies—the backgrounds for the audition with Dunham and a coveted place in the troupe. While there, Kitt holds Dunham's artistry in awe:

> Her choreography was unquestionable. [. . .] [T]he Dunham company meant something in many ways. It stood for progress for the Negro, a step forward in the eyes of every audience that saw us. [. . .] Katherine Dunham had created a better world for many of us, at the same time making the path easier for those who had guts enough to follow. (*Thursday's Child* 79, 85)

Kitt believes in Dunham's mission and the impact it has on society's perception of the Negro body. Kitt knows that, in the troupe, she is part of a team led by a pioneer. Dunham's leadership and choreography overturn America's notions about the Negro woman's body through dance. As a member of her "better world," Dunham chooses Kitt for a number of choreographed dances performed in 1945, including *Blue Holiday* and *Carib Song,* and *Bal Nègre* in 1946.

Nevertheless, Kitt recites a contentious relationship between the choreographer and the student. Although every member receives harsh criticism and expresses discontent with the control Dunham has over them, Kitt feels Dunham personally rebukes her. First, Kitt maintains that her fully developed body and long curly hair irritate Dunham: "You'll never become anything, Kitt, you have too much excess baggage" (*I'm Still Here* 46)—the "excess baggage" being Kitt's breasts.

Perhaps the choreographer has no need for mothering, or for enabling others to mother, so she issues this verbal assault while looking at Kitt's breasts. That Dunham hands out the assault in front of the entire troupe may have been a warning to others who long for the same thing.

In another incident, Kitt, fascinated by Dunham's performance, peeks behind a curtain on a Paris stage and studies the dance interpretations of her instructor. By watching, the young protégé continues her education. Kitt writes, "I wanted to get closer to her, to talk to her and ask questions; I could never really reach her . . ." (*Alone* 93). Kitt apparently wishes to replicate the Cuban dance hall "classroom" experience. Observation and imitation fully initiate Kitt into that new family of peers; she expects both can do the same with Dunham. Her actions, however, are quite different from the unstructured teaching Kitt enjoys in the Cuban and Puerto Rican dance halls. Kitt's gaze infuriates Miss Dunham, "Five dollar fine, Kitty. [. . .] I don't want you watching me. Your eyes penetrate my soul" (*I'm Still Here* 57).

Why does Dunham behave as she does toward Kitt? Both women enjoy public adulation and harvest success. They also share childhood traumas: molestation and domestic abuse. Dunham recounts in her 1959 autobiography, *A Touch of Innocence* (published three years after Kitt's autobiography, *Thursday's Child*), for example, that her father developed an unnatural attraction for her after her mother's death. She endures his fondling of her genitals and his jealous rages over her admirers (266; 281–85). As a teenager, a homeless drunken white man forces her to watch him perform an onanistic act in a Chicago park, as he chants "Jesus Christ. son of a bitch. son of a bitch. son of a bitch" (270–71).

Dunham's responses to Kitt may be viewed through several lenses: outright jealousy of a student's talent; the need for distance between student and teacher; the need for strict discipline and control; or, the need to protect her dance routines from being copied by a star dancer. Perhaps Dunham acts as the stern mother, demanding that the members of her troupe act as adults; and, that empire building in a racist society requires the ability to bear up under assaults; that withstanding strong discipline builds the character and strength so needed in the outside world. Dunham's treatment of Kitt inadvertently prepares Kitt for what she will face in the future. Even Kitt accedes despite Dunham's coldness, she warns her dancers that the world is even more hardhearted. Kitt writes, "Occasionally she would lecture us on not getting discouraged, telling us that the outside world was cruel and hard and that we didn't know how well off we were in getting such training"; "Miss Dunham did indeed create a better world for many of us, making the path easier for those of us who had the determination to follow" (*Alone* 92–93).

In the end, character building does not concern Dunham as related to Kitt. Dunham, I hazard, fears a discovery of her *soul*. For black women to catch each other's eye—to see each other, to take in each other, and to absorb each other—raises the risk of exposure and shame over what the other might see. Kitt's eyes threaten to find that space of pain Dunham suffers at an early age in her life; Kitt's eyes threaten to probe the very depth of her soul. "Soul" translates as Dunham's personal background and history. Kitt fails to understand that if Dunham answers Kitt's appeal for closeness, her instructor might divulge the past that is Katherine Dunham, the person, just as Kitt's stepsister's call divulges Eartha Mae in the hallway at Carnegie Hall in 1974. The discovery of her personal life and its attendant hurt will leave Dunham vulnerable to her protégé, and that information can be used against her at any moment. Kitt, nevertheless, refuses to give up her gaze of Dunham. She continues to watch to the point where the $5 fines compromise her financial stability. Yet, Kitt essentially pays for black art. She endeavors to connect with this black woman who is larger than she—this black woman in whom she could invest her hopes and dreams in dance.

To Kitt, Dunham represents a black woman's body in triumph in a society that so often claims failure for it. Kitt asserts, "I would [. . .] watch [. . .] this beautiful woman extend her fantastic legs into the air with Vanoye Aikens holding her, moving her, lifting her—the most fantastic thing I had ever seen. I was proud to be in the Katherine Dunham Company. I was learning through watching and observing" (*I'm Still Here* 57). The Katherine Dunham Dance Troupe, then, affirms Kitt's own work. By extension, the Dunham/Aikens pair offers an alternative to the uncle/Gracie/Willie triad. Uncle/Gracie/Willie looks on Kitt's body as one to be whipped and scorned. The Dunham/Aikens pair signifies a black woman's body can be lifted up, the legs can move freely, as the body is held up by the strong hands of another. That notion is indeed fantastic. Although Kitt both praises and questions Dunham's demeanor toward her, she also wants the reader to know she has the right to gaze on the magnificence of black art despite her frustration with her teacher's sometimes harsh words.

Kitt challenges not only the rules in the Dunham camp, but also takes up for herself in the midst of the media's opinions of her, as well. Magazine articles featuring Kitt attest to the entertainer's fiery temper. They also illustrate her sharp and intelligent insights, as well as her dissatisfaction over producers' compulsion for her to sing sexy songs. When she is cast as the lead in the Broadway play *Mrs. Patterson* (1954–1955), Kitt blasts producer Leonard Sillman's song choices: "I really sort of resent the notion that I'm a singer of sexy songs. The songs in 'Mrs. Patterson' are really unnecessary. Leonard Sillman won't like it, but I think the play would be better without them" ("Diva to Duse" 61).

Of show business, Kitt says in 1957, "There is a lack of faith in the performer. Overproduction, with elaborate scenery, means that people see with their eyes, rather than with their souls. This is not giving the audience art" ("Talk with the Star" 70). In that same article, Kitt comments on the frustration of being a singer-dramatic actress: "I resent being hired as a dramatic actress and then having to throw in a few songs, as I did in the supposedly straight play 'Mrs. Patterson.' That's commercialization" (70). In another article, "Salty Eartha," Kitt relates her refusal to sing particular songs just to boost record sales. Claiming "Cry" and "Wheel of Fortune" were not her type of songs, Kitt remarks, "That's the problem. Nobody is able to put a definite type on me. All I can do is keep them guessing. I'm a liberal artist" (62).

Kitt takes up for herself as she tries to validate herself as a leading dramatic actress, even though she is part of the vehicle that constructs her image. The media, however, is a means for Kitt to antagonize and critique those patriarchal voices that constrain her dance movements. Using the interview, Kitt agrees to participate in the world of entertainment and relish her performances therein; in the process, her criticisms bring to light the illusions she helps to foster. These illusions, Kitt believes, divert the audience's attention from the artist and her work.

A Hellcat in the White House: Taking Up for Eartha (Mae) Kitt

Eartha Kitt's taking up and talking back, though, would have dire repercussions when she enters the national home, the White House, in 1968. The First Lady, Lady Bird Johnson, sponsors and arranges the Women's Doers Luncheon, an official gathering to address the issues of crime and poverty in the nation's urban areas. She chooses "Crime in the Streets" as the topic, and she invites Kitt on Vice President Hubert Humphrey's suggestion. Kitt impresses Humphrey with her efforts to raise money for Rebels with a Cause, a group of urban youths alarmed with the rise in juvenile delinquency and poverty ravaging certain areas of Washington, D.C. Kitt observes the scene as the guests, including the First Lady, dance around the subject at hand, preferring to sip tea and pose for the news cameras.

Eartha Kitt speaks up. She demands a discussion of poverty and crime as planned; that the voices of the nation's youth and their mothers—who saw the Vietnam War as an inexplicable waste of the nation's cultural resources—be heard; and that the White House take responsibility for the emotional and psychological damage the war has on the nation's youth. "I think we've missed out on something here today," Kitt begins. "I thought the question was *why* is there so much juvenile delinquency on the streets of America [. . . not] how to beautify America" (*I'm Still Here* 232). Lady Bird Johnson returns Kitt's gaze and says, "Because there's a war on [. . .] that still doesn't give us a free ticket not to try to work for better things—against crime in the streets [. . .]" (L. Johnson 623).

Later the gathering assembles. Newspaper reporters, magazine columnists, Liz Carpenter (Lady Bird's press secretary), and later Lady Bird Johnson herself come out in verbal regalia. The comments, articles, reports, and news releases overall design Kitt as a madwoman. In the article "The White House: A Word from Miss Kitt," *Newsweek* implies that Kitt got what she deserved, reporting:

> Miss Kitt raised her hand, and Mrs. Johnson nodded to her, Miss Kitt rose, *puffing* on a cigarette, her eyes *flashing*, "I think we have missed the main point at this luncheon," she declared with some *heat*. [. . .] Mrs. Johnson was visibly *distressed* by the *outburst*. [. . .] Later, Miss Kitt was scarcely in an apologetic mood. (23–24; my emphasis)

President Johnson orders a memorandum of explanation from press secretary Liz Carpenter. According to Lady Bird Johnson's biographer, Jan Jarboe Russell, Carpenter explains to Johnson that Kitt is not to be taken seriously; she is just your average actress seeking publicity to vitalize her career: "Carpenter wrote that Kitt had no 'previous peacenik record' and told Lyndon Johnson that she had married a white man and 'was not well thought of by a lot of people.' Carpenter suggested that the confrontation was a publicity stunt. 'To keep a career going and to be in demand, a performer must stay constantly in the public eye or be forgotten" (Russell 298). In another account, Sharon Francis, an aide to Mrs. Johnson, feels "for a split second [. . . Kitt] might in some way harm the First Lady" (Russell 297). Lady Bird Johnson wonders if what she has just witnessed is a nightmare (L. Johnson 623).

All of these accounts paint Kitt as a contentious wild-eyed black woman full of smoke and heat, the mercenary black actress, and a potential criminal. Although Kitt and *Newsweek* exchange a few words, the entertainer is not invited to the gathering of media "gossip" that swirls about her after the luncheon. Kitt, however, brings Lady Bird into her own written text and holds a one-on-one dialogue with the First Lady. In *Alone with Me*, Kitt takes to task Lady Bird's interpretation of the events as described in the First Lady's own account, *A White House Diary* (published two years after the White House ordeal). For example, Mrs. Johnson notes that Kitt ate very little. Kitt responds:

[Mrs. Johnson] was right. I eat infrequently and very lightly, and only when I'm hungry. I wasn't hungry and, besides, the prospect of participating in a seminar on "Crime on the Streets" wasn't conducive to a hearty appetite. She also stated in her book that I sat and smoked a great deal—which would be unusual for me, for I'm a light smoker; but I didn't count. One gathers from her account of the luncheon that she was paying an inordinate amount of attention to me. Perhaps my chagrin at the way the luncheon was developing was apparent to her; it was beginning to take on all the overtones of the Mad Hatter's tea party. (*Alone* 241)

Part of Kitt's chagrin has to do with the ways in which the other guests behave in light of such a serious topic. According to Kitt:

when we reached our given tables, the ladies were turning the plates upside looking for markings on the bottom. I could understand that: when I look for antiques I do the same. I love the old world things; I love handicrafts; I love the beauty of the old world self-made styles; and naturally the White House of all places was rich in old world history. But the sounds I was hearing as we were being seated were more suited to Hollywood's "Can I have your autograph, Mr. Grant?" Were these women really committed? Were these women really willing to speak the truth of their own feelings, or just there to add to the bullshit? (*I'm Still Here* 230)

Her analogy of the get-together to that of Hollywood points up Kitt's apprehension of the insincere and surface nature of it; the mention of the "Mad Hatter's tea party" puts forth the chaos of the event. The menu consists of seafood bisque, chicken, and peppermint ice cream— "quite a delicious lunch [. . .] a little on the sumptuous side," remembers Mrs. Johnson (620). Mrs. Johnson records the menu right after she tells us that Eartha Kitt arrives late, and "there was a picture [taken] of her and Miss Katherine Peden with me" (620). Mrs. Johnson suggests that no reason exists for Kitt's actions at the luncheon. She serves Kitt a delicious, sumptuous lunch, and makes possible having her picture taken with the First Lady and another guest. Miss Kitt should have been grateful for the opportunity even to be in the White House. Kitt, however, turns the entire affair over on its face.

Russell reports that Kitt's "tirade" takes the First Lady completely aback. "No other First Lady had ever faced down such an explosion of personal rage. Lady Bird was flabbergasted, and asked herself silently, 'Is this a nightmare?'" (Russell 297). To Lady Bird, Kitt is someone to be watched, stared down, and stopped before she does harm; her presence and voice are fearsome. A closer reading of Lady Bird's biography, her White House diary, and Kitt's account, however, raises suspicions. Something more threatening than Kitt's diatribe against the Vietnam War happens at that luncheon, and concerns Lady Bird herself. One can argue that Kitt brings the smoke and heat of the disgruntled masses from the street into the spotless White House—that Kitt brings in the *dirt* and throws it on the White House's rug with abandon. Kitt blames the Vietnam War for the increase in drug use among America's youth. Her thesis is that many of the nation's young engage in drug use to avoid the draft. Mothers are anguished over the thought of birthing boys only to give them over to the government to fight a war. Kitt writes:

> . . . [B]efore leaving for [the] Washington luncheon, I talked with a group called the Mothers of Watts about crime in the streets. The consensus was that the war in Vietnam was one of the biggest problems—both economically and morally. If a young man was law abiding, he was rewarded by being given a gun and the opportunity to kill or be killed in Vietnam. But if he had a record, the armed forces wouldn't take him, and he was deprived of this "privilege." There were few black men—or poor men of any race or color for that matter—who had the cultural background and money to get a college draft deferment. But they could (and many did) get a *crime* deferment!
>
> [. . . . .]
>
> I don't recall, but I may well have said, as Mrs. Johnson reports, that I knew the feeling of having a baby "come out of my guts," and that I didn't go through such labor to have the baby one day snatched off to a war like Vietnam. Such graphic remarks apparently didn't set too well with the peppermint ice cream dessert. (Kitt, *Alone* 240, 246).

As she speaks these words—"reward," "gun," "kill," "black," "white," "men," "poor," "guts," and "snatch off"—Kitt conjures up the entrails of the war into the White House as well as the myriad voices of (black) women from the socioeconomically depressed streets.

Usually, loss in war is termed as "casualty." "Casualty" is a soft-sounding noun and is easy on the ears. Consider White House staff member Joseph Califano's remarks about the war in 1967: "The war worsened in Vietnam. In 1967, nine thousand Americans died and sixty thousand were wounded, more than double the previous year's casualties" (Califano 247). Kitt, on the other hand, vocalizes the gruesome, nitty-gritty of the war: young men across the lines of race are being killed in a most controversial war, and Kitt carries to the luncheon with her their mother's voices. Kitt's tactic connects with culture critic Katherine Kinney's observation of the "bloodiness so characteristic of representations of the Vietnam War" (8). Kinney asserts, "the veteran's authority of experience has come to define the Vietnam War in American culture" (8). Kitt speaks for the women who have given birth to sons, only to have them sacrificed for a bloody conflict. The Vietnam veteran's narrative is one of the lenses through which we learn of the war's atrocities, as Kinney maintains, and Kitt's verbal accusations in the White House supplement that narrative.

Conversely, in the First Lady's eyes, Kitt offends her southern sensibilities in particular ways. As a privileged guest of the First Lady, Kitt's candor sullies Lady Bird's invitation. A veritable changeling—appearing as a well-behaved guest then transforming into a serious sociopolitical critic—Kitt essentially spills the dirt on the White House carpet. This dirt, or a black woman's daring to convey her awareness of sociopolitical cruel realities, disorders Lady Bird's universe. Mary Douglas's dirt theory maintains that misplaced dirt threatens the status quo and, "offends against order" (2). More important, dirt "signals a site of possible danger to social and individual systems, a sight of vulnerability insofar as the status of dirt as marginal and unincorporable always locates sites of potential threat to the system and to the order it both makes possible and problematizes" (Grosz 192). The "dirt" that Kitt spills includes the verbalization of "guts" and "snatch off," and it is an obvious throwback to chattel slavery, a system, according to historian Kenneth Stampp, wherein enslaved women were bred to produce more human property only to have their children "snatched off" for sale at whim (245). In the context of Vietnam, black male children are figuratively snatched from their mother's breasts to serve in this controversial war. Kitt raises up the ghosts of slavery, a memory Russell tells us haunts Lady Bird's childhood home, Brick House. Many a night Lady Bird lays restless in her sleep as the slaves' kiln holds steady in her backyard. Kitt, furthermore, invokes the act of sexual intercourse in its most clinical terms: "labor" produces "babies" who move through the "guts" of a woman's belly. Kitt's "gutter talk" never is articulated in Lady Bird's world.

To understand what really happens at the White House on January 18, 1968, one must go to the childhood environment of Claudia Alta Taylor (also known as Lady Bird). Miss Taylor comes from an ancestral line of prosperous white southerners who practically made East Texas the place it is today. Miss Taylor's mother, Minnie Lee Pattillo, is descended from a line of Scotsmen who settled in America in 1740 (Russell 30). One of her ancestors, "Henry Pattillo, a Presbyterian minister, published the first textbook in the state of North Carolina in 1787" (30). One section of Pattillo's book offers the "Negro catechism," which stresses severe obedience from the Negro to his or her masters and advises never give over to emotion. Her father, Thomas Jefferson Taylor, came to Karnack, Texas, from Alabama in 1899. The Negroes of the county, who comprise more than 50 percent of the population and toil in servitude, call Taylor "Mister Boss." Alice Tittle, Miss Taylor's black nurse and caretaker, nicknames her "Lady Bird" at the time of her birth in 1912. For the rest of her life, Negro servants take care of Claudia Alta Taylor–Lady Bird Johnson (Russell 27, 51).

As for the treatment of white women and their place in society, Miss Taylor grew up in a southern society where grief, pain, and suffering, are borne in silence and never are brought out in the open for discussion. It is incumbent upon a southern lady to suffer these with dignity and without any show of emotion, and "Lady Bird remarks that these tenets are an indication of the 'South's shadowy side'" (Russell 30). Her mother, Minnie Taylor, dies when Claudia is not yet six. The loss is treated as an open secret; no one dares to discuss it. These social mores govern Lady Bird's comportment. In segregated East Texas, everything and everyone have a place. Negro servants who care for the Taylors live in servants' quarters behind Lady Bird's childhood home as is customary. Her father forces Negro women to accept his sexual advances, and he talks about his sexual exploits with them with abandon. Claudia Alta Taylor grew into Lady Bird Johnson out of this life.

Fast forward to the 1968 luncheon. The President makes a surprise appearance in the middle of the first speech. President Johnson extends the standard greeting, thanks the guests for coming, applauds the assembly, and starts to leave the room. Kitt, whose chair practically rubs against the podium, rises from her seat. She stands next to the President and speaks:

KITT: Mr. President, what are we to do about delinquent *parents*—those who have to work and are too busy to look after their children? [. . .] Because taxes are so heavy, both parents often have to work and are forced to leave their children alone.

MR. PRESIDENT: We have just passed a Social Security bill that allots millions of dollars for day-care centers.

KITT: Our subject was crime in the streets; day-care centers were for small children, not teenagers who were forming gangs and terrorizing neighborhoods. [. . .] But what are we going to do?

MR. PRESIDENT: That's something for you women to discuss here. (*Alone* 243)

For a privileged southern white woman, this act is a slander against her heritage. The very foundation of southern decorum on which Lady Bird stands—to avoid a direct address of discord at all costs—cracks. Moreover, Kitt calls for white womanhood to speak from the pedestal on which she has been placed, rather than to stand on it in silence. On the other hand, not only does Kitt come out of the "servants' quarters," but this Negro woman positions herself as an equal partner with her husband-president. She looks him in the eye, poses a question, and expects an answer. Even worse, her husband, the white man–president leans over to Kitt and answers her. Johnson's gesture in answering Kitt is immortalized in an Associated Press photo. Much worse, the President validates Kitt's poser: He throws the responsibility back to "you women." In a backhanded way, President Johnson's verbal acknowledgment confirms Kitt's uneasiness: Get to the issue at hand. That's for what you have assembled here.

The damage continues. Just as Johnson defers to Kitt, so does Mrs. Johnson. The First Lady responds from the podium:

Because there is a war on, [. . .] and I pray that there will be a just and honest peace—that still doesn't give us a free ticket not to try to work for better things—against crime in the streets, and for better education and better health for our people. I cannot identify as much as I should. I have not lived the background that you have, nor can I speak as passionately or as well, but we must keep our eyes and our hearts and our energies fixed on constructive areas and try to do something that will make this a happier, better-educated land. (L. Johnson 623)

These are the most important lines in Lady Bird's response: "I cannot identify as much as I should. I have not lived the background that you have, nor can I speak as passionately or as well. . . ." Kitt's remarks cause Lady Bird to step out from under her magnolia tree—mint julep in hand—and transgress the very tenets her ancestor, Henry Pattillo, laid out more than 300 years before. Not only that, Claudia–Lady Bird–Mrs. Johnson–First Lady admits her own shortcomings in public, and she speaks directly to a Negro woman. Overall, Mrs. Johnson unwittingly recognizes her white privilege. She is ill-equipped to address the real needs that are supposed to be discussed at the luncheon. The luncheon, then, is brought out as the farce that Kitt has perceived it to be. To call for attention to "constructive areas" is precisely what Kitt means to do the entire time. Not only does President Johnson give nod to Kitt's remarks, but so does Mrs. Johnson. This is the unexpected "no good" part Mrs. Johnson has anticipated. Kitt acts uppity.

As bell hooks states, there is indeed power in looking (*Black Looks* 115–31). Kitt enacts such an oppositional gaze and names what she sees at that luncheon. Once one looks back and reveals the character of any thing, the light shines on its true nature. Too, the light shines on the whole, and the culprit is open and vulnerable to its consequences. Kitt has to go. Practically all of her scheduled engagements and performances are cancelled, and she has to find work abroad. Kitt remembers, "In my case, club contracts were canceled or 'lost,' with the contractors refusing to draw up new ones [. . .]. Agents were no longer interested in Eartha Kitt because they couldn't book her [. . .]. I was effectively stopped from performing in the United States" (*Alone* 253–54). Of her actions at the White House, Kitt declares, amid the cautionary voices of her friends, "I didn't *do* anything except voice my opinion" (*Alone* 250).

In voicing her opinion, Kitt does what black women have been compelled to do for ages: take up for themselves and their communities to be raised up and out of the muck and mire of discrimination, oppression, and abuse—traumas that have made for a bruised black sisterhood—and into the land of love and healing themselves. Let us recall Anita Hill's taking up for herself during her testimony of sexual harassment from her former employer Clarence Thomas before the 1991 Senate Judiciary confirmation hearings. Her testimony amid an avalanche of questions brings national awareness to sexual harassment in the workplace. What Anita Hill does for sexual harassment, Oprah Winfrey does for child molestation when she imparts her abuse at the hands of some men in her community on her nationally televised show. Finally, Angela Davis takes up for Joan Little, a twenty-year-old indigent black woman who, in 1974, stabs her white jailer, Clarence Alligood, eleven times with an ice pick for trying to rape her while being held in an all-male jail in Beaufort, South Carolina (Davis, "Joan Little" 74–75). Hill's, Winfrey's, and Davis's actions are love in action—a love that is vitalized by care, psychic nurture, careful talk, compassion, and activism. The element of respect for their black female selves acts as a fundamental current in this love and ultimately promotes a humane care-taking and treatment of others. Cornel West advances the theory of love as necessary to living. In his treatise on nihilism—"the experience of coping with a life of horrifying meaninglessness, hopelessness, and *(most important)* lovelessness"—West believes, "[l]ife without meaning, hope, and *love* breeds a coldhearted, mean-spirited outlook that destroys both the individual and others" (23; emphasis mine).

Kitt's dance in the White House points up incredible interior strength and offers no apology for taking up for herself as a black female activist. A columnist for *Newsweek* interviews Kitt after the White House fiasco and reports:

> Miss Kitt was scarcely in an apologetic mood. Back home in Beverly Hills, she flounced into her house, enthused over a new purple teardrop lamp she had received as a gift ("It's beautiful," she said. "It'll make the place look like a real whorehouse"), called for a belt of brandy [. . .]. "No, I don't think I was rude . . . Yes, I'd do it again [. . .]. If Mrs. Johnson was embarrassed," said Miss Kitt, squirming emphatically in her tan turtle-neck sweater dress, "that's her problem." ("A Word from" 24)

Yes, she said that, and eleven days after the event. Even though Kitt comes to us as an outrageous performer willing to gamble her status in the entertainment industry at the highest level, she unapologetically takes up for her actions. They are her challenges to the national home to make good on its promise to explore the condition of America's underprivileged children living in cultures of poverty. This is taking up for Eartha Mae.

Rejuvenate!, Kitt's last installment in her autobiographical corpus, is a self-help manual wherein Kitt, in her seventies, gives advice on maintaining energy and vitality through proper diet, exercise, and positive thinking. In it, she celebrates her inner capacity to withstand all of her tribulations:

> [. . .] the gods had been more than good, considering my beginnings: ugly duckling Eartha Mae, born out of wedlock and into poverty on a cotton plantation in South Carolina, then given

away because Mama's husband-to-be said he didn't want "that yella gal" in his house. The people she was given to—were they close or distant relatives? She never knew. [. . .] These people were cruel: beating Eartha Mae, poorly feeding Eartha Mae, working her like a dog. [. . .] It was one o'clock in the morning of January 1, 2000, [. . .] I went to bed supremely appreciative for being alive. [. . .] I was grateful, too, [. . .] [t]o still be here and to still be doing, doing, doing—how fantastic! (12–13, 17)

There is Eartha Mae, the poverty-stricken light-skinned child outcast, and there is Eartha Kitt, the popular black woman entertainer who protects Eartha Mae from the threat of destitution. This self-affirmation tells of Kitt's survival, but the litany of facts she still recalls in *Rejuvenate!*'s introduction—illegitimacy, rejection, and name-calling—slips in Kitt's awareness of having been talked 'bout, 'buked and scorned; even more hurtful, called out of her name. Kitt's rehearsals of her life story, however, allow her to document the ways she takes up for Eartha Mae, the community's unwanted child, and defend Eartha Kitt, the entertainer. Each of her narratives erects one more reinforcement for Eartha Mae Kitt who, in all of her Cat Woman arrogance, resists the capillaries of mean-spiritedness and who in the end dances a dance of celebration for fighting for her right to be the awestruck teenager in Katherine Dunham's camp, the risqué wild woman in the world of entertainment, and the hellcat in the White House in the end.

CHAPTER FOUR

Diahann Carroll

The Recuperation of Black Widow–
Single Mother/Womanhood

It is 1968. A stunned Diahann Carroll listens carefully to the "full-scale assault" launched by the ever-popular Harry Belafonte on *Julia*, the new television sitcom in which she is to star (Carroll, *Diahann* 145). The sitcom will break ground: it will be the first time a black actress will take the helm as leading lady in a television program. *Julia* will establish Diahann Carroll as a household name, and her stance against Belafonte will nourish in the actress the necessary confidence to audition for other roles that will have historical significance for her in the future. More important, Carroll anticipates that the weekly program widely would circulate the image of a black mother as the caretaker of her own home and child, not as a maid or a mammy in a white household. The protagonist of the program is Julia, a registered nurse widowed when her husband, a U.S. Air Force captain, is killed serving his country. The program will illustrate how this single black mother manages the tragedy and continues to support her son. For Carroll taking the role would mean a new modern dance of black widowhood and black single motherhood. Carroll recognizes, too, that power brokers are willing to take a chance on the series. She writes, "*[Julia]* was promoted and produced by two of the largest conglomerates in America—20th Century Fox and NBC. I don't think any other show had that kind of production team. It was a new beginning" (Carroll, "From Julia" 101).

Actor-entertainer Harry Belafonte, however, advises the actress to decline the role. Belafonte argues *Julia* shows no regard for the black man. In fact, Belafonte and novelist and essayist James Baldwin strongly urge white writer-producer Hal Kanter to change the name of the show from *Mamma's Boy* to *The Diahann Carroll Show* (later *Julia)* to "refute the canard that black women dominated the males in their families" (Kanter 257). Belafonte is not one to be casually dismissed. Carroll understands full well his ardent commitment to the civil rights movement and his personal relationship with Dr. Martin Luther King, Jr. and Coretta Scott King. Carroll carefully considers Belafonte's arguments. In the comfort and intimacy of her dressing room, the actress reveals in her autobiography *Diahann* (1986) her dismissal of the singer's counsel, believing *Julia's* "middle-class aspect was a positive" (145). She continues, "However *Julia* is presented, she represents another more realistic evolution, purely because of the circumstances of her existence" ("Julia" 58).

The historical and sociocultural environment of the United States in 1968 influences each view. Carroll's preference lobbies for representation of a class of black people that has yet to receive a broad currency in the media; Belafonte appeals for total rejection of a television program offering little or no dialogue on the absent black man in the black household. Both entertainers indeed raise significant issues of representation of black people in the media, but miss the overarching meaning of the sitcom.

To begin with, Carroll's choice to perform in a television sitcom as a black middle-class woman also brings to relief the phenomenon of black widowhood. *Julia* will illustrate how a widowed black mother manages the tragedy and continues to support her son on her own. By extension, *Julia* antagonizes popular belief that households headed by single black mothers imperil the sacred convention of a patriarchal two-parent household. By agreeing to be cast as Julia Baker, Carroll takes the scepter of black widowhood, places it next to black single motherhood, combines the two, and offers America an alternative image of black womanhood in general. "I'd like a couple of million of them (white Americans) to watch and say, 'Hey, so that's what they do when they go home,'" Carroll declares ("Julia" 57).

In 1984, television audiences learn more about the lives of black women when Carroll arrives on primetime soap opera, *Dynasty*. Carroll's autobiography *Diahann* conjointly discloses her unyielding 1980s campaign to integrate the black woman actress into the hallowed mansions of the nighttime television soap opera replete with upperclass white men and their disillusioned but pampered wives. *Dynasty* is an aristocratic world, wherein blacks practically are invisible, are on the periphery, eventually killed, or have short-lived roles. For example, Dora Mae (Pat Colbert) is the black restaurant hostess on *Dallas)* for nine years, yet we only see her when she seats Dallas oil baron J. R. Ewing with his corporate buddies; Patricia and Frank Williams (Lynne Moody and Larry Riley) are the only black couple in the cul-de-sac on *Knots Landing*, and a drunken Gary Ewing (Ted Shackleford) kills Patricia her third year on the show; Julie Williams (Kent Masters) appears as a possible love interest for Karen Fairgate MacKenzie's (Michelle Lee) son, Michael Fairgate (Pat Petersen); and Rosemont (Roscoe Lee Brown) is in the vineyards on *Falcon Crest* for a year. Carroll's groundbreaking characters in *Julia* and *Dynasty* shed light on the multidimensionality of black (female) celebrities.

Julia Baker and Dominique Deveraux—the middle-class nurse and the aristocrat—collectively with Carroll's own middle-class bourgeois background, however, conspire with entertainment and news media powers to de-race Diahann Carroll. Those who create and require maintenance of Carroll's on- and off-screen images in the entertainment world counteract her identification as a *black* woman in America. In other words, Carroll's star quality and success, authorities in film and visual culture believe, separate her from the black race. Black historian and archivist Arthur Schomburg would agree:

> [. . .] by virtue of [the Negro] being regarded as something "exceptional," even by friends and well-wishers, Negroes of attainment and genius have been unfairly disassociated from the group, and [the] group credit lost accordingly. (670)

Carroll stands resolute against this gesture of disassociation, as I will demonstrate, and demands these authorities remember her place in the group of black people, in general, and black women and mothers in particular. Her fortitude embodies what black feminist critic Patricia Hill Collins calls "the importance of self-definition." Collins writes, "When Black women define ourselves, we clearly reject the assumption that those in positions granting them the authority to interpret our reality are entitled to do so" (106–107).

The conflict between Carroll and Belafonte instigates the actress's stalwart assertion of self-definition, an assertion made against the backdrop of the civil rights movement. It is a time when black political leaders are assassinated, and the Vietnam War and the state of the black family preoccupy the nation. In 1965 Daniel Patrick Moynihan releases to the United States Department of Labor his controversial research *The Negro Family: The Case for National Action*. Commonly referred to as "The Moynihan Report," Moynihan concludes "Negro children without fathers flounder—and fail," and that "the measure of family disorganization" within Negro society could be attributed to Negro families headed by women (35). The report not only outlines the historical-political reasons for the disorganization of the Negro family—namely slavery and "an image of the American family as a highly standardized phenomenon" (5); it also cites statistics throughout to illustrate the consequences of the absent Negro man within the home, especially in urban cities.

The assassinations of black civil rights leaders, however, traumatize the nation. On June 12, 1963, a bloodied and dying Medgar Evers drags himself to the front porch of his home after being shot by white supremacist Byron De La Beckwith. Myrlie Evers desperately tries to shield her children as she calls for help. In 1964 in South Africa, Winnie Mandela becomes the matriarch of the antiapartheid movement when the government jails her husband on the prison estate of Robben Island. Prison separates Nelson Mandela from Winnie and their two daughters, Zenani and Zindziswa, for twenty-seven years. On February 21, 1965, Betty Shabazz, pregnant and accompanied by her children, witnesses the murder of her children's father as bullets spray from the audience assassinating her husband, Malcolm X, while giving a speech at the Audubon Ballroom in New York City. On April 4, 1968, Coretta Scott King becomes a widow and single mother of four. Her husband, Martin Luther King, Jr., is assassinated at the Lorraine Hotel in Memphis, Tennessee. These back-to-back traumatic events, coupled with the loss of husbands, fathers, and sons in the Vietnam War, render black America a nation of widows and fatherless children. In 1968 black America's masses groan under death, mourning, and grief.

When weighed with the visuals of the widows of slain civil rights leaders carrying the scepter for civil rights as well as those mothers widowed as a result of war, *Julia,* then, offers an expansive vision of single black motherhood and widowhood. The sitcom especially disrupts the claim published in the Moynihan Report. Institutionalized racism undermines the black family's efforts to construct a cohesive thriving family unit, not the family unit itself. Julia Baker and her young son, Corey, live in an integrated apartment complex in Los Angeles, California—not in an urban ghetto. K. Sue Jewell points out that in the United States is the notion that the black single-parent household is the reason for the entire cultural moral decline. The absentee black father in the black household is the assumed source of rampant delinquency and crime. This absenteeism jeopardizes the two-parent heterosexual ideal; therefore this black family structure poisons the very moral fabric of the United States. Jewell notes, however, a warped view of minorities preceeds this perception, stating, "in many instances, cultural images of African American women and other disenfranchised groups have been distorted and generally uncharacteristic of individuals belonging to this group; yet these images have had a profound influence on other people's perceptions and expectations of African American women" (32). *Julia* and the real-life motion-picture visuals of Mrs. King during her husband's funeral procession and the efforts for self-improvement and childcare on the part of Mmes. King, Evers, and Shabazz as well, contradict these scripts, such as what the Moynihan Report lays bare for the consumption of the U.S. public, and its legislators, as well.

Belafonte's appeal to Carroll to withdraw from the sitcom *Julia* seems contradictory to the advice he offers Coretta Scott King. Belafonte suggests to Mrs. King that she participate in the march for poor people in Memphis scheduled to take place on Monday, April 8, the day before Martin Luther King, Jr.'s funeral. Mrs. King writes:

> The march in Memphis was still scheduled to be held on Monday, as Martin had planned it and as he would have wished. That Saturday morning Harry Belafonte said to me, "I want to talk to you about something that has been on my mind. You don't have to agree, but think about it. I think you should go to Memphis and march on Monday if it isn't too much for you. It would mean a great deal to the people throughout the nation, for you to just be there." Immediately I replied, "I agree. I think Martin would have wanted me to go. I had not thought about it before, but now that you raise the question, I would really like to go. I may even take the children. [. . .] Not that I [. . . could] do what Martin did, but [. . .] in some small way, perhaps I [. . . could] serve as he did, the aspirations of oppressed people of all races, throughout the world." (327–29)

Belafonte advises Mrs. King to appear alone in public, and Mrs. King responds by embracing the nation's grief with her own. Her strength parts the way so that black widowhood and single black womanhood enter the visual media. Her decision to step into the public's eye without the benefit of a husband or protector questions black sociologist Robert Staples claim, "the Black woman actually had little power over the family or society" (Giddings 327). Questioning this statement is indeed one of the services Coretta Scott King offers to the nation and to the world at large. Network television carries visions of the widow into the intimate space of the living room. There, in the private domestic space, a mass audience of black and white Americans witnesses a single black woman continuing not only the care of a nation, but also the care of her personal household. Belafonte's gesture acknowledges the presence of the black woman facilitates the management of national grief. Carroll's blueprint for the expression of black solidarity may not match the political import that the Belafonte/King mission anticipates, however, her strategy is just as valid. The visual configurations against which the actress plays complement those of Mrs. King's. Each distribution of the visual has to do with scripts—written and unwritten—that either exclude black women or, in their inclusion, insist on a certain visual. Black discourses of grief in the 1960s, for example, include the expression of sorrow by major civil rights activists, poets, and novelists over assassinations of civil rights leaders. Generally, the media focuses on the impact the fatalities have on the *masses* of black people, the civil rights movement, and the relationship of the U.S. government to black Americans thereafter. National news articles briefly mention the consequences of death on Mmes. King, Evers, and Shabazz. The masses are allowed a dialogue on mourning and loss in the media, but the voices of the wives and mothers generally remain unheard in terms of the aftereffects of loss of the black father from the home.

In his famous eulogy of Malcolm X, for example, actor Ossie Davis declares, "[I]f you knew him you would know why we must honor him: Malcolm was our manhood, our living, black manhood! This was his meaning to his people" (521). In his controversial collection of essays *Soul on Ice*, Black Panther Eldridge Cleaver writes, "[w]hat provoked the assassins to murder [Malcolm X]? Did it bother them that Malcolm was elevating our struggle into the international arena through his campaign to carry it before the United Nations?" (60). Virtually all of the recent autobiographies written by major civil rights figures and King associates, including Julian Bond's *A Time to Speak, a Time to Act: The Movement in Politics* (1972); Ralph David Abernathy's *And the Walls Came Tumbling Down: An Autobiography* (1989); Andrew Young's *An Easy Burden: The Civil Rights Movement and the Transformation of America* (1996); and Georgia Congressman John Lewis's *Walking with the Wind: A Memoir of the Movement* (1998), record the confusion and despair over the state of the movement after King's death. Lewis, Abernathy, Young, and Bond express personal sorrow over the assassinations of Evers, Malcolm X, and King. None make mention of the state of the surviving family members, or the general emotional, mental, and financial welfare of their children. In Henry Hampton's *Voices of Freedom: An Oral History of the Civil Rights Movement from the 1950s through the 1980s* (1990), Mmes. Evers, Shabazz, and King do speak about these deaths. Their commentaries, however, are couched in the discussion and spirit of the movement and the social platforms on which each husband-leader stood. No dialogue is included about the emotional care of the family on "the day after" the trauma, but an anxiety over strategy, movement continuity, leadership appointment, and the emotional and mental health of the community at large is present.

The episode "The Promised Land (1967–1968)," part of the 1989 PBS video *Eyes on the Prize II: America at the Racial Crossroads 1965–1985* is a visual case in point. Written on the back of the video box is the statement, "[o]n April 4, 1968, in Memphis, Martin Luther King, Jr., was assassinated. Though devastated by the loss of their leader, King's staff struggled to continue the campaign." Next to that statement is a two-inch square black-and-white picture of Coretta Scott King with her son Martin by her side. The caption reads, "Funeral Procession for Martin Luther King, Jr." rather than, "Martin Luther King, Jr.'s widow, Coretta Scott King, and son Martin Luther King, III."

The montage of the funeral procession and the interviews thereafter reiterates my point. As the public hears the news of the assassination, riots erupt across the nation in several major cities, including Washington, D.C. The episode shows aerial and long shots of burning cities, armed guards, and mourners crying in despair. These shots enunciate the sense of absolute turmoil. At the King wake at Spelman College in Atlanta, a desperate camera competes with the crowd to offer a glimpse of Mrs. King and the children as they enter the chapel to view the body. There is one shot of Mrs. King as she bends over the casket to see King. Then, a cut to Mrs. King straining to walk through the crowd to attend the funeral at Ebenezer Baptist Church. After several shots of the dignitaries, the camera cuts to the wagon and the casket, and pans the people. Andrew Young and Daddy King peruse the flowerbed; back to Mrs. King, A. D. King, and Harry Belafonte; extreme close-up of the King casket. Cut to Ms. Marian Logan, Southern Christian Leadership Conference (SCLC) board member. She says, "We didn't know where we were going. Everything was in a state of flux. And our leader was gone and we felt a great void and a terrible sick emptiness. And we all felt that we had to do something that we hoped would be meaningful." Julian Bond narrates, "SCLC was in shock but committed itself to carry out King's [poor people's] campaign" (The Promised Land" 1967–1968). Long shots of bus riders follow; a medium shot of Hosea Williams and Ralph Abernathy leading the mule-driven wagon; a quick shot of Mrs. Belafonte and Mrs. King marching arm-in-arm.

Absent are Mrs. King's thoughts and feelings about the assassination and its impact on her family. The politics of the movement, in particular the question of where do we, the masses, go from here, eclipse black widowhood and black single motherhood. Likewise, the lives of these women are inextricably linked to the images and politics of slain black leaders; they evolve into what I term "professional widows."

Professional widowhood encompasses continuing the political and cultural legacies the slain leader-husband-father initiated. It also requires a commitment to the ideals, hopes, and dreams of those for whom the movement was organized. In the case of the civil rights movement, a vehicle that institutes change in the civil status of minorities on the basic level of human rights, the widow is expected to accept the sociopolitical responsibility along with the movement's current leaders. Part of the philosophy entails moving forward in the face of adversity. We are quite familiar with Coretta Scott King's tireless efforts as the keeper of Martin Luther King, Jr.'s dream. Myrlie Evers-Williams fights for three decades and finally realizes a conviction by a Mississippi jury for white supremacist Byron De La Beckwith for the murder of her first husband—after the first two trials ended with deadlocked juries. She conducts her legal campaign while attending school and raising her three children. Evers-Williams accepts the post of chairwoman for NAACP in February 1995. She successfully polishes the organization's image, and leads it out of debt. Although not as visible as her contemporaries, Betty Shabazz, a teacher and activist, receives a doctorate in education administration. She eventually is appointed director of public relations at Medgar Evers College in Brooklyn, N.Y. She raises six children. The accomplishments made by these widows illustrate their wholehearted agreement to receive the scepter and carry on their husband's legacies with children in tow. There is indeed work to be done the day after.

Carroll and *Julia* enter at this juncture, and within the context of loss and trauma experienced by black women, I consider her interventions into the politics of reading and writing. These technologies facilitate the control over rhetoric disseminated about her in the media in particular and the widespread circulation of images of black women in popular culture in general. Carroll's interventions direct our attention to her behind-the-scenes activities at NBC, where she challenges the script of one of the most influential writer-producers in the television industry at that time, Hal Kanter.

Kanter creates *Julia* after hearing Roy Wilkins, former NAACP executive director, deliver a speech in 1967 on the socioeconomic and cultural status of the black man in U.S. society and the obstacles that inhibited his realization of the American Dream. Wilkins encourages the television industry to "consider more positive and more meaningful ways to support [. . . the NAACP's] practical agenda" (Kanter 254). After contemplating Wilkins's speech, Kanter resolves to create a television show that portrays black people as people—and as people who could be laughed *with,* rather than laughed *at.* With a program such as *Julia,* "sooner or later some of the verities of African-American life would become apparent, some of the myths exploded" (254).

Kanter imagines *Julia* to be a vehicle through which a certain truism about racial dynamics can filter into the American household. During an interview with *Daily Variety,* Carroll recalls, Kanter said, "[w]e're going to tell the truth. We're going to show it like it is" (Carroll 143). From the start, however, the ideal of color-blindness appeals to the writer and, therefore, presents his "bold dream" to NBC with a summary of the story without the mention of color. For his vehicle, he chooses an already popular format: a sitcom set in a female-headed household. Network television premiers four programs in 1968 with the widowed–single mother format. It addresses, however, the absence of the white man in the nuclear family due to death. These 30–minute programs include a narrative about a tragedy that leaves white mothers widowed with children. Hope Lange stars in *The Ghost and Mrs. Muir* (NBC), a comedy drama about a beautiful widow with two small children who is "visited" by a sea captain's ghost residing in her cottage. Lucille Ball again makes popular the zany redhead, now a widow with two teenagers, in *Here's Lucy* (CBS). *The Doris Day Show* (CBS) features the actress of the same name. *Julia* (NBC) starring Carroll, joins the line-up as a widowed black mother, makes clear a reality the sitcom cuts across lines of race.

According to Kanter, the readers "dropped the script in surprise" when they discover on page 12 Julia's retort in an interview with a white interviewer: "Should I have written in bold, black letters on the top of my application, 'I am a Negro'?" (Kanter 255). Kanter's strategy works, and Mort Werner, vice-president of programs for NBC, pushes for the sitcom to premiere on the network. Subsequently, Kanter assumes a paternalistic role saying, "*my* Julia and her son had grown real to me and very dear" (Kanter 256; my emphasis). Within this desire to possess the character, the creation, Kanter decries Baldwin's and Belafonte's suggested name change. "While I respect Baldwin's and Belafonte's points of view," Kanter writes, "this show is not about Diahann, it's about a woman named Julia, so that's what we'll call it" (Kanter 257).

At this time, Kanter also sends word to "Di" to be reminded "her mission is to entertain, not to become the spokeswoman for her entire race. She's Julia Baker, not *Joan of Dark*" (Kanter 257; my emphasis). In a twisted sort of way, the "Joan of Dark" association immediately places Carroll in the role of blackface, or minstrel, whose primary mission is to entertain through the Dunbarian mask that "grins and lies" (Dunbar, "We Wear the Mask" 896). The statement also invokes the fifteenth-century patron saint of France, Joan of Arc, burned at the stake for witchcraft, heresy, and cross-dressing. I hazard Kanter's invocation warns Carroll to know her place inside of popular culture: she is an actress— no, an *entertainer*—first, who plays a character; she is not a messenger for the black race nor is she a part of the group. Kanter, furthermore, finds no direct correlation to the social issues of the 1960s with that of Julia Baker and her story and the actress, Diahann Carroll, as well. Kanter's presumption that he can situate Carroll and manipulate her interpretation of a black character and determine for the actress her mission in the wake of a tenacious civil rights movement, signals a sinister bargain. Kanter is a white and prominent television writer; Carroll is black and female. The writer's statement is an attempt to close off other avenues for representations of the black woman in visual culture and to project on the audience his notions of black life. The Joan of Dark label undercuts Kanter's intentions after the Wilkins speech, when he wonders what contribution he can make to dispel some of the myths about black America and how he "personally could help realize the American Dream for us all . . ." (Kanter 254). Instead the Joan of Dark remark carries forward the myth white people widely held about black people: black men and women are primarily entertainers. What is worse, Kanter's invocation verifies Arthur Schomburg's observation.

Carroll's inchoate clash with Kanter begins here. The struggle for script changes in the dialogue about black women and mothers at the time, and what the black female entertainer is allowed to say about her life unfold via the actress's resistance strategies on the set of *Julia*. Carroll's reading of Kanter's text for television is, in and of itself, subversive, because the privileging of writing, or graphocentrism, has been the primary way European cultures have dominated other peoples. According to feminist critic Barbara Johnson, "[w]hat enslaves is not writing per se but *control* of writing, and writing as control. What is at stake in writing is the very structure of authority itself" (48).

Carroll, Kanter, and *Julia* Backstage

One reading of the actual script demonstrates not only Patricia Hill Collins's "importance of self-definition," but also Carroll's attempt to wrest control of writing from Kanter. This venture, importantly, exposes the authority's imaginings of black life as chimerical. On the set of *Julia*, Carroll scrutinizes the writing for any insensitivity to race. Corey, Julia's son, for example, is to identify as screen legend John Wayne and his white friend (the Indian) is to play dead after he shoots him in a game of cowboys and Indians: "I'm John Wayne and you're an Indian, and bang-bang, I just shot you dead" are Corey's lines (Carroll, *Diahann* 149). Carroll consults Kanter. "Corey cannot say that [. . .] because John Wayne is not the idol of black children. Because black parents don't think of him as a role model. [. . .] I can't be a part of this script" (Carroll, *Diahann* 149). Kanter suggests Roy Rogers, after which Carroll realizes Kanter does not "get it . . ." (Carroll 149). Kanter ignores Carroll's suggestions for script changes; Carroll simply walks away from the script, refusing to shoot the scene. In a rage, Kanter telephones her. "Jesus Christ," rails Kanter, "you can't just take off like that!" Carroll retorts, "Let me tell you something, Hal. *You* can't do it either. We can't do it. It's called out of order. You can't walk out on a problem" (Carroll, *Diahann* 150).

The teakettle whistles from my kitchen, and I welcome a break to chew on this one. I sit curled in the comfort of my papasan sipping a cup of tea in an effort to explicate this passage. With my red pen in hand and a yellow pad, I listen as the monotone of Jungian storyteller Clarissa Pinkola Estés's voice wafts out of my ten-year-old tape player: "To bear the burden of consciousness takes strength," she says as I lay my tired head on the bamboo rim. "Consciousness sends light into corners of your world and the world that many of us would rather not see. [. . .] We feel that it is a burden to see them; we can't bear them [. . .] [but] you have to be able to bear them and bear the sight of them." Is this what Carroll dares Kanter to do? To dare to see and to have the strength to bear the verities of black life—racism, discrimination, the struggle for civil rights, race-consciousness—that he said he wanted to show the world? To be conscious of her identificatory practices inside and outside the postage-stamp world of television? Yes, Carroll invites Kanter to wade in the morass of America's mean-spiritedness; to see it, to bear it, to find creative ways to articulate it. "*You can't walk out on a problem. It's called out of order.*" That Carroll challenges Kanter's script during production of *Julia* marks her battle to control the visual formation of the single black family, the single black mother's voice, and, more important, Carroll's own perception of herself outside of the entertainment industry and inside the black community of parents. Her defiance, too, of Kanter's writerly authority steadies her self-identificatory practices.

Yet, if Corey were to play a black hero, just who would it be? Paul Robeson? The Olympians at the 1968 Olympics, Tommie Smith and John Carlos? Malcolm X? Mohammad Ali (Cassius Clay)? Black Panther Huey Newton? Nineteenth-century slave revolutionaries Denmark

Vecsey and Gabriel Prosser? Since these are the black heroes, why does Carroll not offer to Kanter an alternative? Finally it occurs to me that *Julia Baker* is Corey's hero. Corey lives in a world where his very sustenance comes from his black mother, not from some outside force. Carroll's reluctance to name a hero is an indirect way of explaining in single-parent households headed by black women in the United States, sufficient unto this day is the black mother heroine. The inner workings of maintaining a household in the absence of the black father—regardless of the reason—are in and of themselves heroic. The daily tasks of employment and family care are activities the black child sees his mother perform. These tasks concern survival; they are neither about going off into the wonderland of white heroes and choosing a John Wayne (whose movies were generally about the genocide of Native Americans) to emulate, nor choosing one whose fortune is made on ridicule of black character Stepin' Fetchit, the actor. The aforementioned black heroes are not heroes in the conventional sense, but in the sense that no matter the journey, they carry the burden of representation; they put their lives and careers on the line for the progress of the black race.

As I take another sip of my tea, visions of black children dance in my mind: Yolanda (12 years old); Martin III (10), Dexter (7), and Bernice King (5); Attilah (6), Qubilah (4), Ilyasah (2), Gamilah (7 months), Malikah and Malaak Shabazz (two months in mother's womb); Zenani and Zindziswa Mandela; and Julia's own Corey Baker. I try to imagine what seeing your mother faint after finding out through a phone call that her husband, your father, has been killed must be like; I imagine what having your pregnant mother shield you from a spray of bullets as you watch your father being mowed down on stage must feel like; I imagine how witnessing your mother's terror after your father has been murdered in his own front yard must feel. How does a black child deal with the day after? Who is there to cushion the blow, interpret, and articulate the unholy terror? Who is there to prepare the breakfast the day after? Who will choreograph a dance of images that will uphold the image of the black mother as heroine? John Wayne? Roy Rogers? No. The black mother.

Carroll, Deveraux, and *Dynasty*

Carroll's conflict with Kanter later transfers to an argument for a visual of the successful single black woman. In 1984, at the risk of personal and professional embarrassment, Carroll crashes a Golden Globe after-party of television producer Aaron Spelling to signal her fervent interest in being a part of the *Dynasty* cast, an idea Roy Gerber, Carroll's manager, presents earlier to Spelling. "Well, why not?" Carroll asks. "[*Knot's Landing, Dynasty, Dallas, Falcon Crest*] had touched on just about every other controversial, highly dramatic subject. It was only a matter of time until they overcame their timidity and introduced a black character . . ." (Carroll, *Diahann* 237–238). At that gathering, Carroll says to Esther Shapiro, writer-producer for the soap opera, after Shapiro expresses interest in Carroll's idea:

> Esther, forgive my presumptuousness, but if you don't do it with me, please, please do it with someone. *Dynasty* is an international success, and we tend to forget in America that most of the people in the world are not white. I'd like her to be black because that happens to be me, but should you decide not to go that way, then I beg you to think about an oriental or some other Third World person. (Carroll 240)

The producers choose Carroll, and she enters the wicked and wealthy world of white bitchdom as the "first black bitch on television," Dominique Deveraux (Carroll, *Diahann* 237). Carroll's 1984 side chat with Shapiro, however, distinguishes Carroll as an actress appreciative of the value of the American visual image: it travels across (inter)national borders. The chat is expeditious because Carroll's suggestion not only broadcasts the myriad changes that have occurred on America's sociopolitical and cultural post–*Julia* and civil rights scenes, but the Carroll–Shapiro conversation also brings forth the need to show a cross-cultural representation of women in power. Carroll's plan both acknowledges and anticipates several events. Indira Ghandi, re-elected as Prime Minister of India in 1980; Corazon Cojuangco Aquino, elected Prime Minister of Pakistan in 1988; and Aung San Suu Kyi, Burmese human rights activist and 1991 Nobel Peace Prize winner illustrate the global rise to power of women. Corporate America integrates its boardrooms by recruiting black women into their corridors. Black women such as Jill Nelson, is the first black woman to write for the *Washington Post*, and Bari-Ellen Roberts, is the first black (woman) Vice President at Chase Manhattan Bank in the Global Trust Division; Myrlie Evers-Williams, widow of slain civil rights leader Medgar Evers, is the first black woman to be appointed to the Los Angeles Board of Public Works in 1988, and later is elected the first woman to chair the NAACP in 1995. The Deveraux-Carrington partnership continues this trend.

In addition to the strides women made in leadership and in the boardroom, technology closes the cross-cultural gap in communication.

Lawrence Roberts's pioneering efforts in web communications technology in the 1960s eventually facilitate a speedier intercultural exchange with people from around the globe. The Internet blossoms in the 1970s, and by the 1980s, the web and electronic mail open up alternative lines of interchange. With the click of a mouse, Americans can converse with a woman in Poland or send a financial report to a CEO in Bangladesh as a result of Microsoft technology. These technological advances, as well as the social and political progress engineered by women around the world, generate a cognizance of the worldwide diversity of women.

As an actress navigating through the politics of the visual image, Carroll believes the internationally popular *Dynasty* the perfect vehicle to project to the world a picture of itself. Specifically, Carroll extracts from the personalities of powerful black women in entertainment to compose that of Dominique Deveraux, and the character's composition is an international one. Bricktop, the famous black hostess of her own club *Chez Bricktop* in Paris tops the list. "She knew everyone and could pick up the phone and call dozens of important, titled people all over the world and Dominique had to have that kind of power," Carroll recalls (*Diahann* 242). Carroll also feels Dominique should have a dash of Regine's flair, the celebrated black Parisian nightclub owner who founded the world's first discotheque in Paris, and "the monumental power" of Suzanne DePasse, the dynamic film producer and assistant to Motown founder Berry Gordy. When Dominique Deveraux arrives in America's living rooms, she presents herself in the "best, most imperious and elegant voice, full of authority, haughtiness, and class" (243). Carroll again makes history as another first, and rightly discerns a broader, more global picture supported by an (inter)national population in love with the nighttime soap opera. She expects the television industry to offer up images and story lines complementary to her own world that indeed is not a predominantly white one.

While writers and casting directors recognize Carroll's broad range and cast her in diverse roles, she wins roles in stories about the lives of white characters in which white actresses originally are cast.

Claudine (1974) proves another challenge because the film depicts a single black mother surviving on welfare with six children in a Harlem ghetto: "Everybody involved in the production felt I was wrong for it, for the same reasons I had heard before *Julia*—I was too chic, too much of a jet-setter, too far removed from the gritty reality of Claudine's world" (Carroll, *Diahann* 200). Carroll's rehearsals as a teenager after she heeds the advice of her black teenaged peers to abandon her goody-two-shoes image and don a more inclusive sartorial style prepare her to consider in-depth Claudine's predicament (discussed later herein). Conjointly, Carroll appreciates the strong influence the absence or presence of parental guidance can have on the life of a young black woman, as well as the privileged lifestyle her parents afford her while growing up. Carroll remembers:

> I have known this woman all my life. We grew up together in the same neighborhood. She was one of those girls who married too young and had babies too fast, and now that her middle years were upon her has to live with the consequences of her mistakes. Who can say for certain—if I had had different parents and hadn't been blessed with some talent, I could easily have become Claudine. [. . .] I couldn't wait to put aside the couture gowns and to work without glamorous makeup. (Carroll, *Diahann* 200)

Same Time Next Year (1977) opens with Dick Van Dyke and Carol Burnett; the film version features Alan Alda and Ellen Burstyn. Carroll "decided to take the chance" to play the characters originally played by Burnett and Burstyn (Carroll, *Diahann* 226). In a review in the *Los Angeles Times*, staff writer Sylvie Drake remarks, "[Carroll and co-star Cleavon Little] bring to the roles a sensitivity and human dimension not so readily perceptible in past productions. [. . .] As a team, Carroll and Little turn in the richest reading yet of what has always been a threadbare script" (10).

In the 1982 stage production of *Agnes of God*, white actress Elizabeth Ashley originally is cast as Dr. Livingston, the psychiatrist assigned to investigate a murder in a convent. After seeing the production, Carroll badly wants to play the psychiatrist. She feels, however, that "because of the color of [. . . her skin] and the fact that [. . . she] had never done a drama, [. . . she] would never be given the opportunity" (Carroll, *Diahann* 234). Later, the producer of the show, Ken Weissman, approaches her about filling in for Elizabeth Ashley. It is only a week's run, and Carroll loves the character so much thereafter that she offers to pay the white actress's salary if she will take one more week of vacation. Ashley agrees. Carroll writes:

> I was so happy performing this difficult and challenging role that when the week ended, I didn't want to give it up! I wanted to keep on playing it. I wanted that more than anything in my life! [. . .] I paid [Elizabeth Ashley's] salary for that week—it cost me several thousand dollars, but I would have paid more just to be able to do the play again. (236)

Of Carroll's performance, Geraldine Page (who plays Mother Superior) observes, "It's enormously different. Diahann's such an opposite type person, and the part is so wonderful it makes sense both ways. Diahann is very withheld and dignified and the emotion sort of comes out at the end; she's very laid back, so it kind of sneaks up on you" (Bennetts 6). Carroll responds, "I never thought for a moment [. . . my performance] would be the same; we're different human beings, and one brings to any role the sum of one's life experience" (Bennetts 6). According to Carroll's niece, Susan Fales-Hill, "This was a historic moment, a black woman replacing Elizabeth Ashley, a noted white actress in a major dramatic role that was not written for a black woman" (*Diahann Carroll A&E Biography*).

In the 1995 stage production of *Sunset Boulevard*, Carroll interprets the lost world of silent pictures that white actress Gloria Swanson immortalizes on film in 1950. The actress assumes the role of Norma Desmond (played initially by white actress Glenn Close and, later, veteran actor Betty Buckley in the Los Angeles stage production), and the character is another addition to Carroll's litany of challenges undertaken to not only expand her own horizons, but also the visual stereotypes usually accorded black women in the media. About her performance, John Coulbourn of the *Toronto Sun* writes, "Carroll breaks new and exciting ground, waltzing through a host of Webber's trademark anthems with elegance" (43). In a special interview for the *Detroit News* after her 1995 Toronto performance, Carroll relates to Kenneth Jones she saw:

Norma . . . [as] a symbol of loss and rejection, and those ideas dwarf any star actress who plays her. But [Carroll] hates the idea of a colorblind world in which nobody sees the vibrance and variety of life. When a colleague once said he does not think of her as black, she rebuffs him. Ignoring her color, she says, "is about dismissing everything that I am. I'm walking around. What do you mean you don't see me as Black? What have you done to me? Where is my skin? Where is my hair? My face? You can't do that." (4C)

Carroll's embrace of her Blackness in the face of the colleague's de-racination of her accompanies Terry Eagleton's definition of ideology and goes hand-in-hand with Roland Barthes's critique of myth. The concept of *ideology*, according to Eagleton, "obscure[s] social reality in ways convenient to itself [and] frequently takes the form of masking or suppressing social conflicts [. . .]" (5–6). Barthes's critique holds that meaning before myth has a presence and a biography; it is rich in history and memory. Once meaning becomes form, and myth latches on to meaning, and history and memory are hemorrhaged out; meaning becomes ahistorical as it "leaves its contingency behind; it empties itself, it becomes impoverished, history evaporates, [and] only the letter remains" (Barthes 117). Barthes continues, "[t]he form has put all this richness at a distance: its newly acquired penury calls for signification to fill it. . . . But the essential point in all this is that form does not suppress the meaning, it only impoverishes it, it puts it at a distance, it holds it at one's disposal" (118). Ideology and myth, then, create a diversion from history and memory.

This diversion is shown in Carroll's narrative of a power meeting between Carroll and Kanter pre-*Julia*. At that meeting, Carroll and Kanter discuss race. By this point, Kanter believes Carroll can breathe life into Julia because she will be able to recall instances of racism that she has suffered in the past:

> KANTER: You must remember some indignities that happened to you in the past?
> CARROLL: I had heard that one before. It is often assumed that once a black person achieves a little success, all the problems that come with the color of your skin automatically disappear. What do you mean, in the past? The day before I left New York I waited on Fifth Avenue for an hour before a cab would stop for me.
> KANTER: Oh, well, that's just New York for you. It happens to me all the time.
> CARROLL: Really, Hal? Do they slow down for you, stick their heads out of the window and shout, "I ain't goin' uptown, baby!"? (Carroll, *Diahann* 138)

That Kanter and the colleague do not see Carroll as black underscores the influence of Barthes's form—celebrity, entertainment, publicity, beauty—and how form repudiates an awareness of history. I contend Kanter situates her in what bell hooks terms "universal subjectivity (we are all just people)" (*Black Looks* 167). In turn, because of her status as an established star, Kanter perceives Carroll to be a part of the cultural and racial norm and is, therefore, as star theorist Richard Dyer notes, ordinary (*White* 3). Dyer maintains whites talk about themselves as people, as part of the human race, rather than as people marked as "white." He writes, "[I]n Western representation whites . . . above all are placed as the norm, the ordinary, the standard" (*White* 3). Dyer also explains the star phenomenon promotes the middle-class bourgeois ideal founded on the myth of success: U.S. society is sufficiently open for anyone to rise to the top. This perception supports the sociocultural view that racism does not exist. Similarly, Kanter presumes Carroll's membership in the entertainment elite inoculates her against the practice of racism. Carroll refuses to entertain these cavalier assumptions. Her response to her colleague suggests that for him to make invisible her blackness means stripping her of her being (meaning); ignoring her parents; denying her culture; rejecting the black teenage women in the high-school bathroom (discussed later herein); and dismissing the importance of self-identification. (*"What have you done to me?"*) What Carroll says is that even though she is an acclaimed actress respected by her peers; even though the culture of entertainment has honored her work via coveted awards; even though she performs across the genres of film, television, theater, supper clubs, and musical comedy; even though she is a stylish and elegant, financially sound, black woman dubbed the "Black Jacqueline Onassis"; in the United States, her body still comes charged with history. (*"Where is my skin? Where is my hair? My face?"*)

At the restaurant, the institution of nourishment, Carroll throws on the table Kanter's unacknowledged privilege of whiteness. A taxi driver who does not stop for Kanter is very different than one who passes by Carroll. Carroll trumps an effacement of her history and memory—*"you can't do that"*—just because "form" happens to be the vehicle through which she is marketed. Carroll, then, disengages herself from myth and affirms her place in the black community. James Baldwin agrees the presence of the Negro brings with it the presence of all that America is; the Negro presence walks and talks, and in these movements America's history is dispensed back to itself. Baldwin writes, "the image of the Negro breathes the past we deny, not dead but living yet and powerful" and "it is a sentimental error, therefore, to believe that the past is dead" (Baldwin 28–29).

Kanter prefers to assume a wondrous unnuanced America but Carroll's retorts rend the mask of "innocence." In the context of the history of blacks in the United States, in general, and the civil rights movement, in particular, America is not good, sweet, and kind to its black people; America's black people have to be killed, lynched, beaten up and hosed down before they are declared U.S. citizens. These are the realities of American life for which Carroll demands consideration. Yes, Carroll is a fortunate black woman; she knows all of the right people; she rubs elbows with the President and the First Lady, John F. Kennedy and Jacqueline Bouvier Kennedy. In other words, Carroll has done everything *right*. The actress, however, rightly acknowledges good fortune fails to eradicate racism from her life, nor does her "genius" separate her from the black race. Carroll intuits no matter how much she achieves in the United States, she still is read as a "nigger" by a cab driver on a New York City street corner. The privileged entertainment career fails to shield Carroll from racism and discrimination in the United States.

Dress Rehearsal for Change

Let us rewind to another behind-the-scenes battle Carroll wages. Carroll has to convince her agent that in spite of her glamorous image, she can transform herself into the character Julia and prove to Kanter she is right for the part:

> AGENT: Well, the truth of the matter is, Hal Kanter doesn't really want to see you. But he's talking to every black actress he can find.
> CARROLL: Why isn't he anxious for me to have the role?
> AGENT: He thinks you're too sophisticated, Diahann. You represent glamour and elegant nightclubs, and couture clothes, and that's not the image he wants to project. He's going for a different audience.
> CARROLL: But I am an actress. I hope my range is a little broader than that. Can you send me the script? I'll read it immediately. (Carroll, *Diahann* 135)

In his autobiography, *So Far, So Funny: My Life in Show Business*, Kanter contradicts the agent's claim. He writes, "Dave Tebet of NBC suggests Diahann Carroll. I did not know the lady or her work, so a meeting was arranged for lunch in the Beverly Hills Hotel's Polo Lounge. There I met Miss Carroll who was chic, beautiful, warm and delightfully witty enough to overcome her proclivity for arriving a half-hour late, which, I was to find, was almost early for Di" (256). Kanter prefers a pretty unknown black actress, but the studio wants a "name" (256). Kanter relents and settles on Lena Horne, so we know that Carroll's image could not have been an issue (256). What is more interesting is that Kanter says he never met Diahann Carroll when she is suggested to him and is unfamiliar with her work, which is why an arrangement is made for the singer-actress and the writer to meet. At the Polo Lounge at the Beverly Hills Hotel, Kanter makes a minor reference to her glamour: she is "chic, beautiful, warm and delightfully witty" (256). On the other hand, the A&E Biography *Diahann Carroll* (1996) claims Kanter indeed judged Carroll too sophisticated for the role. Why the contradiction?

We have to visit the events that lead up to the agent's call to understand the inconsistencies. A year prior to Kanter and Carroll meeting, Tebet, an NBC executive, approaches Carroll about moving to California. Carroll refuses the offer because "Hollywood made [. . . her] so uncomfortable":

> CARROLL: I don't think so, Dave. Like the song says, "Hate California, it's cold and damp. That's why the lady . . ."
> TEBBETT [*sic*]: Well, would there be any circumstances that might change your mind?
> CARROLL: For how long, Dave?
> TEBBETT: I'm not sure. Suppose it was for three, four, or five years?
> CARROLL: Dave, are you serious? What *are* you talking about?
> TEBBETT: I don't really know yet. I just want to find out if you'd consider it.
> CARROLL: Well, it would have to be something that I'd love.
> TEBBETT: Okay, well, let's see what happens. I'll talk to you soon. (Carroll, *Diahann* 133–35)

No doubt the agent is conscious of Carroll's dislike for Hollywood, and, in all likelihood, Tebet and the agent have spoken about the subject. I would suggest Kanter reviews Carroll's filmography and footage from her television appearances on *The Danny Kay Show, The Carol Burnett Show, Hollywood Palace, The Dean Martin Show,* and specials with Frank Sinatra to acquaint himself with her work. We may reasonably assume Kanter expresses his reluctance to Tebet and the agent after his review.

One thing is certain, however: an agent knows the temperament of a client. Carroll's agent comprehends Carroll wants to perform as much and as often as possible (Carroll, *Diahann* 134), and her desire to do so far outweighs her objections to Hollywood. With that in mind, the agent appeals to the performer in Carroll, and he wraps the appeal in that bane of existence for all actors: rejection. The strategy works. Carroll remembers:

> That's all I had to hear. Tell me I'm not right for a part, tell me you *don't* want me, and I'm yours. I'll do pratfalls, I'll do handstands, I'll do anything—but please tell me you love me. Sud-

denly, I was very interested. [. . .] It wasn't so much that I wanted the part; I wanted to be wanted for it. (135)

As is obvious in the interchange between Carroll and her agent, Kanter's reluctance to consider Carroll for the part is predicated on the actress's persona, namely her haute-couture glamorous image, on- and off-stage. Notice the inference to high culture and low culture in the dialogue. Kanter does not want to see Carroll, nevertheless, "he [. . . was] talking to every black actress he [. . . could]." Carroll is haute couture, or above the black masses. Kanter's sense of the interference of Carroll's image with his vision of a middle-class black woman, and by extension the vision held by (white) television audiences about black women, is a remarkable assessment.

This appraisal puzzled me. What exactly does Kanter mean that Carroll is too elegant and glamorous? If any one can fit the bill Carroll can; she epitomizes the black middle class. Along that line, I remember how strongly Carroll's upbringing mirrors my own, and how I identify with the mother-daughter relationship while reading her narrative. Carroll writes:

Unlike many mothers in my neighborhood, every morning my mother made breakfast for me—a hot cereal to "give me energy and keep me healthy." Respectability, achievement, hard work—those were the values my parents lived by. [. . .] Every night before I went to bed she neatly laid out my clothes for the next day—the freshly ironed white middy blouse, the navy blue skirt, the polished oxford shoes and little white socks folded down at the ankles. And every night she set aside time to dress my hair—applying Vaseline, then wrapping each curl in pieces of brown grocery bag paper so that I would have curls just as nice as Shirley Temple's. It was my mother's way to prepare me for life. . . . (Carroll, *Diahann* 9, 11)

I study her pictorial autobiography and visit the websites dedicated to her, paying close attention to her fashion and style at the time. She wears finely tailored suits on her presidential visits with John F. Kennedy and Lyndon B. Johnson in the 1960s; her wedding dress is exquisite; her intricately detailed black lace dress accentuate her appearance on the *Garry Moore Show*; she wears a flowered satin sheath and pearls at a Student Nonviolent Coordinating Committee (SNCC) meeting with Marlon Brando, and a bouffant pillbox hat and tailored suit at the Golden Globe Awards with Fred Astaire and Barbra Streisand. I reflect on the fashions of the time the women in my community wore, specifically the women in my church. I remember my grandmother, my mother, my aunts, and their friends dressed with gloves, pearls, lovely jewelry, and beaded hats and purses. Every one of them could have had a meeting with the president or walked the stage of an awards ceremony. When I peruse Carroll's stage wardrobe, I think about my own mother's party gowns, draped in organza, silk, satin, velvet, and lace; the moiré and satin poie-de-soirs and gold and silver evening shoes. Carroll's stage mannerisms and her gestures bring back memories of the performances of each soloist in my church.

Just who is the black middle-class woman in Kanter's mind? There is an obvious black and white difference of perception here. From a sociological standpoint, Baldwin believes the Negro woman's "relationship to all other Americans has been kept in the social arena. [S]he is a social and not a personal or human problem. To think of [. . . her] is to think of statistics, slums, rapes, injustices, remote violence; it is to be confronted with an endless cataloguing of losses, gains, skirmishes" (Baldwin 25). A black woman is the "old lady who lives in a shoe," with so many children she does not know what to do. What she does is burden taxpayers. She is a parasitic welfare queen and something of an unsolved problem that tantalizes U.S. society.

Or, she keeps house. In the culture of entertainment, households subsist on a diet of black personalities in programs that feature black maids. These personalities move from the silver screen to radio to television. The 1939 radio program *Beulah* stars none other than Hattie McDaniel, who plays a maid in the Henderson household. The show moves into America's living rooms via television in 1950, with Ethel Waters in the role, and in 1952 with Louise Beavers as maid. Amanda and Lillian Randolph join this chorus of roles in domestic servitude. These women perform in shows such as *The Laytons* (1948), *The Danny Thomas Show* (1953–1964), and *The Great Gildersleeve* (1955–1956). Ruby Dandridge (Dorothy's mother) plays a housekeeper in *Father of the Bride* (1961–1962). Personalities such as the sophisticated classical pianist Hazel Scott (host, *The Hazel Scott Show*) and actress Ernestine Wade (Sapphire in *Amos 'n Andy*) show an alternative to portraying maids, but their images are only the proverbial drop in the bucket of visual images of black women that permeate U.S. television culture (Hill 3–6). What, then, does Carroll's overall image represent to a visual establishment (in particular Kanter)? That Diahann Carroll is dubbed "the black Jacqueline Kennedy" no doubt accounts for Kanter's dismissal of her.

We can explain Kanter's actions, but Carroll's response to the agent's call uncovers a hunger and neediness so great that Carroll will contort her body to receive the public's love. What does this mean in the sociohistorical and cultural context? Seen through the lens black sociologist E. Franklin Frazier offers, Carroll appears to unmask an inferiority complex that Frazier believes is endemic to the black bourgeoisie, a class to which Carroll belongs. In his groundbreaking book entitled *The Black Bourgeoisie*, Frazier writes:

> the masks that [. . . the Black bourgeoisie] wear to play their sorry roles conceal the feelings of inferiority and of insecurity and the frustrations that haunt their inner lives. [. . .] Likewise, their feelings of inferiority and insecurity are revealed in their pathological struggle for status within the isolated Negro world and craving for recognition in the white world. (213)

Frazier contends that this performance of blackness causes the quotidian operation of inferiority and insecurity; it is a sickness the black woman carries with her as she operates in a society that constantly excludes her. It is a craving to be found worthy to live in a white society. We can argue that Carroll's expression is but a desperate call for acceptance in the culture of entertainment. We have to examine, however, the extraordinary leitmotifs of Carroll's story. Carroll's hunger is not just about race or class if it is at all. Her hunger is fed from childhood trauma, parental choices, and peer pressure on a young black teenager, which Carroll reveals in her autobiography. We have only to visit Carroll's account of her childhood to understand the formation of that hunger and neediness out of which she works.

Carol Diann Johnson is born on July 17, 1935, in the Bronx, New York. When Carroll is not yet two years old, her parents, John and Mabel Johnson, are a struggling young couple who had migrated north in search of work "to make a better life" for themselves (Carroll, *Diahann* 14). To offset their financial hardship, the Johnsons are forced to leave Carroll with one of her mother's sisters in North Carolina so Mrs. Johnson can supplement the family's income. Separating the family is a choice made out of shame and humiliation as her mother becomes employed as a domestic. "Sending your wife to work as someone's maid or cleaning woman meant you couldn't support your family and weren't a real man. I knew [. . . my father] felt a sense of shame," explains Carroll (*Diahann* 14). Carroll brings to light the societal stigma placed on domestic employment; the inference also is that regardless the class, practically the only employment a black woman could expect was that of a domestic. After being left, Carroll represses her feelings of abandonment, even though she "didn't see or hear from either [. . . parent] for over a year" (14). The experience leaves her so devastated, explains Carroll:

> that [afterward] I was too terrified to sit on the toilet. [. . .] For months I behaved like an animal—whenever I went to the bathroom, my mother had to cover the tile floor with newspapers. [. . .] But [. . . the experience] explained so many things in my personality – the need to be good so that no one would leave me; the need to make those who loved me prove it; the need to be led by those who took care of me. (14–15)

At age twenty-eight, after one of her therapy sessions, Carroll confronts her parents about this traumatic event. Her mother denies it, and her father screams, "Don't call this house again!" (*Diahann* 15). Several phone calls later, her mother relents, and through sobs and tears admits, "I left you. I left you. I had to. There was no other choice" (16).

Her parents were a working class black family who, through fierce ambition and early sacrifice, along with "respectability, achievement, [and] hard work" later realized their middle-class aspirations (Carroll, *Diahann* 9). Mr. Johnson works as a subway conductor at the Department of Transportation for the city of New York, while her mother stays home to take care of her. Her parents afford her many luxuries amidst the "mostly black families headed by working parents, by people struggling every day to survive" (Carroll, *Diahann* 9). She learns the piano and attends the theater, and there are roller skates, a new bicycle, a closet full of striking dresses, and a children's library. Her father drives the newest model Chrysler and owns a brownstone in New York; Mrs. Johnson spends her day "caring for [her daughter's] needs, [her] wants, and sometimes [her] demands" (9). When she cringes in embarrassment while being dropped off to school in the Chrysler, Carroll writes "[my parents] were so proud of their accomplishments they couldn't really understand my embarrassment" (9).

At age ten the acclaimed Abyssinian Baptist Church, pastored by the charismatic Adam Clayton Powell, features her as a soloist. Mrs. Johnson fashions her to be so "different" that the girls at Benjamin Stitt Junior High School (one of the roughest schools in Harlem) kick her and spit at her, grab and pull her hair, and yell and curse at her mother. Fales-Hill remembers her aunt's classmates consider Carroll "too prissy, too pulled together; she was beaten up on the one and supported on the other with people saying 'you go do what you do and represent us nicely with your pressed hair and your white gloves'" (Carroll *A&E Biography*).

After one of the many schoolyard attacks (during which she fought back), the rough girls call her into the "intimacy" of the toilet and tutor her on the etiquette of the street: "Listen, we just want to talk to you," the first one says. "Look you're not really all that square, but you can't dress this way. As long as you look like Miss Goody Two-Shoes, you're looking to get your ass kicked every day" (Carroll, *Diahann* 9). In spite of the meticulous care Mrs. Johnson gives her daughter—white gloves and pressed curls contained by Vaseline—Carroll commences a performance of "pratfalls and handstands" in the community of her teenaged black peers:

> [. . .] after the attack at school, when the girls let me know that different was not better, I did my best to try in little ways to fit in with the other kids. I saved my lunch money and, for $4.99, went to Miles Shoe Store and bought a pair of high-heeled black shoes, which I hid in my book bag so I could change into them before classes began. I left the house with my socks folded neatly at my ankles, but before school began I unrolled them and fastened them with rubber bands. And one day I finally convinced my mother that it was okay to let me carry my books loose in my arms rather than haul that neat little book bag. I even messed up my hair after I left the house, and tried to recurl it around my fingers before I returned home. These were small things, but they made me feel less alone among the other kids. (11)

Her participation in the conference call in the girl's bathroom allows her to become a part of the group. Through these "costume changes," Carroll initiates a "broad range" of characters for which she would later inform her agent she could be cast. Carroll wants to fit in, yes, but more important, her desire is an acknowledgment of a world from which her parents cannot shield her. She concedes the voices of the masses of black women cannot be overlooked, and she negotiates between two worlds: the insular environment of her middle class home environment and the more open space of street culture.

This negotiation correlates with the decision to go against Belafonte and informs her love for the character Claudine, a single black mother on welfare in Harlem depicted in the film *Claudine* in which Carroll stars. She put these experiences to use, as the trajectory of her career illustrates.

Let us remember, however, that the civil rights and Black Power movements and the music of the 1960s conspire to buoy Carroll's interventions. Recall, too, this is after the House Un-American Activities Committee and its blacklist, so the risks Carroll takes at the time will not have a detrimental effect on her career. As *Julia* airs, a reporter criticizes Carroll for her support of the black nationalist group, the Black Panthers. Carroll does not agree with the macho rhetoric that circulates among the ranks in the group, but she fully supports their agenda to "give dignity, education, and economic opportunity to young blacks [. . .]" (Carroll, *Diahann* 146). Carroll sponsors a fund-raising dinner in Southern California for Shirley Chisholm, the first black woman to run for president of the United States, and, in a bold move, extends an invitation to Huey Newton, founder of the Black Panther Party (146–47). The Godfather of Soul, James Brown, blasts the airwaves with the black national anthem, "Say It Loud, I'm Black and I'm Proud." This is the vibrancy and the variety that Carroll interjects into the American television landscape.

As I prepare to close this chapter, something kept nagging me to stay with it. There is more going on here, I thought. So I crawl over to my bookcase and pull out my 1993 anniversary edition of Martin Luther King, Jr.'s "I Have a Dream" speech. In that speech—one of the most famous speeches in the history of American oratory—the civil rights leader voices his desire to see black and white hands joined in the efforts to create a color-blind nation: the sons of former slaves and sons of former slave owners; black boys and girls and white boys and girls; black men and white men, Jews and Gentiles, Catholics and Protestants. King envisioned a time wherein his "four little children [. . . would] one day live in a nation where they [. . . would] not be judged by the color of their skin but by the content of their character" (23–24). And yet, Carroll demands that the color of her skin be recognized. What is to be made of Carroll's stance in light of this 1963 speech? In the ardor for a color-blind brotherhood, on one level, King imagines integration would eradicate segregation. On the other, the speech does not address another movement that speaks for the liberation of black people from white oppression: black nationalism. Gary Peller sees this exclusion as the ideological root of the struggle for civil rights. Peller notes, the "repudiation of race-consciousness" was the price paid for the intense struggle for the "national commitment to suppress white supremacists" (127). Carroll, then, interjects race-consciousness into the dialogue. Conjointly, Carroll's yearning to become a part of white television sitcomdom is a dance with integrationism. So, in a small way, Carroll bridges the gap, or conflict, between the integrationism and black nationalism. The two can coexist, or at least touch each other in some way.

I have talked about the trajectory of Carroll's career and how her reading of sociocultural scripts enable her to extend the interpretation of roles for which white actresses at first are considered. Carroll's broad range extends the image of the black woman: she is the enterprising welfare mother and widow and nurse; she is the sophisticated and aware corporate executive; an investigating psychiatrist in a convent of white nuns; she is the aging angst-ridden silent-screen actress; and, she is the troubled daughter who wants answers to a pain that has accompanied her for years. Through everything in her life and career, Diahann Carroll is a social, cultural, and political activist.

Carroll maximizes her television arrival in 1968 and 1984 with the publication of her autobiography *Diahann* in 1986, which reveals the behind-the-scenes media politics she negotiates in the turbulent 1960s via *Julia* and the glitz of the 1980s "me" decade through her characters Julia Baker and Dominique Deveraux, respectively. Unlike Belafonte, who strongly suggests she remove herself from *Julia*, Carroll's strategy throughout her career is to "chang[e] the dispositions and configurations of cultural power, not [to] get [. . .] out of [them]" (Hall 168). Not only a black feminist move, Carroll's decision to proceed with each project also inaugurates a cultural plan that queries prescribed casting decisions made across genres of television, film, and stage during the progression of her career.

When the last exegesis is drawn from Carroll's narratives of specific tactics she uses to uphold the importance of self-identification in film and visual culture, one other aspect comes to light. Diahann Carroll acts out a fierce love for blackness. On one hand, this love, and each loving act, reinforce her identification with the black race and ministers group credit to black women. As a result, loving blackness (hooks, *Black Looks* 9–20) fortifies Carroll in an industry wherein the systematic manufacture of the visual image ahistoricizes the black actress and can threaten self-annihilation. On the other, loving blackness agitates for an expansion of the vision of black women by the white image-makers— Hal Kanter, Esther Shapiro, and the news media—and by black men in entertainment such as Harry Belafonte. In every enactment of loving blackness, Carroll delineates safeguards for self-identificatory practices not only for herself, but also for the community of black women. These safeguards recuperate, restore order, and thereby leave open a space for a holistic articulation of the lives of black women in visual culture as the trajectory of Carroll's own career illustrates.

CHAPTER FIVE

Mary Wilson

Taking Care of the Business of Girlfriends through Autobiography

It is a tawdry irreverent mess that February day in 1976 when Florence Ballard is laid to rest. The relentless flashing of photographer's bulbs stimulates the assembly of people at the New Bethel Baptist Church in Detroit, Michigan; they behave in such a boisterous fashion that the Reverend is tempted to put his Christian principles aside to calm it down: "Please, people, show some respect for the dead," the Reverend C. L. Franklin implores. Police hold the crowd back. "Here comes somebody!" someone shouts, pointing excitedly as cars pull up in front of the church. In one aisle inside the church sit two women: one grief-stricken, the other itching to take the microphone. "This is unlike any funeral I have ever attended; my God, that mob!" Mary Wilson observes. Just then, the other woman, a wiry fur-clad figure, traipses up to the podium: "Can I have the microphone, please! Mary and I have something to say." Wilson reluctantly joins Diana Ross to whom she has not spoken in months. This is the same Diana who entered with Wilson and Ballard the rarefied world of entertainment named "Diane," later changed to "Diana" by Motown's CEO Berry Gordy to correlate with his vision of her as a star. "I was furious that I was being dragged into this. My grief was personal and private. I didn't want to get up but I was so taken aback by Diane's words that I felt I had no choice," Wilson recalls (248).

Wilson demonstrates through Ross the fanatic nature of fame, how fame draws out a mob's mentality without deference for the private life of the entertainer, and how a celebrity becomes a public entity when the public and private merge. Ross says, "Mary and I would like to have a silent prayer. I believe nothing disappears, and Flo will always be with

147

us." Ross represents total investment in notoriety—even at the death of a former friend, Ross insists on being the star of the show. To Ross, Flo is a "thing" rather than a dear friend who helped to solidify the popularity of the Supremes. Wilson nevertheless depicts the pull celebrity has on her when she answers Ross's demand to preserve the façade of a supreme black sisterhood and accompany her to the podium.

The drama continues. Onlookers groan against the outstretched arms of the police to catch a glimpse of Ballard's coffin. The desire to see the funerary box is so great that all of Ballard's floral arrangements "were thrown out to the mob" to keep them at bay. "[T]he only proof that the flowers had ever existed," remembers Wilson, "were the bare wire and Styrofoam [sic] frames left lying on the sidewalk" (248). Florence Ballard's passing signals to Wilson that the dream three black teenagers had fulfilled while living in Detroit's Brewster projects has been stripped down to the "bare wire" and "Styrofoam frames" of memory. The essence of who these women were—the flowers—are hurled to a virtual mob still craving the image (past and present) of these women with whom they have grown up in the neighborhood, in concert halls, at the sock hops, and on television.

Wilson, mourning the loss of her friend, remains the last witness at Ballard's final resting place. Everyone else—Flo's family, Diana Ross, and the Four Tops (the pallbearers)—saunter back to their cars after her coffin settles firmly at the bottom of the grave. "How did three talented little girls come to this?" a bewildered Wilson wonders over the moist brown six-foot cavern. "What turn of fate made one friend a household name, while the other struggled for years in poverty?" she laments. Finally, "When did our dream die?" In a bittersweet farewell to her friend and colleague-in-song, Wilson promises, "Don't worry, Flo. . . . I'll take care of it" (249). Ten years later, Wilson initiates the African tradition of remembering the dead by publishing her autobiography, *Dreamgirl: My Life as a Supreme*.

The women studied up to this point, however, almost exclusively are solo turns in the dance. Wilson's text is not a single movement but a carefully arranged dance of minimovements that incorporate the biographies of the late Florence Ballard, her best friend; Diane/Diana Ross; and Motown CEO Berry Gordy. This dance movement is significant for two reasons. First, *Dreamgirl: My Life as a Supreme* joins the black women's renaissance of the 1980s wherein novelists such as Toni Morrison (*Sula*) and Alice Walker (*The Color Purple*) delve into, via fiction, the ways in which black women navigate through girlfriends and relationships once a rupture has occurred. Second, Wilson's dance bares a whole new family structure and dysfunction she locates in the corporate House of

Motown. Motown is a family wherein she and Florence dance to the beat of intrigue launched by patriarch extraordinaire Berry Gordy and the intensely ambitious Diana Ross, Gordy's obsession (his baby) and personal favorite of the Supremes (Gordy 195, 289; Ross 123).

A brief mention of two critical movements in U.S. literary history is essential to analyzing Wilson's autobiography. In light of the rise of black feminism in the early 1970s and the subsequent blossoming of the black women's literary renaissance in the 1980s, Wilson's narrative takes on an added significance. Now we have the tools for reading Wilson's autobiography in a more meaningful way. Black feminism joins the collective struggle for black self-determination and self-identification during the civil rights movement and at the close of the era. While the majority of black female authors articulates multiple issues relating to black women's experiences, including motherhood, the black family, and the connections between sexuality and spirituality, several novels, along with Wilson's autobiography, probe the intricacies of black women's friendships.

In Toni Morrison's novel, *Sula* (1974), for example, Sula Mae Peace and Nel Wright unwittingly contribute to and witness the drowning of their childhood friend, Chicken Little. Film and visual culture critic Kwakiutl Dreher states, ". . . the fact that Nel and Sula agree to make [the accident] a memory all their own casts a spell on the friendship. Boundaries are broken, and the relationship [between the two young women] becomes fraught with conflict, assumptions, and misunderstandings" (79).

Another novel surveying black women friendships is Alice Walker's *The Color Purple* (1982). Walker studies the intimate bond between Celie, a poor black woman, and Shug Avery, a blues singer and Celie's husband's lover she has to nurse back to health. Eventually, Shug and Celie leave for Memphis to start a clothing business. Germaine, a young man of nineteen, attracts Shug and Shug begs Celie to allow her one last fling with him. Celie explains in a letter to her sister Nettie:

> Last year, say Shug, I hired a new man to work in the band. [. . .] Oh, she say. He little. He cute. Got nice buns. You know real Bantu. [. . .] By the time she finish talking bout his little dancing feet and git back up to his honey brown curly hair, I feel like shit.
>
> Celie, she say. All I ast is six months. Just six months to have my last fling. (248)

Sula and *The Color Purple* characterize the connections black women establish, how unions are breached in varying ways, and thereby threaten to vitiate the support system on which they rely. Walker and Morrison not only evaluate the rifts among black women, but they also lay out black women's ingenuities as they work through changes. Wilson's *Dreamgirl* drops into this whirlpool of literary activity and, as a celebrity autobiography, adds one more dimension to black women's storytelling. Wilson examines the dynamics of black women's friendships as they perform in public and private. As Wilson brings to full focus the inimical effects the Berry Gordy and Diana Ross dyad has on the Wilson and Ballard partnership, she investigates more broadly the strict consociation among three women dependent on each other for sustenance of star identities and economic welfare.

Wilson, in consonance with Walker and Morrison, scrutinizes the alarming psychical and emotional contusions formed when the black woman's support systems are torn asunder. Berry Gordy acts as a surrogate father to Wilson, Ross, and Ballard in the same vein as MGM's Louis B. Mayer; the teenagers are Daddy's little girls. Patriarchy is not limited to white men as Wilson's text demonstrates. Gordy rearranges the group to suit his business interests and, effectually, disrupts the bond of black sisterhood.

The Supremes enter the national scene in the 1960s and the group members become superstars whose choreography hinges on each member's commitment to harmonize—in musical performance, fashion, social comportment, and with each other. The *supreme* image parades before admiring fans and advertises a tenacious young urban black sisterhood constructed in the House of Motown. Wilson makes known that Gordy's and Ross's maneuvers interrupt the smooth movement of the dance and set off a major shift in power dynamics among the women in the group—a change for which the Supremes initially neither is originated nor its members equipped to handle. By extension, the changes Gordy instigates undermine the cohesive structure of the organization and activate an identity crisis—coupled with emotional and mental distress—which compel Wilson and Ballard to scramble for internal and external coping strategies. Ross manages by aligning herself with Gordy. Wilson assumes a chorus line of roles: mother, protector, and counselor for Ballard and conciliatory member in the Supremes. Ballard, instead, orchestrates an outrageous womanish dance in the vortex of the crisis. In the end, the Supremes break apart, but they are reassembled into a vocal group designed to showcase a star on the shoulders of the group: *Diana Ross and the Supremes*. Ross assumes her place at the helm; Wilson remains and strives to finesse her position as Cindy Birdsong is cast to replace Ballard. Ballard, instead, disassociates herself from the Supremes by signing Motown's release agreement without legal counsel. Although

Ballard signs the agreement, the document itself is Berry Gordy's push to dance her out onto the back lot of the stage and into obscurity. Hopefully, in his mind, Ballard will disappear.

The Motown family, according to Motown historian Gerald Early, however, touches the hearts and minds of black people, who understand the value of family:

> The family myth resonated in two ways for Motown: First, as applied to an ostensibly black family, the Motown myth was particularly pleasing to blacks for whom "family" and "unity" are nearly fetishistic affections [. . .] fraught with political and metaphysical meaning generated by memory of oppression. [. . .] Second, the family myth meant that Berry Gordy was not merely a CEO, a boss, a leader, or even a visionary but that he was a father, an older brother, an uncle, a coach, a teacher, a guardian, an authority figure motivated by something other than making money from his acts. And the acts [. . .] became his children, his brothers and sisters, his wards, his companions and not simply his employees. (30–31)

Wilson confirms a dysfunction festers in the House of Motown as she unravels and rends the veil covering the myth of the Motown family through Ballard. The Motown myth, Early maintains, once uncovered, brings into high relief the feelings of discontent among other musical groups on West Grand Boulevard: "[S]ome felt [. . . the Motown family] was a myth that was nothing more than self-serving hypocrisy" (31). In the early years, Motown artists believe themselves a part of a company that sponsors racial uplift and encourages black expression without exploit. Their commitment to black expression during the civil rights movement, according to Early, "undoubtedly fostered the sense among many that Motown was not a privately owned enterprise which, in fact, it was, but some sort of cooperative venture" (31). Gordy admits, however, "Power—its uses and *misuses*—is something that has fascinated [him]" (7; my emphasis).

Gordy's Motown appeals to black teenagers who have nothing more than dreams in their pockets and the courage to want to express them. Ballard, Ross, and Wilson have little (if any) business sense, yet they strongly believe in the house on West Grand Boulevard just like other "sibling" groups. Wilson implies that Gordy takes advantage of their youth, their inexperience, and the trust the black families put into Gordy's enterprise. Gordy does deliver. He gives back to them what they see on television and on the silver screen—an image in the middle-class mold. Hitsville churns out the bulk of the black shining stars of the moment, and each artist holds fast to the possibility of membership in the Gordy camp with fierce tenacity. Gordy forces no one into his family. Yet his decision to grant membership into his "home" means an assumption on the part of its members that they will be treated fairly. In her autobiography, however, Wilson documents the silences and the betrayals, including her own, over the company's treatment of her and Ballard. In the process, Florence Ballard's voice rings throughout, a voice that goes silent on February 22, 1976, when Ballard is thirty-one. Ballard—founder of the Primettes, which later blossoms into the Supremes—is the member of the Supremes who suffers the most because her womanism crosses the grain of middle-class notions of black women. Wilson takes care of those issues via her dance on the white page. She focuses on the apparent wrongdoings and paints a picture of the perpetrators; she really does not have to discuss her own debasement in explicit terms. The inferences she makes highlight her own humiliation and, consequently, the others look even worse.

Wilson's autobiography does more. *Dreamgirl* is a story about the management of identities shaped in relation to one another—with each woman counting on the other for self-knowing, survival, and, ultimately, celebrity, fame, and stardom—and the consequences thereof. Wilson's text illustrates the hyperinterconnectedness among three black teenagers from the Brewster projects (government housing in Detroit) who practically come of age as women via stardom during the explosive 1960s. This is significant because the 1960s for black people are about group mobilization and stripping away convention. We learn through Wilson, nevertheless, Hazel Carby's inessential quality of black womanhood operating on the common ground of entertainment. The text also delves into the agony of the forceful disengagement from the virtual Supreme "family" each woman faces at the burgeoning of the black feminist movement.

Wilson's autobiography documents Ballard as one of the founders of the Supremes and, thereby, releases her from the threat of obscurity. Wilson, instead, reintroduces Ballard to the public as a black female entertainer who confronts the most commanding and powerful black patriarch in the music business, one who she presumes derogates black sisterhood. She takes care to describe Ballard's parents, including Ballard's mother's size, skin color, and hair length; she names each of her eleven brothers and sisters; gives the reasons for the Ballards' migration from the south to the north; lists the characteristics of the Ballard family; and, includes a write-up of where the Ballards live and the type of row house they occupy. Much less space is devoted to the Ross family, however, and not one of Diana's five siblings is named. Her accounts of Gordy remain in the business arena. Wilson's narrative gives Florence Ballard a past and a place in music history beyond that of the Supremes and far away from a limited memory of her as a tragic figure. It is virtually a literary obituary.

Throughout her text, Wilson preserves her role as interpreter for Ballard, and this enables Wilson to express vicariously through Ballard her own reactions and responses to Gordy's intentions after the Supremes gain prestige. Several factors make *Dreamgirl* a significant text. By telling her story along with that of Ballard's, Wilson attempts to come to terms with her own ardent investment in fame, stardom, and the Motown supreme image she eventually trades, as we shall see, for Florence Ballard, her best friend. Second, Ross's biography interfaced in *Dreamgirl* brings forward the female component of the exploitation of black women in the music industry; nepotism is not purely a masculine enterprise. Third, entries describing Berry Gordy instruct us to be mindful that patriarchy is not the sole domain of white men in the entertainment business. More important, Wilson's text declares the vicissitudes of black womanhood. Here Wilson complicates the reasons that black feminist critic Barbara Smith's essay "Toward a Black Feminist Criticism," published in 1977, gives for an essential black womanhood. Smith believes that the black woman enjoys a host of commonalities that materializes via a common language and cultural experience. She writes:

> The use of Black women's language and cultural experiences in books *by* Black women *about* Black women results in a miraculously rich coalescing of form and content and also takes their writing far beyond the confines of white/male literary structures. The Black feminist critic would find innumerable commonalities in works by Black women. (164)

In other words, according to Smith, there is an *essential* black woman with a language, history, and culture that cohere into a universal experience. This essentialism, rejoins Hazel Carby, however, "reduc[es] the experience of all black women to a common denominator and limit[s] black feminist critics to an exposition of an equivalent 'female imagination'" (10). She maintains that essentialism threatens to ahistoricize black women's experiences. The history of slavery and oppression of peoples of African descent link black women to each other; however, the interaction with and in these circumstances differs for each black woman. Thus, while the Supremes present the image of solid black sisterhood to the public through television, print ads, and interviews, Wilson's text negates this portrait of solidarity manufactured in the House of Motown. In addition, she highlights how black women in entertainment deploy numerous strategies to engineer, maintain, and repair their own subjectivities.

Finally, Wilson carries on the African diasporic tradition of remembering the dead. As storyteller, she acts as a West African griotte—the caretaker of her and Ballard's contribution to history-making in the music business. As griotte, Wilson's remembrance of Ballard, in effect, "inton[es] the [. . .] name of the deceased, reminding the mourners [. . .] what the person who died accomplished" (Hale 56). Although the griotte has its origins in oral tradition, Wilson enacts an African pattern in the Western tradition of the written word and thereby gives Ballard a living biography. *Dreamgirl* is a contemporary text; yet, the autobiography demonstrates an African cultural continuity retained much in the way the enslaved Africans in America kept memories alive of traditions, customs, and rituals through storytelling. Remembering Ballard, as has been shown, begins with death.

The Draw of Motown

Motown: that prosperous family of entertainers at 2648 West Grand Boulevard in Detroit, Michigan. Unlike Lena Horne's relationship with Louis B. Mayer, Gordy's assembly-line approach to the girl groups at Motown gives birth to an assembly of "Daddy's girls": the Marvelettes, Martha Reeves and the Vandellas, and the Supremes. In the 1965 article that announces their debut, "The Supremes Make It Big," Ross exclaims, "Hitsville U.S.A. is just one big happy family. I know it sounds corny but Gordy is like a father to us. When we're on the road he's always calling and bugging us about taking our vitamins, wearing warm clothes and getting to bed on time. If that isn't a father, then I don't know what is" (84). As a father figure, Gordy contrives a sort of family, but one with all of its familial dynamics, including the formation of self-identity, parenting, jealousy, sibling rivalry, and betrayal.

Gordy fashions Motown as the clearinghouse for the distribution of black culture, and, through the Supremes, he also designs a template from which America's teenagers—black and white—can pattern themselves. Young girls also could emulate these supremely composed young black women. On my elementary school playground, for instance, where awkward children swing from monkey bars with their Buster Brown saddle shoes dangling in the air, squeals coming from the swings, as some of those saddle shoes threatened to touch the clouds, and the see-saw moves to the rhythm of made-up sing-song nursery rhymes, away from the noise, a cadre of young girls assemble. With right foot forward, hand on hip, and hand raised, they demand that somebody stop in the name of love. The index finger moves accusingly from left to right to ward off another heart breaking as they chant the advice to be sure and think it over. All the while, in another corner, a second group sings of love and an annoying itchin' in the heart that just is tearing it apart. As hips swing and heads bob, the school's nuns glide silently by. This is the one activity they do not interrupt. Their silence seemingly indicates that they understand the itchin' of the heart and the heartbreak. I now imagine that, perhaps, in the quiet of their off hours, they secretly watched the Supremes on *Hullaballoo, The Ed Sullivan Show, The Red Skelton Show, Mike Douglas,* or *The Tonight Show*, pledging to say ten Hail Marys and Our Fathers afterward.

The Supremes and their music captivate everyone, and the three young women loom large as a glamorous trio of sophisticated, modern, and beautiful young black women. As on the schoolyard playground, these women bring into America's living room—via *Ed Sullivan* or *Mike Douglas*—a young dignified black womanhood. The Wilson, Ballard, and Ross image joins that of Horne, Dandridge, Carroll, and Kitt; the Supremes, like those women before them, arrive under the auspices of racial uplift that exact adherence to a middle-class definition of ladyhood. According to popular culture historian Suzanne E. Smith:

> Motown's preoccupation with public image, proper etiquette, and general decorum stood in direct relation to these older philosophies about black respectability and black culture. The company sought to produce the black music of Detroit but also to package it in such a way as to not contribute to any racist stereotypes of African Americans as uncouth or uncivilized. Motown marketed a product that proved that black popular culture could "uplift the race" on a mass scale; it could be both "of the people" and dignified. (121)

On-screen and offscreen, Mary Wilson, Florence Ballard, and Diane Ross exhibit disciplined bodies with contained, safe mannerisms: hands firmly planted by the side; be-wigged well-coiffed heads bob ever so slightly; right foot in front of the left in a model's pose; and impeccably tailored fashions of the day. They are delicate ladies, and with all that rages within the group, Gordy choreographs a rarely compromised beautiful supreme dance.

The flowering of Wilson's and Ballard's sisterhood occurs long before Gordy's choreography, however, as the women develop a "strong, instantaneous affinity" prior to the creation of the Supremes (Wilson 35). Wilson paints Ballard as a vibrant, voluptuous, inventive, and, more important, insightful young black woman:

> [Flo was a] pretty girl, with [. . .] fair skin, auburn hair, long legs, and curvaceous figure. [. . .] Compared to the rest of us, Flo looked like a movie star. Even without make-up Flo's face was perfect, her big brown eyes perfectly balanced with her full, sensuous lips and valentine-pointed chin. Because her hair was relatively light, everyone called her "Blondie." . . . [H]er voice was magnificent. [. . .] (27)

In our visual culture, image is everything, and Wilson makes known that of all of the group's members, Ballard has the movie-star quality essential to gaining the public's approval (like Horne and Dandridge had); her talents and abilities unquestionably are apparent. This physical appraisal of Ballard, moreover, authenticates her friend's membership in the Supremes, and Wilson's portraiture of Ballard shows her friend has every qualification to belong in the Supreme family.

By composing Ballard's features on the white page, Wilson testifies to the compatibility she and Ballard have as well as to the fact that she *sees* Ballard. For her, the late singer exists in a vibrant and essential way. Their participation in the popular sphere of the talent show cultivates a rapport long before Motown enters their lives. Comparable to the television talent show of the twenty-first century, *American Idol*, these eager and persistent teenagers display individual raw talent with the hopes of being discovered by scouts at a local talent show. On one of these occasions, in 1958, Wilson and Ballard meet in a scene that has the elements of a Harlequin romance novel: Wilson's detailed sketch of Ballard, the dreamy walk home with Ballard, inattention to time, the reluctance to part company and the closeness, are common characteristics of popular romance novels. The enthusiastic fourteen-year-old women congratulate themselves for singing in front of an audience. They are engrossed in the conversation, time passes idly by, and they walk home together combing through every detail of the night's performance. As with many teenagers who bond, they make a pact to contact each other if one is asked to join a group. Wilson remembers, "[a]fter lingering outside my building for a while, we reluctantly said good-bye. There was a bond between us. We could not have known that it would last a lifetime" (27).

This description of their first meeting historicizes the singers' sisterhood and the long-held admiration Wilson has for her friend. Later Ballard keeps her promise and asks Wilson to audition for a sister ensemble to be part of the Primes, a very well-known male group. They both audition, along with another teenager, Betty Travis. A member of the Primes invites Diane Ross to audition also, and the four become the Primettes. Ballard's loyalty to the pact made in 1958 demonstrates for Wilson her trustworthiness, but this trust will be tested by the enormous success of the Supremes.

Another quality Wilson attributes to Ballard is insight into the music business, a quality that emerges early in their career. After performing at many talent shows and sock hops, the Primettes win the Detroit/Windsor Freedom Festival amateur contest in 1960, and their victory earns them an invitation to audition for Motown. The possibility to be recording artists excites Wilson as each young woman delights in her achievement. Ballard, the more astute member, asks, "Isn't Motown the record company that cheats its artists?" Ballard is mindful of the rumors of "shady dealings" being circulated about Motown, and she cautions the group to be wary of where they place their talents.

Wilson, as well as other teenagers in the community, knows of Motown's "crafty" business dealings and Ballard's criticism is valid; yet, despite its reputation, the group relents and joins Motown because, "[Motown] was the newest company and seemed most open to fresh young talent" (53). Wilson also describes Ballard as courageous and perceptive, qualities she displays when a dramatic shift occurs in the group's arrangement. Much to Ballard's and Wilson's disappointment and surprise, in 1963–1964 (when Ballard renames the Primettes the Supremes) Gordy christens Ross the lead singer without any discussion. Wilson writes that Gordy interrupts a studio rehearsal to announce, "I know everybody in the group sings lead, but Diane has the more commercial voice, and I want to use her as the sole lead singer" (142). Wilson presupposes that Gordy's interest in what is financially sound for business prompts this move. From Gordy's standpoint, Wilson's and Ballard's voices fall short of "crossover" potential for the white market. In his mind, Ross's talent will propel the Supremes from an exclusive rhythm-and-blues sound into the wider more commercial arena of pop music. Gordy thinks Ballard's and Wilson's voices are too fat and brassy. Ballard, in fact, is fat all over: her big voice and voluptuous body overwhelm the girlish lyrics and melodies Gordy's songwriting trio of Brian Holland, Lamont Dozier, and Edward Holland write for the group. Ballard's gospel undertones echo the soulful sound of the already popular Aretha Franklin, rather than contribute to the new pop sound Gordy is seeking. The rearrangement stands to bring in the economic gains the CEO wishes to realize. Wilson, however, hints at a more poignant discovery: Gordy's decision signals the beginning of her and Ballard's exploitation not only by the CEO, but also by Ross and the songwriters. Wilson writes, "[t]he bigger we got, the less anyone at Motown wanted to tamper with what was beginning to look like a sure thing" (143). In other words, no one would question that Gordy overturns the original arrangement under which the Supremes were formed whereby each singer would share the spotlight.

Diana Ross exacerbates the growing tension by exploiting Gordy's blatant favoritism toward her. Even though she admits, "[Gordy] played favorites and set up an unhealthy internal climate," she rationalizes her privilege in the group: she is the superior singer and the more regal of the group:

> I didn't wiggle my hips or bat my eyes. I wasn't interested in manipulating men by bumping or grinding [as Mary Wilson did]. [Mary] was the sexy one; Florence was much more stand-offish; I was always interested in elegance and the music. [. . .] My gift was being able, simply and honestly, to express the emotions of a song. For that reason, my voice worked best as lead singer on the kind of material we used. [. . .] (92–93)

Ross believes she is endowed with special flair and skills and, therefore, is entitled to take charge. In her mind, Ross has qualities admired by the public: honesty, simplicity, and a willingness to give herself over to the audience. She also has the musicality to enhance the material considerably. Wilson and Ballard, conversely, project surface, more temporal characteristics of glamour that run along the lines of personality rather than star quality. What stings, however, is that Ross not only implies a lack of talent within Wilson and Ballard to lead, but also that both singers fail to deliver the music. Ross can. In essence, Wilson and Ballard neglect to do their job. Gordy's assessment of their talent and Ross's feelings of entitlement together pave the way for Ross's ascendancy to stardom. Although both Ballard and Wilson are upset, they later become disoriented as they comprehend, "[l]ittle did we know that neither of us would ever sing lead on a Supremes single again" (Wilson 143).

Gordy's arrangement happens without mediation and leaves both women to interpret for themselves the devastating about-face that will materialize. Social psychologist Wade W. Nobles maintains crucial to managing the inevitable changes that occur in life, mediation in families has to take place. He writes:

> The family's ability to mediate the conflicts and other concrete conditions affecting its members provides a strength or support

so obvious that it barely warrants explication. Clearly, the abilities to provide family members with concrete and pragmatic help and to engage in interpersonal relations around problem solving and decision making [. . .] constitute a critical strength of African American families. (90)

Gordy disturbs the initial structures supporting the Supremes' family unit since these structures uphold Ross, Ballard, and Wilson as equal partners in the supreme family. The CEO clearly neglects to offer the requisite "concrete pragmatic help" to Wilson and Ballard, and this particular black family, therefore, fails to signify as one of critical strength.

Once preferential treatment is accorded Ross, Gordy releases an avalanche of unmediated confrontations as well as nonsupportive behaviors by him and Ross. Ballard protests. "An injustice was being committed, and Flo wasn't going to tolerate it," Wilson declares (194). Wilson acquiesces to the decision, but makes known her feelings of resentment through Ballard. Certainly both women have more than enough to feel angry about. Wilson and Ballard share dressing rooms whereas Ross enjoys her private space apart from the other members; logistical changes such as scheduling rehearsals and performances are shrouded in mystery, and neither Wilson nor Ballard can determine if Ross or Gordy or both initiate these modifications. Gordy sends Ross, not Ballard and Wilson, for grooming outside of the in-house school of etiquette headed by Maxine Powell. Music historian and critic Arthur Kempton notes:

Once Gordy saw the indications of her stunning trick appeal, Diana became his preoccupation. [. . .] He sent her for a five-month course in grooming at the John Powers School for Social Grace, where she was given a practical education in acting like a white girl: how to sit, stand, talk, eat, and laugh, whether she was in public or in polite company. Gordy attended personally to her making, both as a performer and a public image. (283)

The CEO's efforts pay off as the media begin to notice Diana as the spokesperson for the group. Wilson recollects, "In Flo's mind this was unfair, and her resentment began to consume her. . . . It was apparent that neither Diane nor Berry [Gordy] gave a damn about what we wanted, and Flo made no bones about feeling betrayed and lied to" (189–90). Wilson makes no direct mention of the emotional backlash the deal between Gordy and Ross has on *her*. She instead embeds her frustration in the third person "we," sandwiched in between Ballard's expressions of unfairness. Wilson's concentration on the effect Gordy's decision has on Ballard signifies the powerlessness of both women and the overwhelming influence of notoriety. The best Wilson can advance is an "I'm-doing-the-best-I-can" attitude, while Ballard resorts to alcohol and food to mitigate her pain. Wilson enumerates the times she and Ross step in to save Ballard from herself. Tardiness and drinking become serious problems for the Supremes even though Wilson hides alcohol from Flo. Wilson, frustrated, admonishes Ballard to be on time for press conferences. The following dialogue ensues:

> BALLARD: Honey, I am not working myself to death to make Diana Ross a star. . . .
> WILSON: [W]hen Flo said "Diana" the bitterness cut through me like a knife. But, girl, I said, can't you see that you are only making yourself look bad? You should have heard Diane carrying on. She was trying to get Berry on the phone, and you know she's going to tell him everything. Why are you doing this to yourself?
> BALLARD: Because I don't give a damn about Diane or that jive Berry, [a]nd don't think for a minute that they give a damn about me or you! (194)

This scene illuminates the disparate strategies the three women exercise in navigating a corporate decision that Ross has been privileged to participate in making. After this agreement, Wilson concedes what Ballard already has: that Gordy relegates them to the position of "glamour prop" to carry out his and, eventually, Ross's agenda to make her a star.

The parsing out of each woman's strategy makes vivid Wilson's literary subtleties. At first glance, Ballard's behavior connotes a jealous, out-of-control, self-destructive cast-off. A more incisive reading of Wilson's structure of the scene unearths an incensed but clear-sighted performer. Ballard intuits that Gordy and Ross cannot carry out their agenda for *Diana Ross and the Supremes* without the Supremes, otherwise the CEO just would disband the group. The group gains international fame and bypasses the popularity of other Motown girl groups, namely Martha Reeves and the Vandellas and the Marvelettes. Gordy cashes in on the Supremes' celebrity by fashioning a star in Ross. The ingredients for making the group successful have to remain in place, namely the social etiquette of Maxine Powell, Motown's in-house talent doyenne. Powell ensures the Supremes continue to cultivate a "unique and very sophisticated style" (Wilson 151) embroidered with elegance and grace. If each member maintains the Powell panache then *Diane* can transmute into an incandescent star, *Diana Ross*. Gordy renames Diane *Diana* because the former "seemed a little passive for what [he] saw in her. *Diana*. That was a star's name" (Gordy 147).

This transmutation, Ballard discerns, rests on making the Supremes an opaque background against which *Diana Ross* can hypershine. It also requires that Ballard and Wilson remain unnamed and subsumed under the title *The Supremes*. The vectors of power, then, confuse subject positions that once were static and solid. Instead of a group partnership wherein each member shares equally the division of labor, the individual of Diana Ross gains a front and center position. Ross's stardom, then, would come at Ballard's and Wilson's expense. Gordy is the corporation that relies on a product—The Supremes—to distribute his new product—*Diana Ross and the Supremes*—to the public. Implicit in Ballard's answer to Wilson's question, "Why are you doing this to yourself," is Ballard's indirect declaration, "I'm damaging the product I know Gordy has to have to promote Ross to stardom."

Ballard's reaction to Gordy and Ross is visceral and much more forceful than Wilson's. Wilson apparently accepts the arrangement but she coaxes us to understand her anguish over the group's reorganization. In the previous dialogue, Wilson's careful use of "the" with the noun "bitterness" rather than that of the proper noun (Flo's) leads the reader to infer that Ballard's calling out "Diana" brings Wilson's own resentment to the surface. Importantly, Wilson refrains from contradicting Ballard's assessment, which suggests her passive agreement with her. Ballard insists on the destruction of her "product" self (which in turn displaces her from the group) and leaves Wilson in an interesting philosophical position. Wilson consistently lets slip the subtlety of her protest to the arrangement by framing Ross's phone calls to Gordy within her own discourse with Ballard. This careful literary device allows Wilson to lay out the subtlety of her objection. She then can place blame on the lead singer and the CEO for the destruction of the integrity of the group without actually pointing the finger at them.

Wilson's literary subtleties continue as she outlines the entrenchment of the team of Gordy and Ross. The following scene occurs at Detroit's Twenty Grand nightclub in front of other members of Motown. Part of Ballard's defiance is to gain weight, and many times Diana's choice in costumes for the group has to be changed because Ballard cannot fit into her own. Wilson recalls:

> Berry said, "I agree with Diane. You have to do something about your weight. You are much too fat." "I don't give a damn what you think!" [. . . Flo] replied. Then she threw her drink in

his face and stormed out of [the Twenty Grand]. Though Flo
had never been comfortable maintaining The Supremes' glamour-girl image, she had enjoyed it at first. Lately, however, she
had come to regard it as phony and fake, and the rigors of tour-
ing, of being a star, seemed to overwhelm her. (194)

Wilson's excerpt broadcasts how Gordy and Ross subvert the concept of a black sisterhood, which Ballard notices. What is created out of
Ballard's heartfelt desire to express talent and a part of the self in a girl
group, and her ability to share the lead in it, has been tainted. While
everyone, including Wilson, to some extent prefers to sidestep Gordy's
and Ross's machinations and see Ballard as an overweight and out-of-
control group member, Ballard, in turn, throws the drink of the betrayal
in the face of its perpetrator.

That Gordy and Ross try to control Ballard's body through public
embarrassment only encourages Ballard to assert agency over it. She is
adamant in her desire to control the output of her labor. Wilson shows
through Ballard how she uses these "tools" to break through the illusion
of stardom and the glamour image that accompany it via the popularity
of the Supremes. Ballard could not "give a damn"—or anything else for
that matter—because her initial agreement to give meant an equal sharing of the labor between black women. What she ultimately receives
instead is a "phony and fake" contract of sorts.

No one else in Gordy's organization takes responsibility, but Ballard
courageously does. Wilson is determined to show the ways in which
Gordy cannot control Ballard because she sees through Gordy's schemes.
Her keen sight is something from which Gordy cannot escape but
through which Wilson can project her own dissatisfaction. At every turn
in her dance on the white page, Wilson shines Ballard's light on her own
perceptions of events and occurrences. Ross and Gordy establish a close
relationship, which later would produce a child. This aspect sets Ross
further apart from Wilson and Ballard and gives her much more leverage
with Gordy. Diana does not have the same personal dance "contract"
that Ballard and Wilson have so she can ally herself fully with Gordy.
Wilson observes that neither Gordy nor Ross owes Wilson and Ballard a
thing. Without the kinds of investments Ross has with Gordy and the
commitment he in turn gives to Ross, both begin to treat Wilson and
Ballard as cardboard props for Ross's impending stardom.

By contrast, Wilson determines to go along with the new configura-
tion of the group. Wilson defends her behavior by explicating in her "I
was born in" narrative the strategies she learns to manage familial turmoil. To place Wilson's childhood story next to her Motown story is to

regard Mary Wilson separate and apart from her celebrity. We get a broader sense of Mary Wilson the individual. Mary Wilson was born March 6, 1944, in Greenville, Mississippi, to Johnnie Mae and Sam Wilson. Mr. Wilson relished the fast life of gambling and parties, to the financial detriment of the family. He often took trips to St. Louis and Chicago to satisfy his appetites. The time eventually came when Mrs. Wilson deals with her husband's love for the fast life and how it overshadowed his interest for his family. Unemployed and with only a few dollars of her own, she reluctantly gave Mary to her childless youngest sister, I. V., and her husband, John L. Pippin, who worked in the auto industry. Mary went to live with her aunt and uncle (whom she refers to as her parents) in Detroit, and her mother returns home to Mississippi to restructure her life.

At first, the nice middle-class house with his-and-her cars (a brand-new dashing Chrysler for John L. and a classy Chevrolet for I. V.) gave Mary a sense of safety. I. V. took great pains to see that Mary had the finest clothes and shoes in the way Diahann Carroll's mother treats her. Wilson writes, "as far back as I can remember, I felt like a miniature fashion plate" (12). Over time, however, the idyllic atmosphere changed to confusion for Mary. I. V. would lose her temper with Mary for not doing things exactly right, or over the "daily trauma" of getting her hair fixed. I. V.'s inflexible nature traumatizes Mary who starts to wet the bed and develops feelings of confusion and bewilderment. More significant, she develops "a fear of authority and a reluctance to speak out" (12). For example, Mary and a neighborhood friend decide on a whim to raid I. V.'s "fabulous new wardrobe of brightly colored dresses" (15) and strut through the neighborhood looking cute. During a routine inspection of her clothes, I. V. saw to her horror that several of her new dresses were soiled (the kids had been slurping on watermelon and strawberry pop). I. V. and John L. discover the culprits, and proceed to whip them. They punish Mary further by shunning her. I. V.'s behavior has long-term effects on Mary's personality. Wilson writes, "Based on what I saw as my parents' anger over the incident [. . .] I learned a lesson that stayed with me for the rest of my life: to maintain peace, no matter what the cost" (17). Her upbringing influences every decision she makes in the House of Motown, but we learn early in her autobiography that Wilson has been cast out of a family once via I. V.'s and John L.'s shunning and that she will never let it happen to her again.

Wilson applies this defense in her dealings with Gordy, Ross, and Ballard. A close inspection of Wilson's text does not reveal any retorts, debates, or confrontation on her part. When Gordy tells her she does not have the talent to sing lead, for instance, she is devastated and uses years of music therapy to heal the wound and rebuild her confidence. When Diana undercuts Wilson and Ballard, Wilson casts an icy smile. Ballard complains about Ross; Wilson upbraids her—"cool down," she advises, "stick it out," and wait for the situation to resolve itself.

This mechanism of silence, however, dishonors Wilson's friendship with Ballard. It originates a compromise with which Wilson has to come to terms in Motown's living room during the "let's kick Ballard out" bull session with Gordy, Ross, Wilson, Ballard, and Ballard's mother. Wilson writes:

> When I arrived I found Flo and her mother, Diane, and Berry. We sat in the living room, where there was a huge grand piano. Diane and Berry sat together, Flo and her mother sat together, and I sat to one side by myself. (198)

At that session, everyone involved hears how Ballard's behavior jeopardizes the Supremes, and how "she had been messing up and was not upholding her end of the deal" (198). Throughout, Ballard is quiet. Only Mrs. Ballard speaks for Flo, as she looks straight at Wilson: "But Mary still wants Flo in the group. . . ." Wilson answers, "Mrs. Ballard, Flo no longer wants to be in The Supremes. Yes, I want her with us, but she no longer wants us" (199). Her reply comes after she contemplates whether to defend Ballard and bring to light the duplicity both women experience at the hands of Gordy and Ross. Wilson does not see what good a defense will do, but believes Ballard wishes Wilson to rescue her from the Supremes. Ballard's response, according to Wilson, "was frighteningly cold and distant. She was detached, yet seemed satisfied with the outcome" (199).

One other kind of betrayal takes place after Gordy's evaluation of Ballard's behavior. After the "intervention," Ballard legally disassociates herself from the Supremes by signing a release agreement drawn up by Motown's attorneys. In that agreement, Ballard:

> [. . .] irrevocably bargains, sells, assigns, transfers and sets over to Motown all of Artist's right, title and interest in and to any and all royalties, commissions, fees known or unknown, which would otherwise have become payable to Artist pursuant to the First or Second Recording Agreements. [. . .] [Artist agrees] she does not now have and never has had any interest in [The Supremes] tradename or any rights therein. (*Florence Ballard Chapman v. Diana Ross et al.* 291)

In one way, Ballard's signature on the Motown document specifies the drastic measures artists take to have artistic control, even if it means a ponderous emotional and professional suicide. In another, the singer's sharp riposte severs her completely from all rights due to her having worked as a member in the Supremes and Motown.

The legal document restrains Ballard from ever identifying herself as "a former member of the Supremes" (*Chapman v. Ross* 291). The wager Ballard contracts ultimately results in her "death" as a Supreme as well as a conclusion that she is a tragic figure in the history of Motown. But why does Ballard, the insightful member of the group, sign away all of her rights, even, in some sense, her history in the Supremes? All of her actions leading up to the "intervention" complicate interactions within the Motown corporation and the Supremes. Why acquiesce now after a period of talking back? One explanation is that the session grants Wilson a forum to speak out on Gordy's assessment. His and Ross's tactics cause the schism in the group. Ballard's and Wilson's friendship made after that talent show in 1958 is tested in that meeting; Mrs. Ballard's direct look cues Wilson to take the reins. Up to this point, Ballard bears the burden for both women in her public displays of rage against the collusions of Gordy and Ross. Through her body and voice, Ballard verbalizes the truth for her and Wilson, knowing full well the cost. It is Wilson's turn to carry the load, and all along Wilson has ignored Ballard's call to her to remember the "original contract" of black sisterhood made in 1958 on her doorstep. Wilson's response, however, connotes a silent agreement with Gordy and Ross: that Flo's behavior is not in retaliation against Gordy's and Ross's scheme, but the "acting out" of a disgruntled group member who has set in motion her own designs to destroy the most lucrative and popular black ensemble in the history of music.

Even though she places herself outside of both groups (Gordy and Ross; Mrs. Ballard and Florence) the session copartners Wilson with Ross and Gordy—not that Wilson salivates over stardom like Ross, but such is her identity with the Supremes that she does not want to risk her membership. The Supremes are not just a group to which she belongs; it is her identity. Wilson assuredly informs Ballard of her position by using the third person plural, *us*. Wilson's narrative, however, is compelling for what it does not say. She indicates only that Ballard leaves, not that Gordy dismisses her from the group. Ballard withdraws in silence after Wilson's response—and on Wilson's words—not Gordy's. The inference is that Wilson—(un)knowingly—breaks the bond made between her and Ballard after that talent show in 1958, and Ballard knows it.

Wilson, Ballard, and Ross manage the precarious situation of being consigned to stage props in contrasting ways, and we bear witness to the consequences of each woman's choice. Wilson's text, however, opens a broader analysis of their choices. Ballard stages a radical wild womanish dance and smoothly segues into Alice Walker's paradigm of womanist behavior. Walker would agree: Ballard, indeed, is "outrageous, audacious, courageous, [and] willful"; a serious womanist demanding greater knowledge "in greater depth than is considered 'good' for one" (Walker xi). The displaced singer's womanism works against the tenets of Powell's social etiquette in the public and private spheres. Powell's standard exacts rigid faithfulness to the code of ladyhood with its middle-class myths and ideals. A lady stands straight, refrains from coarse or crude language, controls her anger, and speaks softly. Horne, Carroll, Dandridge, and Wilson adhere to their ladyhood images, even if they do not fully embrace them. Kitt sings risqué songs and sets (white) men on fire with attraction for her but she does so in the image of ladyhood. All of these women perpetuate the image of ladyhood.

Ballard disrupts the Supreme image in public and private; Ross and Wilson stand by the ladyhood ideal. Ballard's womanism catapults her up and over black ladyhood and into the realm of the neo-black womanhood many black women in the 1960s welcomed. For example, in 1963, Cicely Tyson wears cornrows, a West African hairstyle, on the television drama series *East Side/West Side* (dir. John Berry). Tyson's cornrows shun the white standard of beauty and shock cadres of black women who believe straightened hair facilitates an assimilation into mainstream culture. In 1966 the Black Panther Party appoints Kathleen Cleaver national communications spokesperson. In the political arena, Shirley St. Hill Chisholm brings an entirely different image to national politics as the first black woman to be elected to congress in 1968. Her slogan? "Fighting Shirley Chisholm—Unbought and Unbossed." Tyson, Cleaver, and Chisholm defy institutional racism, discrimination, and oppression and set out to transform the racist attitudes of many white people. Ballard's dance of resistance compares with the womanish performances these activists choreograph. There is a difference nevertheless. Tyson, Chisholm, and Cleaver perform in a real world of hard and true facts; Wilson's text delineates a powerful world of illusion within which Ballard's activism as well as Wilson's compliance occur—a world that nurtures Wilson's conformity and spews out Ballard.

Wilson conforms to Gordy's blueprint for the Supreme's comportment, but her autobiography dances a womanist dance. Wilson's autobiography and (mini)biographies of Ballard, Ross, and Gordy locate the intra-racial compelling forces—black women versus black women—that cause internal confusion and dissension within groups, and the eventual implosion of them via psychological abuse and the illusion of entertainment. The Supremes must circulate the harmonious image Motown manufactures, however, and in the process deny access to the public Ballard's and Wilson's rebellion against another type of oppression. As a womanist and neo-black woman, however, Ballard shines light on the illusion and the creators of it; we see how these elements operate in layers in the house of Motown.

The illusion of entertainment runs rampant throughout this house, and it is the constituent that contaminates it. Wilson's narrative demonstrates how its illusory nature makes this "home" dysfunctional, unreasonable, and in the final analysis, deadly. Ballard is an activist—a real person—in the trumped up make-believe house of entertainment. In essence, Wilson shows up the fallacy of the value of ladyhood and the limitations of its conventions on black women who cannot and simply will not conform to it. Wilson has to dance twice as fast while occupying the central position of mother and protector. In the meantime, she cannot betray the identity she has nurtured for approximately ten years through practice, discipline, and hard work. She is a black woman in the entertainment industry who, like Ballard, does what is necessary for her own survival. Wilson's strategy enables her to maintain whatever power she has. Ballard's dance is one in which Wilson cannot participate because doing so would mean her own destruction. In essence, Wilson pulls two teams, and this illustrates phenomenal strength on her part. All black women have been caught in a position wherein they have had to make difficult decisions simply to maintain themselves. This especially plays out during the time of the civil rights movement—at the time of Gordy's reconfiguration of the group—wherein black women exert themselves against detrimental constructs and illusions or negotiate how to deal with them. Ballard and Wilson, fundamentally, try to make meaningful changes in the distorted world of entertainment.

Managing Success and Managing Lives

Ballard's "antics" announce what Michael Dawson terms "linked fate." Dawson maintains, "A construct of *linked fate* is needed to measure the degree to which African Americans believe that their own self-interests are linked to the interests of the race" (77). The exploits of the individual African American bear on the entire race. "Linked fate" is antithetical to the western ideal of rugged individualism and the "pull yourself up by your bootstraps" mentality. Rather, the concept is connected to the

African heritage that features the communal responsibility to members. Ballard and Wilson hold firm linkages because they never lose step with the community. As we shall learn from their fan narratives, Ballard and Wilson yearn to do something more with fame.

As agents of culture, Ballard's and Wilson's hands-on redistribution of fame circulates it back to the community from which it comes as does Lena Horne by listening to Count Basie's counsel and Eartha Kitt by standing in for America's poor. Initially, the Supremes carry great influence among America's youth. For example, in a 1966 advertisement in *Ebony*, Motown announces, "The Motown Sound . . . is the official music of the modern generation. . . .'The Sound of Young America'" (only Ross's face appears in the advertisement; "Motown Sound"). The Motown sound dominates teen school dances. It is wholesome, and any girl teen could form a group and belong, as we did on my school's playground. Ross notes, "It's incredible how much influence we have on young people. . . . So many older people can't make contact with them" (Miller 424). These entertainers perceive that their status as stars inspires audiences, and that the "little ones" initially choose them. "The viewing audience anoints this one and ignores all those others," Jib Fowles warrants. "[I]t is only reasonable," he continues, "that stardom should happen this way, for it is the public that the star serves. In a real sense the star is employed by the spectators, who in turn reward the star handsomely" (63). In other words the viewing audience makes the star and, according to Fowles, making stars is a democratic process. Gordy's business decision, however, inverts Fowles's theory. Wilson's text indicts Gordy for his undemocratic ways and highlights Gordy's inversion of the process by foisting Diana on the public.

The entertainer is part of a machine, however, and this machine is interested in the promotion of the star as an individual as Richard Dyer avers (*Heavenly Bodies* 7). This promotion elevates the individual above the masses to make the star unapproachable and unavailable while remaining, nevertheless, visible. Here is where Gordy and Ross clash with Ballard and Wilson:

> . . . soon Berry was criticizing both of us. "Mary, you know I think you're making yourself too available," Berry said. I knew he wasn't referring only to the fans; he thought I had too many boyfriends, too. "You should be more like Diane—untouchable, unreachable. You're getting too familiar." This kind of accessibility, as limited as it was, irked Berry to no end. The more Flo and I dealt with the fans, the more Berry complained about it. [. . .] (Wilson 187–88)

Gordy wants the star to be apart from the masses. For him, the individual is accessible only through an image that perpetuates the illusion of entertainment. His strategy staves off the threat to profitability of the commodity, an advantage ordinariness compromises. If the image is perceived to be ordinary, what is the public's incentive to purchase it? It impels the image-makers to maintain a distance between the star and the consumer because the nature of popular culture is contingent on the whims of the public.

Gordy, without considering, falls short of understanding the full meaning behind his critique of Ballard and Wilson. How could Wilson and Ballard comport themselves as untouchable and unreachable when Gordy and Ross have a personal agenda? Ross makes herself and remains a confidante and business partner to Gordy. Gordy relates his feelings for Ross in his autobiography:

> Diana meant more to me than she could ever imagine. It is absolutely true that at one time I was obsessed with her. In the heyday of The Supremes I saw the butterfly emerge from the cocoon and I was dazzled. She was magic and she was mine. Diana was willing to let me make her a star and I knew she had the talent, drive and stamina to go the distance. [. . .] I loved her because she gave everything to our mission. (195)

Gordy essentially crowns Ross the equivalent to a First Lady. Could Wilson and Ballard compete? To be "more like Diane," Gordy will have to make Wilson and Ballard mean more to him than they would ever know and undergo name changes as does Diana (from Diane).

These things fail to happen, and the partnership between Gordy and Ross makes for an uneven playing field. Fan culture, then, assuages the pain and cedes Wilson and Ballard some control over the representations they remit to the public. Theirs is a type of ownership of public veneration. The enthusiastic consistent patronage of the fans sustains them in an inconsistent entertainment culture. Wilson and Ballard can lean on the fans for support in their management of in-house Motown events over which they have no control. Fan and star reciprocate adoration. Gordy's criticism, then, attacks the one thing Wilson and Ballard cherish as their own.

One of the most important aspects of membership in the Supremes Wilson makes known in her dance on the white page is the element of fandom. The Supremes enjoy their public achievements as a sister-girl group. Until 1964 the Supremes are dubbed the "no hit Supremes." They have not produced a single that would reach *Billboard*'s Top Ten since their recording careers began on February 15, 1961. Ross expresses the group's frustration to Gladys Horton, a member of the Marvelettes, who assures her, "Don't worry, Diane. [. . .] You all will get a hit record. It just takes time, you know" (Wilson 135). What Horton, Ballard, and Wilson do not expect to accompany a hit single is an abrupt change in group dynamics. Ross's crossover voice singing lead on "Where Did Our Love Go," "Come See about Me," and "Baby Love" catapults the Supremes to the top of the music charts. Gordy, too, rests comfortably in the security of his choice.

The group tops the national and international music charts, and make *Billboard*'s Top Forty in 1966 with "My World Is Empty without You." "Stop! In the Name of Love" garners a 1965 Grammy nomination in the Contemporary Rock & Roll Group Vocal Performance category. They make seven appearances on the *Ed Sullivan Show* in 1966 and several product endorsements for *Supreme White Bread*, *Coca-Cola*, and *Arrid* deodorant, all the while gathering a host of fans. In fact, according to Motown historian Gerald Posner, "75 percent of all of [Motown's] releases hit the charts in an industry in which companies averaged only 10 percent" (158). In 1964 "Baby Love" was the first Supremes hit to top the British charts. The busiest of all the groups that signed with Motown, the Supremes make their first covers on *Ebony* and *Jet* magazines. In the debut article, "The Supremes Make It Big," *Ebony* mentions, "the three chirpers are intelligent, friendly, witty and, as Mary explains it, 'average [normal] girls'" (81). Another *Ebony* article, "The Supremes Are Tops," hails the trio as "pretty-as-you-please young ladies [and] the world's foremost vocal trio" (153).

The Supremes prove to be major crossover artists. Edwin Miller, a writer for *Seventeen* magazine—the periodical that appealed to white female teenagers—interviews the teenagers and writes the article "Off the Record with the Supremes." In the article, Mary, Florence, and Diana talk about working hard and keeping focus; about participating in after-school activities such as choir; about exchanging clothes, learning, weight gain, and makeup; and, the most important, about being popular and a part of a group. Ross recalls in that same interview, "We were thirteen or fourteen when we started singing together, and we were the most popular girls in school. Everybody envied us. They would say, you're in a *group*! To be in a group was the biggest thing that could happen to you" (Miller 280). Of the group Gordy recollects, "All three girls had qualities so unique I'd often think: 'If they could make us feel the way we do, what could they do to the world at large?' My belief in them sustained my hopes during three years of flop after flop" (147).

Ross's wholehearted acceptance of Gordy's preference for her, however, causes a tear in the seam of the sisterhood cultivated prior to the group's popularity. Even worse, Ross's and Gordy's intimate liaison gives Ross an inequitable advantage over the other women. "Through everything," Wilson said, "what really kept us—especially Flo and me—going, were the fans" (186).

Wilson, Ballard, and Ross direct the phenomenon of fandom associated with their success in various ways. An interpretation of each woman's choice draws out an additional manner in which Wilson's autobiography antagonizes Barbara Smith's theory of the essential black woman. Familiarity threatens to make the group commonplace among the public Ross and Gordy reason. Wilson and Ballard, on the other hand, designate the public domain of fandom a life-support system. They want to learn about and mingle with the fans to the point of familiarity.

Each woman privately endures personal break-ups with lovers and the attendant stress, as well as the psychological disquietude resulting from Ross's promotion to lead. Wilson's Fan Narrative illustrates that while the Supremes give something to the fan, the fan also provides Ballard and Wilson a break from group discord. The reciprocal relationship narrows the gap between the star and the masses of fans invoking the belief that success is possible. Wilson gives an up-close look at the fan community as it works for her and Ballard:

> [. . .] fans like [our most ardent fan] Tony—who were always well behaved—were permitted to see us. There was a lot of competition among the fans, and the fact that it was friendly made it no less serious. The fans divided themselves into two groups: the B fans—just anyone—and the A fans, like Tony, who always got through. Within the fan community the As were stars in their own right (so the As told us), and one reason they were allowed to be around us was that it was known that a good A fan would throw the other fans off our trail. We were rarely mobbed, but could always count on a lively, vocal contingent of kids and teens waiting for us wherever we went. (187)

The role of the A fan is to relieve the star of unwanted attention from the B fans (but the B fans bestow their adulation on the star, as well). The Supreme Fan Community, with its built-in hierarchy, is an extension of the security systems Motown provides for the Supremes. Stardom, more important, reproduces itself through the fan—"[fans] were stars in their own right." Associating with the star via fan labor stimulates this reproduction. The fan's success in securing the A status rests on his or her resourcefulness in locating the object(s) of desire. Fan culture is not necessarily a hodgepodge of starstruck teenyboppers. This fan community is an organized "contingent of [serious] kids and teens," or a national network ready to give unbridled admiration, attention, and respect to the star. Fan devotion, then, proffers a type of stability for Wilson and Ballard as both women negotiate their participation in the Supremes amidst the ongoing turmoil.

The dedication the Supreme Fan Community has for the Supremes, likewise, calls up Wilson's memories of the hustling she, Flo, and Diane did to be received into the House of Motown as bona fide artists in the early 1960s. "I was touched by these shows of affections, especially from the little ones," Wilson writes. "It took a lot of stamina to stand outside a stage door, sometimes in freezing weather, just to catch a glimpse" (187). As young teenagers, the Primettes hunger for entry into the Motown family:

> We [had] agreed that it would be in our best interests to go to Hitsville each and every day after school. Even without a manager, we were rehearsing on our own. [. . .] We were convinced that someday Hitsville would have to give in and record us, and we wanted to be ready. Every day we would hitch rides with friends to West Grand Boulevard, and the four of us would meet outside the lobby. [. . .] [Motown] was still one of the few places in Detroit a young musician or singer would make a buck or get the chance to really succeed. (57–58)

Berry Gordy remembers, "[t]he girls were making friends with producers, trying to get gigs singing background for other artists" (147). The group's determination runs parallel to the enterprising fan's efforts to touch all that the Supremes represents to them: the American work ethic. One's labor, persistence, preparedness, and trust in one's abilities comprise the tenets of this principle. Being "touched by the affection" invokes the memories of when Wilson, as a "little one," craves to be something other than ordinary and to be a part of an event in music history that is special, happening, and positive for other little ones.

Wilson's knowledge of the inner workings of the Supreme Fan Community affirms an interrelationship with the fans. Ballard personally asserts this communal link and wants it to apply to the group as well. Ballard's interaction with the company of admirers demonstrates her agreement to lend to the public the image of black success as made in a capitalist society. Wilson writes:

All of us would sign autographs, but Flo and I would stay out and talk to the fans. Flo also made the younger fans her little pals. [. . .] Hundreds of times I saw her standing outside a stage door. [. . .] "How long you kids been standing out her? You must be hungry. Let's go get something to eat." Flo would always be beautifully dressed, and on winter days her long fur coat would sort of billow as she marched along briskly, looking like a Pied Piper with a couple dozen young kids jogging behind her. She'd . . . order pizza or burgers and sodas or cocoa for everyone, then sit with the kids for a while. Once they were engrossed in their snacks, she'd slip out the door. (187–188)

Fans are an integral part of entertainment. Their veneration of images and the products the image produces is the linchpin of longevity in the artist's career. As barometers used to measure popularity, fans contribute to the artist's financial success. They consume the artist's product. The fan culture creates, then indulges, the artist. The fan, therefore, seeks a return on its investment: the artist's autograph. There is fashioned between the fan and the artist "the most extensive, formidable relationship of modern times" (Fowles 155) via the autograph. The autograph is like a signature on a contract. A quasi-transaction, the autograph implies an artist and fan partnership actualizing a particular goal. Better than the autograph is physical contact.

Ballard and Wilson, aware of this partnership, honor the contract the autograph initiates by talking to, getting to know, and feeding the fan. Ballard appreciates the appetite of the "little ones" and the value of taking time with them. This value she learns from her father. Jesse Ballard, Sr., ". . . spent hours on end singing and playing the guitar for his [eleven] kids, and he taught Flo to sing," writes Wilson. Unlike Dorothy Dandridge's mother and Eartha Kitt's aunt, "Mrs. Ballard took pains to see that her children were safe and secure. There was real love and caring in that family. . . . [N]o matter what happened, they all stuck together" (29). Ballard, then, recognizes the importance of giving time to the youth; she feeds their desire to see, feel, and touch the arm of black success; she understands the longing of black youth to be a part of it. By eating with them, Ballard continues her father's tradition. What is more, Wilson and Ballard make memories for and pass down legacies to the next generation of fans. Ballard allows them some access to her symbols of success—her image and her fur coat. This interaction with the fans assigns a specialness to the fan and confirms that dreams are reachable.

Gordy's disapproval of Ballard's and Wilson's interaction with the fans also explains his need to control not only their images, but also their labor. His push to supervise the image automatically spills over into a need to discipline the activities of the body that furnishes it. The Supremes become hot commodities in the Gordy enterprise, or "the family," which require his exclusive hands-on management of their talent. Period. Even though the women have grown up, so to speak, by the time they make their first hits, the Supremes, on contract, belong to the Motown family. They still are under, therefore, the strong arm of Gordy's supervision. According to Motown historian Gerald Early, Gordy exhibited an "intense paternalism" (31). Gordy's admonition to Wilson to elevate herself above the masses is not only his way of keeping the created product fresh and new for public consumption, but it is also Gordy acting his role as a parent-father-guardian and, more radical, a "pimp" protecting the street value of his investment. Interestingly, prior to Motown, Gordy had "a few girls" on John R Street known as the red light district in Detroit, Michigan, alleges his former wife Raynoma Gordy Singleton (Singleton 43). While he expressed revulsion over what the "motherfuckers down there do" (44), he nevertheless "was familiar with its chapters and verses" (Kempton 199).

Wilson relates the serious outcomes of Gordy's strategies; she exposes those decisions that contribute to the eventual downfall of the Supremes. She reveals the consequences of Florence Ballard's audacity to resist Gordy's and Ross's treatment of them, and of her own earnest inclinations. Wilson's adjustments say something about the singer's own determination to stay in the group. By projecting her experiences through Gordy, Ross, and Ballard, Wilson, in turn, takes ethical responsibility for her sins of omission against Ballard's promptings, as well as for her efforts to maintain "peace" in the not-so-Supreme family.

Wilson's dance stages a struggle on a level that the ordinary spectator cannot see. If Wilson had not written her autobiography and had not weaved in Ballard's biography, we, as an audience would hold the glamour shots—the images of perfection—of the Supremes to be the "truth" of who they are. *Dreamgirl: My Life as a Supreme* depicts the world of entertainment as a dangerous one; it is ruthlessly make-believe, and some black women in it are susceptible and sometimes powerless to withstand the duplicities made by heads of corporations and by other black women themselves. The autobiography is by a black woman telling her sister's story. In turn, Wilson enacts a very African pattern of remembering the dead; remembering even though her friend was dishonored. In the end, Wilson carefully replaces the flowers on the bare wire and styrofoam frames thrown to the mobs of adoring fans at Flo's funeral.

Wilson's dance on the white page takes care of it for Flo.

CHAPTER SIX

Whoopi Goldberg

The Black Woman
Celebrity Tell-All Iconoclast

Whoopi Goldberg opts for a descriptive discussion of scatology, feminine hygiene, and sex in her autobiography *Book* (1997). Along the way, Goldberg sprinkles in delightful vignettes about her family and home and provocative political insights as well. Goldberg selects, so to speak, a "spread-eagled" approach, exercising a kind of agency in relation to her body, given that her body represents at least a potential source of pleasure for her. What are the implications of *Book*? *Book* is a politics of language, and it compares interestingly to the tantalizing language Dorothy Dandridge and Diahann Carroll use in their autobiographies *Everything and Nothing: The Dorothy Dandridge Tragedy* (1970) and *Diahann* (1986). Goldberg's politics of language claim a powerful stance in linguistic territories set aside for men. Generally, "locker room" talk, for example, is in the exclusive realm of the masculine wherein men generally brag to each other about their sexual prowess and exploits. Goldberg's celebrity autobiography jockeys for a space of linguistic equality as she moves her text into a landscape reserved for men.

Comparatively, Goldberg, as a star, challenges Hollywood's prescription for stardom and this challenge complements if not explains her performative autobiographical text. Black women who desired stardom in the film industry no doubt have to fit a particular idea established by it. As film historian Donald Bogle notes, the 1940s and the 1950s usher

An abridged version of this chapter appears in *Popular Culture Review* 17.2. (Summer 2006): 45–54.

175

in an era of glamour. "During this era," he states, "Hollywood had very set notions about beauty standards, to which all female stars were expected to conform. It became almost a generic beauty look [. . .]" (Bogle, *Dorothy Dandridge* 122). This "generic beauty look" becomes a mainstay and still operates, although modified, in contemporary entertainment culture. Popular white actresses of the past such as Greta Garbo, Marlene Dietrich, Jayne Mansfield, and Marilyn Monroe dominate the scene and set the standard for the white screen goddess just as contemporary white actresses Nicole Kidman, Kate Hudson, Charlise Theron, and more recently Scarlett Johansson do today.

Any black woman in entertainment desirous of stardom has to emulate the industry's "set notions about beauty standards." Dandridge embodies the star image in the 1940s and 1950s, and Carroll carries it out as far as possible in the 1980s. Whoopi Goldberg, however, slashes Hollywood's standard look in the 1980s and 1990s and, in its stead, offers the public a personality and star image Audrey Edwards, editor-at-large of *Essence* magazine, terms as "[t]he dark-skinned, dreadlocked, gap-toothed, hoodoo-acting woman [. . .]" (58). Goldberg gives the public a dose of her "hoodoo" act at the 1993 New York Friars Club Roast in her honor. Ted Danson, Goldberg's then-boyfriend, Hollywood actor, and master of ceremonies, "roasts" her in a tuxedo and, most blasphemous, in blackface! An excerpt from his "tribute" to her reads:

> This morning I was shaving and wondering what I was gonna say this afternoon, and Whoopi was giving me a blow job. [. . .] I know comparisons are odious but, uh, I gotta tell ya, black chicks sure do know their way around a dick. I suppose in all fairness, that's because white girls get toys at Christmas. (Dougherty 230)

In her closing remarks at the roast, Goldberg says:

> I give good head. I make no bones about it. Those of you who have had it know I'm telling the truth—and that's why [Ted] got me [. . .] 'cause he knew how to elongate that cumming. (Dougherty 233)

More jarring (?) is Goldberg's admission that she wrote Danson's skit and suggests he wear blackface.

The discourses Dandridge, Carroll, and Goldberg use in the description of intimate relationships in their autobiographies illustrate the con-

trast among the three women entertainers. The overall narratives of bedroom romps in *Everything and Nothing* and *Diahann* emerge fairytale-
like. The language carefully wraps and secures each woman's privacy.
Second, Dandridge and Carroll carry forward the legacies of ladyhood
and ladylikeness. These legacies include the aspects of delicateness and
caution in speech and action. Dandridge and Carroll keep the integrity
of their own ladyhood images. Along the way, their autobiographies cast
the prominent men of Hollywood as spectacles, idols, knights in shining
armor, and even wolves in sheep's clothing.

In her autobiography, Dandridge relates how she "studies" Aus-
trian-born director Otto Preminger over champagne in her apartment
while contemplating the lead in the film *Carmen Jones* (dir. Otto Preminger 1954). The depiction of romance with the prolific filmmaker is
most subdued. Dandridge recalls, "[b]y one or two o'clock in the morning, we had consumed much champagne. My hand was in his. Otto
talked on in a warm, accented way, gently, in words I don't clearly recall
. . . [b]ut this was a man. He was physical, all-male—no problem there.
. . . That night I became his girl" (172–173). Dandridge affirms Preminger is "all-male"—insinuating she inspects his penis. She finds "no
problem there"—she identifies the penis and indicates an erection she
validates as pleasing and functional. Becoming "his girl" in the end signals she and Preminger consummate their relationship. It is the perfect
denouement to this erotic event.

In *Diahann*, Carroll tells of her first meeting with black screen idol
Sidney Poitier:

> The door opened. He stepped inside. My life changed. The first
> thing I saw was a man who moved like an animal, an incredibly
> beautiful self-confident, jet black man with the satin skin of a
> panther. [. . .] His presence was so mesmerizing, his whole bear-
> ing so unashamedly sexual, that I was totally overtaken by the
> moment. [. . .] I must have crossed and uncrossed my legs a hun-
> dred times as he went around the room saying hello. Finally, it
> was my turn. (75)

Carroll remembers how she and Poitier would stay up an entire night
laughing and talking and making love (122), but Carroll writes no
explicit language about the lovemaking.

Carroll's narration charges Poitier with animal eroticism and mag-
netism. The striking particulars of the scene operate as sexual
metaphors for the female genitalia and sexual intercourse: "The door

opened" (vagina); "he stepped inside" (sexual intercourse); "my life changed" (orgasm). Carroll's emphasis on Poitier's physiology is interesting in view of the foundation of Poitier's screen success. During America's integrationist period, Poitier represents to Hollywood and to white America the safe, controlled, and intelligent Negro—a necessary paradigm to quell white fear of black masculinity. In essence, Poitier's controlled cinematic image gives the film industry a safety net against the virility of the black man. But what are we to make of Carroll's references to Hollywood's black darling in terms of animal imagery? Even though her references immediately bring to mind the historical incantations that the black male is but a savage, brutal beast, Carroll nevertheless subverts Poitier's muted screen persona; she cloaks him in sexuality and sensuality, within and against racial stereotype. In a way, Carroll's gender and race privilege her to situate Poitier in such a vigorously sensual manner. The specific image of a panther attributed to Poitier symbolizes a virile and erect big black dick present for Carroll's visual and, more specific, personal gratification.

The Preminger and Poitier portraitures invert Laura Mulvey's exemplar that outlines female film spectatorship as "active/male and passive/female." Mulvey asserts, "[t]he determining male gaze projects its phantasy on the female figure which is styled accordingly. In their traditional exhibitionist role women are simultaneously looked at and displayed, with their appearance coded for strong visual and erotic impact so that they can be said to connote *to-be-looked-at-ness*" (62). Instead, Dandridge and Carroll enact bell hooks's "oppositional gaze," whereby the black female spectator affirms agency in the experience of looking. hooks declares, "[s]paces of agency exist for black people, wherein we can both integrate the gaze of the other but also look back, and at one another, naming what we see" (248). The authors' written "I" (eye) enables Dandridge and Carroll to perform as desiring subjects rather than as desired objects. The act of black women looking back and naming what they see empowers them as agents of the gaze. Dandridge preempts authority from the powerful white director Preminger; Carroll restores sexual prowess to Poitier's staid cinematic persona.

Whoopi Goldberg's *Book* unabashedly exposes the personal areas Dandridge and Carroll refuse to discuss. As an autobiographer, Goldberg casts the most delicate "private parts" into the public sphere with reckless abandon. The comedienne's aggressive exhibition of the penis and vagina places sex and the myriad performances of it front and center for her audience. Goldberg announces on the inside flap of the dust jacket that she intends to skirt "ladylike" discretion: "I tell you, in my own inimitable way, how uproarious and provocative this book is, how out there, and cutting edge, and whatever else I can think to throw into the mix." This brazen spontaneity is Goldberg's signal of her intention to perpetuate the renegade image she institutes at the onset of her film career. Edwards asserts, "[Goldberg] . . . who is by turns both sexless and sensual . . . retains the skewed worldview of the comic, with a loopy disdain for convention and a wry 'screw you' attitude when it comes to considering what others may think" (58).

Book's dust jacket presents the comedienne with an unconventional look that fails to match what Bogle refers to as the Hollywood standard of beauty; yet the text showcases a sensual and thoughtful Goldberg. In a visual culture that traditionally adores and reveres the looks of white womanhood and, subsequently, of those black actresses and entertainers who possess white features (such as Halle Berry, Jada Pinkett-Smith, former Miss America Vanessa Williams, and song-stylist Alicia Keyes to name a few), Goldberg is a virtual iconoclast. *Book* allows Goldberg's nisus to construct her own version of Hollywoodism and to interject an identity. Both of these fly in the face of Hollywood convention. In other words, *Book* gives the black and white film and visual culture establishment the middle finger.

Goldberg's literary move is not without historical precedent. According to literary critic Françoise Lionnet's analysis, Zora Neale Hurston's autobiography *Dust Tracks on a Road* (1942) complements the spirit of Goldberg's *Book*. Lionnet states Hurston refuses to conform to conventions of self-portraiture (that is, linear narrative recounting the events of a life). Hurston prefers to inform the reader of her life "or, to be more precise, how she [. . . had] become what she [. . . was]—an individual who ostensibly [. . . valued] her independence more than any kind of political commitment to a cause, especially the cause of 'Race Solidarity' . . ." (Lionnet 114). Although Hurston does not come close to using the outrageous literary strategies Goldberg applies, *Book* dances with Hurston's spirit. Goldberg wantonly disregards convention and claims an independent spirit. These qualities devise an autobiographical text that complicates our notions of celebrity and the written texts celebrities may produce.

Goldberg's autobiography defies the conventions of celebrity autobiography in almost every respect. An analysis of the narrative techniques in *Everything and Nothing* and *Diahann* discloses that Dandridge and Carroll manage a safe distance from their readership, thereby preserving images of the black screen goddess in the white goddess ideal. The alluring photos on the front and back dust jackets display Dandridge and Carroll as epitomes of beauty, dignity, and exquisite black ladyhood. Carroll, for example, is photographed most seductively. The book's title *Diahann* is emblazoned in uppercase bold red letters on the front dust jacket.

Goldberg breaks the mold beginning with the dust jacket. The text's title and the name of the author appear embossed on the spine rather than on the front cover. The extreme close-up iris shot of Goldberg's dark brown face and dark berry lips on the dust jacket presents her looking directly at the reader, sans smile. On the back cover, the extreme close-up head shot exhibits Goldberg winking at the reader with a Cheshire cat smile; her dreadlocks are splayed in nimbus fashion.

The musical term "Riffs"—the title of the table of contents—signals Goldberg's main intent: to be raw, direct, and to the point. Yet, interestingly, Goldberg gives the reader no visual access to her full body: there are no family or celebrity photos within the text. Her denial of visual gratification forces the reader to visualize through the author's narrative sketches and through the narrative techniques of naming, detailing, and description. In effect, we absorb Goldberg through words and ideas only, and they are unaccompanied by high-gloss publicity photos and her body. Thus, of her own volition, Goldberg skirts a construction of celebrity glamour-girl image made standard in autobiographical texts written by black women in entertainment.

The riffs of particular interest are "Wind," "Head," "Sex," and "Dick." In the aggregate, these sketches give voice to those activities and desires that usually are articulated only within the private sphere.

In "Wind," Goldberg undertakes a discussion of the bodily function of farting; the anus and all of its characteristic effluvia are addressed: "We all fart, right? [. . .] But we don't like to talk about it [. . .]. Why is that?" (7). The sketch moves forward with a discussion of fart venues (elevators, buses, cabs, subways, and under the bedcovers); fart etiquette ("You shouldn't be allowed to drop one of those silent killers and not claim it," 10); and, fart sounds (power dumps or slow and silent). "Head" and "Dick" deliver an unabashed excursion into the obnoxious proclivities of (white) men in bathrooms with Goldberg as witness to the performing penis. She writes, "No one wants to be found out during the oh-baby period. Men [. . .] don't leave their crusty underwear on the floor, they don't piss in the sink. Yes, men actually piss in the sink" (29).

"Sex" is a treatise on the pros of masturbation, and the beauty of satisfying the body's sexual desires follows. She writes, "We all do 'feel good' things to ourselves, or to our partners, and that's cool as long as we're all consenting adults about it. Whatever feels good, you know" (119). Consider this sketch: "I was once married to a guy who couldn't give head to save his life. I was busting to tell him, 'Get a Life Saver and put your tongue through it, motherfucker. That's all you gotta do" (117).

These vignettes can be dismissed as Goldberg performing stand-up comedy; after all, she is a comedienne. Examined within a larger historical context of popular culture, however, Goldberg's literary venture begs for a more critical review. The black woman's vagina is considered only for its ability to accommodate the black penis for breeding purposes during the slave regime and for its availability to the white colonialist penis. In the case of Sarah Bartmann, an African girl displayed in a cage half-naked as the Hottentot Venus in England and Paris, the black woman's vagina becomes the site of medical curiosity by European physicians and scientists as it is exhibited in the realm of popular culture. Bartmann's genitalia is prodded, probed, and ultimately dissected after her death as nineteenth-century European anthropologists and medical doctors scramble to prove differences between black and white women, and, in particular to prove ludicrous theories regarding black women's inherent lasciviousness. The black woman's vagina, then, is a space of male entitlement. The vagina, moreover, is but an attachment to a body, a piece of flesh for the deposit of semen. It is an organ for the reproduction of chattel in the slave economy, an organ of pleasure for others, and a specimen for study and display over the course of time.

Goldberg reclaims the dismembered pieces of black female genitalia. She dissects then parades it in full view of the reader. Goldberg critiques the sexual performance (and lack thereof) of her male lovers and boasts of her sexual skill at the Friars Club roast. Her critique intrigues the reader because the men to whom Goldberg has been married, and with whom she has been linked publicly, are white male actors: Lyle Trachtenberg (former husband), Ted Danson, Timothy Dalton, and Frank Langella. *Book*, then, complements the popular tabloids, "outing," in a manner of speaking, the private (and gross) activities of popular actors. Although Goldberg refrains from directly naming the actors, she piques our curiosity over the author of these behaviors. Are Danson, Dalton, and Langella the obnoxious men who piss in the sink? Which one is skittish about performing oral sex? Does Ted Danson wear crusty underwear? Did Whoopi convince Tractenberg to use the lifesaver to "play around down there" (117)?

In the riff "Sex," Goldberg gets serious about masturbation and oral sex as alternatives to sexual intercourse:

Former Surgeon General Joycelyn Elders took a lot of shit for
suggesting masturbation should be taught in schools, but
what's wrong with that? People lit into ol' Joycelyn for saying
masturbation was a viable way for young people to experiment
sexually without the risk of infection or pregnancy, but it is.
[. . .] If we're gonna tell our kids to abstain from sexual intercourse, then we owe them some alternatives. [. . .] And why
stop with masturbation? Let's teach them how to do it to each
other too. (119)

Goldberg's critique of the Clinton administration's and the public's disdain for Surgeon General Elders's recommendation that masturbation
serve as a conduit to safe sex reminds us that seventeenth-century Puritan
principles still govern America's stance on sex in the twentieth and
twenty-first centuries. Her assessment of the public's reaction to the Surgeon General's recommendation as well as her conclusion that we "owe"
America's youth another possible choice for self-gratification, campaign
for the public to consider America's youth as a group worthy of real dialogue. Encouraging an adolescent to "just say no" to sex is easy; encour-
raging masturbation, however, takes sheer nerve to discuss on a national
level because the act comes historically charged with negative connota-
tions. Goldberg declares "[w]e still carry a lot of fucked-up Puritan baggage about [. . .] masturbation" (119). The diaries of Puritan Michael
Wigglesworth, for example, reveal his anxieties over his desires to mas-
turbate and those uncontrollable night dreams. He laments, "I find such
irresistible torments of carnal lusts or provocation unto the ejection of
seed. [. . .] The last night a filthy dream and so pollution escaped me in
my sleep for which I desire to hang my head with shame [. . .]" (4).

Major minister and personality of the Puritan era, Cotton Mather,
warns adolescents against "unclean" behavior: "Beware of having light
thoughts about some sorts of *Uncleanness* wherein many young people
have been so infatuated as to excuse themselves. There are abominable
self-pollutions [. . .] " (Elliott 36).

The language of these Puritan texts illustrates that Goldberg rightly
detects the Puritan's legacy of attitudes on sex inhibits our ability to
have an open discussion about masturbation. Masturbation bears a
negative linguistic history; it is an abominable unclean self-pollution
performed in private. For Goldberg, Elders's recommendation to the
nation in public brought up these Puritan beliefs. Yet, even though
Mather deems masturbation obscene, Emory Elliot notes, "[t]he very
fact that Mather felt free to speak out openly on the subject and even to
preach an entire sermon on it at a later date indicates a more open

atmosphere of discussion of the problem that in itself probably helped young people" (36–37). Goldberg suggests Elders's public support for educating young adults on the benefits of masturbation is her gesture (like Mather's in the pulpit) to have that "open atmosphere of discussion" of the problem of teenage pregnancy. In Goldberg's estimation, the "shit" Elders took and her subsequent dismissal closed down the opportunity for real and honest dialogue with America's youth about alternatives to traditional sex.

Goldberg, indeed, revels in the discussion of sexual politics, yet she is also unequivocal in her rhetoric on politics and race relations. The riff "Trust" forms a link with the political climate of the 1990s and Bill Clinton's presidency. "Trust" also queries the public's preoccupation with the alleged sexual exploits of U.S. past presidents at the expense of more important aspects of the president's overall performance:

> I don't care how many people our presidents have slept with. It doesn't take away from who they are or what they're about or what they might accomplish. [. . .] It's just part of the human package. [. . .] Do we believe in what [. . . President Clinton] stands for, and in what he's trying to accomplish? Or do we just slap another scarlet letter on yet another person just to help us to feel a little better about ourselves? (17, 23)

This richly comedic treatment recognizes the naturalness of sex. It also offers that the power of the mind overrides the supposed power of sex. Goldberg, furthermore, points to America's hero-worship and its disallowance of human frailties. Thus, Goldberg undermines the perceived potency and magic of sexual intercourse, which "suddenly" transform people in power into reckless human beings.

Although Dandridge and Carroll specify rough instances in their autobiographies, these women tell their stories with quiet reserve and distance, sans raunchy intimacies. Goldberg's narrative style, however, insists on the reality of living rooted in the basic rituals of our physical presence. The "in your face" narrative makes obvious that contained within life's neat little packages is the urge to fart in the most unlikely places.

Goldberg pulls back one more panel of life's experiences and could be imagined shouting: Hey, it's MY body, and I'll show it if I want to. Yeah, I was born and I'm living, but on my journey I get laid, menstruate, and wipe myself after I defecate and urinate. And, guess what? You do too, so let's go to our own locker room and talk about every itty-bitty detail! Why should men have all the fun? Her position as a comedienne gives her license to open these personal packages, and to add those "riffs" that we want to leave unpacked. Goldberg tells us that underneath the deodorant, our stench accompanies us wherever we are.

Of course no one wants to smell or see the stuff that Goldberg has thrown at us, but that is just the point. Because we do not want to, we almost never do, and thus a whole set of human desires, foibles, problems, accidents, painful situations, and illnesses are masked under the smiling assertion that everything is fine, nothing smells, and no one is hurt. More often than not, society pretends that no one is going crazy.

In "Word," Goldberg jockeys for the desensitization of racist terms such as "nigger" and "hymie"—pejorative terms used to signify the African-American and Jewish communities:

> Take the word nigger. Now, I've never been a nigger. Don't really know what a nigger is. [. . .] Maybe other people have thought that I was a nigger, but that's their definition. And yet people hear the word nigger and they run from it, or they're stopped by it, or they get an attitude about it. Why? Is it because deep down, you feel it's true? If that's the case, then why is it okay if a person calls himself a nigger? Does that make it a term of inclusion, and if so what exactly are we including ourselves in? (184–185)

She continues:

> [Jesse Jackson] came out and called New York "Hymie-town' and people were ready to light him on fire. [. . .] Hymie-town should not have been an insult, because there is no Hymie-town. Maybe there's Hymie Smith, you know, but there's no Hymie-town. (190, 191)

These vignettes are surprising. For Goldberg names seem to have no history or power in their invocation. Goldberg obviously recognizes the efficacy of words because she wrote *Book*. The written word is efficacious, and Goldberg's invocation of Hester Prynne's punishment in Nathaniel Hawthorne's classic *The Scarlet Letter* in her discussion of Clinton bares evidence that Goldberg understands the harmful impact of labeling, branding, and naming: As critics Ferdinand M. De Leon and Sally MacDonald claim, "[t]he labels we use affect how others perceive us and how we see ourselves; [. . .] they are used by those in power to define the rest even as they struggle to define themselves" (65). Correspondingly, Maya Angelou poignantly chronicles the distaste black people have in being called anything other than their given names. A white employer with a lazy tongue regards Angelou's name too difficult to pronounce and cavalierly assigns her another name. Angelou retorts, "[e]very person I knew had a hellish horror of being 'called out of his name.' It was a dangerous practice to call a Negro anything that could be loosely construed as insulting because of the centuries of their having been called niggers, jigs, dinges, blackbirds, crows, boots and spooks" (109). In other words, labels such as "nigger," "hymie," "spic," and "kike" come charged with history.

Certainly Goldberg's celebrity status affords her the luxury to disregard these words, but I hesitate to conclude she is so insensitive that she wants to disavow their harmful effects. Given the complexity of her work and what we know about her career, that she would be oblivious to her situation and to the power of her words seem unlikely. One of the criticisms of "political correctness"— do not utter "nigger" but say "the 'n' word" instead—is that it does not solve the problem of racial hatred but merely creates more hypocrisy and secrecy (that is, a person does not speak the word but still thinks it). I think Goldberg asks, which is better? Maybe—just maybe—we are better off knowing that Jesse has a problem with Jews or that Mark Fuhrman and many other white Los Angeles cops hate black people. Maybe she is saying we would all have fewer intestinal problems if we could fart in public. Maybe she suggests that we express our prejudices so that they can be addressed and answered. The invocation of the Puritans in America ("In the Puritan days, we dragged adulterers into the streets and put 'em in the stockades and posted a big old sign next to them describing their crime: FOR UNLAWFUL CARNAL KNOWLEDGE," 183), Goldberg reminds America of the violence in our nation's history because a group of people was labeled and punished. This labeling causes communities to virtually implode.

Goldberg's *Book* no doubt complicates the general public's idea about public notoriety and the projection of African-American female celebrity image in the genre of autobiography. Goldberg's discourses endow *Book* with a different quality of storytelling, separate and apart from the sugarcoated portraits Dandridge and Carroll present. The conjoining of scatology with sensible advice about sex is evidence of Goldberg's efforts to construct a more comprehensive African-American female. Somehow, *Book* restores Sarah Bartmann, expands the dialogue Dandridge and Carroll begin, and permits women to engage in bawdy language. It's okay. Dandridge and Carroll manage to retain the perfectly assembled Hollywood persona at the end of their texts, and this complies with the film culture's building of entertainment images. Together, the language of Dandridge, Carroll, and Goldberg asserts a black woman's power in looking . . . and . . . talking.

Conclusion

The Dance Finale:
What Have We Here?

Midnight. I am completely drained from a stint in the library that involved eight hours of roaming the musty stacks and pounding away on my laptop in an impersonal wooden desk in the library's reading room. I place my keys on the kitchen counter as I roll my weary, worn shoulders back to unleash them from an overburdened backpack. I need a drink. As the black quilted nylon straps slide down my arms and past my hands—leaving a zippered clump of forest green in the corner somewhere in my living area—I saunter over to the refrigerator and reach for a much-appreciated bottle of water. Uncapping the bottle initiates my midnight ritual. I grab a moist cold remote that somehow made it into my refridgerator's vegetable bin, and plop myself down in front of the television.

Just as I take the second long gulp of the icy water, however, I suspect this is no ordinary night. I have come to the end of my journey with six remarkable black women. Tonight calls for a cup of Taylor's of Harrogate tea. A splash of half 'n half, a sprinkle of sweetener, and I am good to go. I resettle into my papasan with the remote. As soon as I am about to press "power," the women come, one by one.

Lena . . . Dorothy and Little Dottie . . . Eartha Mae and Kitt . . . Diahann . . . Mary and Florence . . . Whoopi. . . . Just a dancing across my mind every which a'way. Tonight is not a night for television. It is a night for something else. . . .

I course through my album collection, and nestled between *The Mills Brothers Greatest Hits* and the Barbra Streisand *Broadway* albums, I pull out that Kitt collectible album. Although I do not have Lena Horne's *The Lady and Her Music* album (and I dare not call my friend and ask for it back), I do have *Lena Horne and Harry Belafonte Interpret Gershwin's Porgy and Bess*, compliments of a dear friend and colleague. Of Carroll, I have only her autobiography.

With my steaming cup of golden tea, I rest in my papasan chair, holding Carroll's book close to me. The spoken words of Kitt's first cut, "Après Moi," float through my speakers. Such attitude! How bold! Kitt has taken the reins of control in this relationship. What a voice! Kitt is so deliciously arrogant, so confident in her delivery. Her rhythms undergird her sauciness. There's "C'est Si Bon," "Cross at the Crossings," "Let's Do It," "An Old Fashioned Girl," the erotically charged "Santa Baby," and, of course, the fabulous "Uska Dara" (Ooooooh, those Turks!).

The stylus lifts the needle from the vinyl and I put on some Lena and Harry. Lena envelopes the words with a lush southernness in Gershwin's "Summertime." The phrasing, her breath control, the way she interprets that song: It is so . . . personal, so . . . determined, so . . . sophisticated, so . . . Lena. Lena delivers the thick and stifling hot of a southern summer's night on Catfish Row. This woman is something else! My my my my my my. . . . *See, I told you! Love, Dad.*

As Lena sings, I peruse again Carroll's autobiography and dust jacket. Draped behind all that sable and silver lamé is a woman who has earned every diamond in that starburst ring; she has earned the hand on the hip and those partially opened lips. She has said enough and worked behind the scenes. She can hold herself any damn way she pleases!

I turn to an untreated section in her text. It is the part wherein Carroll critiques *Julia*. Even though she is drawn to the sitcom because *Julia* presents a black woman with a desire to make a place for herself and her son in the world, a desire for decent housing, employment, and education for her son; even though she feels Kanter and NBC have a finger on the moment; and even though she identifies with many of the conversations the script calls for her to have with her son, Carroll nevertheless detects, "the attitude toward every other meaningful issue the script touched on—a woman alone, a woman on a job, a woman who's a widow raising a child—was equally mild. *Julia* was a terribly mild statement about everything—period" (136). Uh huh, I think. Carroll and I share the same opinion of this show, albeit mine is a bit more radical. Carroll and I bond in the recesses of my papasan.

This is what black celebrity autobiography does. It gives performances more panache, more meaning. The life story illuminates the performance; it brings out its color and bestows on the viewer a cloak of understanding the visual cannot give. To understand a black woman entertainer's life is to grasp her full meaning, to comprehend more fully each nuance, or to regard in a particular way or with several meanings in mind. In a particular way, we regard Horne, Dandridge, Kitt, Carroll, Wilson, and Goldberg as black female entertainers whose careers span decades. We might catch a glimpse of them on television, in a film, during an interview, or during an awards ceremony. Or we may be reminded of them, as Halle Berry advises us to reacquaint ourselves with Dorothy Dandridge and George Clooney reminds us of Hattie McDaniel. Black celebrity autobiography, in any case, coaxes us to understand or to hold up the black woman entertainer and stand with her through her story.

Black celebrity autobiography joins the continuum of black autobiography. More often than not, the mask of stardom, accompanied by fame and fortune, precludes these texts from study in the context of black self-determination and black self-expression. Yet from *Lena* to *Diahann* to *Book* these black celebrity autobiographies open up our thinking and discussion about black female resistance to oppression and discrimination they dance to in a variety of arenas. Behind every sequined gown, fur coat, and diamond ring, behind the glitter and the glamour that are part and parcel of entertainment, behind every character on celluloid, and behind every publicity shot are battle scars—even grave sites—that tell stories of each woman's survival.

. . . and the Women Dance: Lena Horne

As Dyer notes in his exegesis of the star, " . . . what makes [stars] interesting is the way in which they articulate the business of being an individual, something that is, paradoxically, typical, common, since we all in Western society have to cope with that particular idea of what we are" (*Heavenly Bodies* 18). With each consultation with her peers in the community of entertainment, as well as with her family members, resulting in an endorsement of her, Horne perceives the power of the image and the star, and their power to move spectators. She grasps the star's function in the film industry: to create myth, magic, and the desire for the unattainable.

Horne's star status in the strictest sense is "typical" and "common" since MGM provides her with the requisites, though minor, for the cultivation of a star, most notably the long-term contract. In 1944, she is the first Negro to appear on the cover of a movie magazine, *Motion Picture*. The glamour photographs, which invoke sensuality through flowing and revealing gowns and come-hither poses (an image perpetuated through the close-up in celluloid) embellish her in the minds of the Negro and white film spectator. As part of the labor force in the economy of visual culture, Horne stars in films as either sexy vamp or sultry singer. As a star, she joins the ranks of well-known white stars such as Bette Davis, Joan Crawford, Katherine Hepburn, and Elizabeth Taylor. These instances designate Horne as a usual star.

Horne's tenure at MGM, however, is by no means ordinary. Quite the contrary, as has been discussed, Horne's arrival in Hollywood and talk of stardom with Count Basie and her father, Teddy Horne, after her audition with Louis B. Mayer activate a distinct racial, cultural, and political dynamic her white counterparts do not experience. Horne assumes the precarious dynamic of the burden of representation. This burden brings not only the intense scrutiny of the Negro race, but also a vicious dismemberment on celluloid. Horne remembers, "It was an accepted fact that any scene I did was going to be cut when the movie played the south. So no one bothered to put me in a movie where I talked to anybody, where some thread of the story might be broken if I were cut" (Peck X3). The conscientious attempts of a film society and culture to cut her out of the cinematic master narrative and its resultant alienation fail to prevent the actress from realizing a career that has endured.

The singer-actress never is nominated for an Academy Award; that honor went to Dorothy Dandridge; nor does MGM develop film properties for her comparable to those of Crawford and Davis. She is known mostly for one song, "Stormy Weather," and two films: *Cabin in the Sky* and *Stormy Weather*, the latter made at 20th Century Fox. Lena Horne, however, transmutes the star and the symbol into a static and fluid image. The image is fluid in the sense that for all of its magic and myth-making potential for the general public, the star shape-shifts into the symbol when confronted with race. Marilyn Monroe and Lana Turner are stars and symbols, but they are symbols of things, attitudes, and values. Once Horne enters the picture, she turns into the symbol of a community and an entire race of people, and she accepts the scepter with forethought and grace. Horne also recognizes the artist's complicity in the making of the image. She writes, "[t]he image I have chosen to give [the audience] is of a woman they can't reach [. . .] just a singer" (*Lena* 128). Horne peels from celluloid her mass-mediated image, and demands a reckoning with Lena Horne, the tenacious, dignified, and informed performer and, by extension Lena Horne, a member of the Negro race.

Dorothy Dandridge

Any study of Dorothy Dandridge's narrative *Everything and Nothing* must be situated in the context of the advances made by the dance of Hattie McDaniel and Lena Horne in the Hollywood system from the 1930s through the 1950s. The landmarks they made inaugurate momentous precedents to which Dandridge and numerous other black actresses are indebted. McDaniel's Academy Award nomination by members of the Academy of Motion Picture Arts and Sciences (AMPAS) and win in 1940 makes it even conceivable to the Hollywood community of actors and the film-going public that a black woman ever could be nominated for the prestigious award. This is what actor-director George Clooney alludes to in his acceptance speech at the seventy-eighth Annual Academy Awards. Even more accompany the nomination: Dorothy Dandridge is the first black woman to attend the Academy Awards banquet, an AMPAS occasion from which McDaniel is barred at the time of her nomination. The most coveted accolade in the film community is the Oscar—the bronze statuette members of AMPAS award to an actress for giving her "best" in the dance on celluloid. The Oscar is an exclusive club whose nominees before the 1940 Academy Awards, are white actors and actresses. McDaniel, then, opens the way for Dandridge and a host other Oscar nominees and winners to participate in AMPAS on a level other than actress and laborer (Mapp). On March 30, 1955, Dandridge walks the hallowed red carpet as the second possible member in the Oscar club of privilege.

McDaniel and Horne forge crucial ground in Hollywood for black women in celebrity culture, but their advances fall short in significant ways. McDaniel acquires entry into the Oscar community as Best Supporting Actress, but Hollywood restricts her to a dance of the mammy, cook, and maid supporting roles. Horne indeed takes to task white patriarchy in Hollywood, but she never is able to solidify her position as a female star in the film industry. Dorothy Dandridge's personal and professional strides made in Hollywood fully integrate the black female entertainer in the microcosm of entertainment culture.

Her nomination for an Oscar for Best Actress; her marriage to Harold Nicholas; and her close ties with the Hollywood white male elite, namely John F. Kennedy's brother-in-law and actor Peter Lawford, film director Otto Preminger, and co-star Curt Jürgens, catapult her in the top tier white Hollywood strata. Then, again, in every one of Dandridge's movies, her characters are a part of the cinematic narrative rather than a mise-en-scène filmed to be cut from the film's storyline as had Horne's appearances. Dandridge's marriage ceremony to Nicholas in 1942 includes the Black Hollywood elite, and the partnership ties Dandridge to the Black community of actors contrary to Horne's relationship to it. She boasts friendships with Bill "Bojangles" Robinson and Herb Jeffries (the "Black Singing Cowboy" of Hollywood's Black westerns). Her light skin and ultra-sophisticated look make easy her crossover appeal in segregated Los Angeles; white actors and actresses feel at ease socializing with her.

The Oscar nomination furthermore, produces Dorothy Dandridge— the first black actress to present the Oscar to a colleague. Premier entertainer Bob Hope introduces Dorothy Dandridge on March 30, as "The only girl in the history [sic] to get me to go to the opera, Carmen Jones in person Ms. Dorothy Dandridge." Dandridge knows full well the magnitude of the night, and states, "If I seem a little nervous, this is as big a moment for me as it will be for the winner of this award. For Film Editing. In Hollywood. *On the Waterfront* Gene Milford" (*Dorothy Dandridge: "An American Beauty"*).

In the whirlwind of accomplishment, however, Dorothy Dandridge slips from the mind's eye of the public and into the ash heap of forgetfulness. On September 8, 1965, the Los Angeles coroner pronounces Dorothy Dandridge dead. She only has $2.14 in her bank account. So buried is she in obscurity that as a young black woman, I learn of her by happenstance in the hallway of high school. That attempt in 1974 to excavate the life of Dorothy Dandridge in the corner room of a high school study hall foreshadows the literary and visual enterprises to unearth the all-but-forgotten black star in the 1990s.

I queried, however, a series of things as I compare the HBO story to that of her autobiography. First, Berry's project is based on *Dorothy Dandridge: An Intimate Portrait of Hollywood's First Major Black Film Star*, a biography penned by Dandridge's long-time manager, Earl Mills. Why do the producers not draw on Dandridge's *autobiography*? Second, both the film and Mills's text neglect to establish her mother and stage-mother as the tenacious forces behind the construction of Dorothy Dandridge, the star. Third, these stories obscure the routine physical abuse Little Dottie suffers for years at the hands of her appointed stage-mother, Auntie Ma-ma. In addition, Mills asserts, "I'm quite sure that if Dorothy had appraised her life carefully, she would have chosen her childhood years as the best" (25). Dandridge, however, makes clear in her childhood narrative the abnormality of her upbringing. Berry's project, as well as Mills's, center on the sexual aspect of the abuse, not on the everyday occurrence of physical abuse Little Dottie suffers as does Dandridge's autobiography.

Dandridge ends her autobiography trying to find the meaning of Paul Laurence Dunbar's poetry in her life. "Several times . . . I have picked up [Dunbar's] *Complete Poems* and looked inside, as if trying to get a glimpse backward or find a ray of light for my own experience since [childhood]" (Dandridge 229). Dunbar, she concludes, "captured the nitty-gritty of American Negro life" (229). The nitty-gritty for Dandridge involves telling the story of Little Dottie who copes with abandonment, exploitation, and ill-treatment. Her story, indeed, is one of an existence in chaos. In the end, I believe, Dandridge succumbs to those things that shape her life from the beginning.

In her 40s, bankrupt, divorced, pursued by the Internal Revenue Service, and sometimes dependent on friends for food, Dandridge "chased a will-o'-the-wisp called a Comeback" (Dandridge 222). By this time, she is addicted to prescription drugs and her performances are so erratic, many managers threaten to fire her. During one performance, Dandridge is depressed to a state of paralysis: "I couldn't stand and had to be carried. Face, arms, and legs were frozen. Four physicians thought I would never walk again. A standby took over for me that night" (224–225). The only thing left for her to do is to dance on the white page.

Even then, Dandridge's best friends determine that her story is not worth the dance. Dandridge, however, tells her story within this whirlpool of personal ataxia and pandemonium, and as a night of pill-popping and champagne-swilling droned on, she thought to "either kill [herself] . . . or die of attrition then and there—simply will [herself] to death" (226). These thoughts of death visit her after her own friends deride the only thing she can call her own and could not be taken from her—her story—not during her time in the film industry. In her adulthood, practically every support system she creates and tries to maintain collapses.

Dorothy Dandridge dies at age forty-two in 1965, but not before she leaves us with her story of a girl called Little Dottie. "Let outsiders decide whether my life, my work, my motherhood, my quest for security, my friendships were so reprehensible, so poor a human story," she declares (Dandridge 226).

Eartha Kitt

Eartha Kitt joins Toni Morrison in her critique of the intra-racial dynamics in the black family. An examination of her texts brings to bare the practice of verbal, sexual, and physical abuse within the black community, just as Morrison does in *The Bluest Eye, Sula,* and *Paradise.* Through her we learn of the cultural continuities that play out among members of the black community. Black self-determination neither is exclusive to the binary of black versus white, nor does it imply only a struggle against oppression instigated by dominant powers. It also involves the investigation of how some black communities continue slavery's legacies.

Also important to Kitt is her realization of the nation's misunderstanding of her feistiness even though her attitude instigates bad press in both the black and white media. To take-up for herself against these accusations and judgments, Kitt writes four autobiographies. Three of Kitt's autobiographies (*Thursday's Child* [1956], *Alone with Me* [1976], and *I'm Still Here: Confessions of a Sex Kitten* [1989]) are written or published before and after major episodes in her life. *Thursday's Child* is published two years after news articles appear in the *Time* and *Ebony* magazines. Producer Leonard Stillman casts Kitt in Broadway's *New Faces of 1952*, where her legendary performance of "Monotonous" stops the show for a year. *Alone with Me* is in print eight years after the 1968 Women's Doers Luncheon at the White House. She performs her acclaimed Carnegie Hall concert two years earlier and President Jimmy Carter invites her back to the White House in 1978. That same year, she stars in the Broadway musical *Timbuktu* (for which she earns a Tony nomination). *I'm Still Here* emerges after the black feminist movement, and major interest in African-American literature—including celebrity autobiography written by African-American entertainers—takes hold in the mass-market media.

On one hand, this litany of publication dates is significant in that it reveals something about Eartha Mae, the communal outcast, and Eartha Kitt, the sultry entertainer. Retelling her story over time, however, Eartha (Mae) Kitt asks the reader to listen to her and to understand that she is a black woman who practically has had to vault over a nuclear and national community's mean-spiritedness. Kitt comes to us as an temerarious performer willing to gamble her status in the entertainment industry at the highest level. Her texts do not dismiss her arrogance, but point to reasons for it. And we understand.

Diahann Carroll

Carroll's decision to accept the role of Julia Baker and challenge Kanter's script illustrate the actress's willingness to take the scepter of black widowhood and black single motherhood, combine the two, and make visible a holistic image of black womanhood through the medium of television. According to popular culture critic John Fiske, television, as a medium, acts as a cultural agent as it produces, provokes, and circulates meaning (1). Interestingly, Carroll negotiates for her "new black women" in the arena of television. Television generates closeness and familiarity; people tune in after dinner and before retiring for the evening. The residue of a night's program, the actions of a particular character, or both remain fresh in the minds of the viewers. Carroll's image, then, cues the American television viewer to think about black women in new ways. With the media's primary focus on black leaders of the 1960s' civil rights movement, the voices of the black woman as widow and single mother remain largely ignored.

Conjointly, the media's preoccupation with the ghetto during this time feeds the American television viewer with images of poverty-stricken black men and women, and poor black single mothers with illegitimate children living on welfare. The focus on the ghetto also helps to cultivate the belief that *all* black people exist in the culture of poverty and illegitimacy. Robin Means Coleman contends, "*Julia* can be seen as a reinvented mammy stereotype. Julia was portrayed as a docile, content servant (in service in her capacity as care-giver or 'regulated'" (90). Carroll notes, "critics thought that *Julia* was a cop-out. Blacks didn't really live like Julia, they said" (144). Carroll goes on to note that the television writer for the *Saturday Review*, Robert Lewis Shayon, writes an attack on the show (Coleman 90). According to Carroll, Shayon believes, "[*Julia's*] plush, suburban setting was, 'a far, far cry from the bitter realities of Negro life in the urban ghetto, the pit of America's explosion potential'" (Carroll 144). But in her resolve to take the part, Carroll unwittingly asks: Why is it that talk of the black race is invariably about blacks and violence and downtrodden blacks in poverty and in the ghetto? Why is the black single mother not respected as the primary caregiver? *Julia* is a widow whose husband—the father of her child—is killed. Why do we not question that aspect of black life?

Sometimes critics and scholars are so preoccupied with finding the stereotype that they miss other more important issues that would make for a more open interpretation of a particular show. Film critic James Snead enters at this juncture, waving his "code of stasis" flag. Snead's study chastises film critics for their fixation on the stereotype. This fixation proffers a code of stasis that cuts off any other lines for interpretation. Snead asserts, "Onscreen and off, the history that Western culture has made typically denies blacks and black skin of historical reference, except as former slaves or savages." He continues, "The black—particularly the black woman—is seen as eternal, unchanging, unchangeable" (3). In other words, the role of a caregiver or healer a black actress assumes in visual culture automatically associates her with the mammy figure, as Coleman posits. Here, we need to remember, the character Julia Baker spent years in medical school studying and practicing to become a nurse. To qualify to handle the human body in that capacity, Julia Baker had to take tests to become certified. The war makes her a single black mother and her son a fatherless child after her husband serves his country. Black Americans live like Julia; black mothers are widowed as a result of war and violence; black mothers are possessed by a dogged determination to have a better life in the United States. These factors cut across lines of class. *Julia*—for all of its suburban plushness—challenges the common notions about the living conditions of black men and women. Not all black people are victims of poverty, crime, and drugs. These social diseases exist, but they are not the totality of black life.

Black life is not a monolith. Carroll's push for Dominique Deveraux on *Dynasty* furthers her campaign to show the breadth of experiences in the lives of black women. Television audiences who perhaps remember her on *Julia*, then, carry with them visuals of not only a resilient and resourceful widowed black mother, but also, audiences absorb an independent, affluent, and prosperous black woman executive.

Mary Wilson

In the 1970s, word got out about an impending breakup and Ross's "ruthless campaign" to be crowned the lead singer of the sterling group, the Supremes. Rumors of her cunning designs to be lead singer reminds me of several incidents on my school playground. These involved either a playmate's insistence on singing the lead or the anxiety over someone wanting to leave the group for whatever reason. I remember the animosity it caused between us: "Why does *she* always have to be out front?" some of us grumble. "If she leaves what will happen to the group?" Rumors spread that Ross, along with Berry Gordy, orchestrate the breakup at the expense of the other members. Circulating among the public is the most notorious rumor that Gordy fathers Ross's first child, Rhonda, and that Ross marries California public relations executive Robert Ellis Silberstein to cover it up. Two more infamous reports surface. First, the responsibility for Florence Ballad's dismissal and her ultimate personal demise rest exclusively on the shoulders of Ross and Gordy; second, Ross extends her influence on Gordy after her departure to derail the future success of the Supremes. If true, the latter works.

A college friend and soror of mine returns home to a small reception. We celebrate her successful stint in the chorus of the original premiere of the critically acclaimed Broadway musical, *Dreamgirls* (1981). From the article in *Ebony* magazine "Dreams Come True on Broadway for Young Stars in *Dreamgirls*" (Bailey), we know the play is based loosely on the life of the Supremes, and we are eager to hear *everything* about her experience in the show. We gather around her, anxious to listen to her stories about the big, big world of Broadway; about how she manages the bright lights of New York; and, more important, whether she has seen any stars.

"Oh, yeessss!" she graciously answers. "Mary Wilson came backstage. . . ."

"Mary Wilson?" I interrupt, with a wide-eyed gasp, "You mean, THE Mary Wilson of THE Supremes?"

"Yes," she smiles understanding my awe. "THE Mary Wilson. She came backstage, hugged some of us, and marveled, 'How did you know? How *did* you know?'"

Five years later, Wilson's autobiography *Dreamgirl: My Life as a Supreme* hits bookstores. The Ross and Gordy dyad plays itself out within the text, along with stories of jealousies, alleged career sabotage, and intense personal pain and suffering. Gordy's arrangement, I sadly conclude as I close the book, ultimately assaulted the integrity of the group, thereby compromised the Ballard/Wilson relationship. Wilson's earlier question, "How *did* you know?" is a validation of sorts.

Wilson is neither a first in the sense that Dandridge, Carroll, and Horne are, nor does she have the career former Supremes lead singer Diana Ross has. Wilson's book is a postmortem apology to Florence Ballard. In a way, what has been discovered, or what we know, is *Dreamgirl* is Wilson's journal of penance for her silence at a time when her best friend needs her voice. Although Wilson may feel responsible for a betrayal of Florence Ballard, her account of the dysfunction in the House of Motown exposes the forces effecting the relationship between the three women. It also exposes the fragility of that bond. Along the way, Wilson also recognizes that her identity as a teenager and performer is caught up in being a part of the Gordy family, and so she purposefully ignores Ross's and Gordy's schemes. The funeral at the end of *Dreamgirls* really highlights the stark realization of the death of the black sisterhood shaped after a talent show and under the stars—one that stardom later jeopardized.

Whoopi Goldberg

The comparison of *Book* with that of *Everything and Nothing* and *Diahann* not only highlights Goldberg's off-beat comedic linguistic style; the comparison underscores the disparate times within which each woman lived. Dandridge and Carroll grow in popularity during a period in which black women hold "ladyhood" in high regard, specifically the 1950s and 1960s. For decades black women in the United States labor to disengage themselves from the derogatory images that characterized black women as loose, lascivious, sexually promiscuous, and sexually deviant beings. These appropriations arise out of the era of slavery to justify the rape of enslaved women and out of anthropological and medical studies abroad as well. "Ladies" refrain from coarse language, are well-coiffed, and matters of the boudoir are discussed delicately if at all. The majority of black women in entertainment during Carroll's and Dandridge's time dedicate themselves to projecting an image antithetical to those earlier propounded by dominant culture.

Whoopi Goldberg offers up provocative wisdom and biting wit through humor and opens a literary space for black women to talk about their sexual exploits. Her brazen dialogue complements the uninhibited aura of the sensational gay 1990s that boast a dramatis personae of scantily clad entertainers such as Jennifer Lopez, Janet Jackson, Li'l Kim, and Destiny's Child, along with the charismatic President Bill Clinton. In this "let it all hang out" era, Goldberg seizes the opportunity to critique numerous key issues that are indeed "hanging out" in American popular culture during that bodacious liberal time: adultery; race relations, identity, and naming; teenage pregnancy; safe sex; and so on. Goldberg preserves her "hoodoo-acting" image and further encourages a novel approach to reading (watching) black women in entertainment.

Common Ground

Although these entertainers handle racial discrimination and family dynamics in disparate ways, the common thread that binds Horne, Carroll, Dandridge, Kitt, Wilson, and Goldberg is their determination to be the women they perceive themselves to be. Each entertainer dances on the white page to make her dissatisfaction with the status quo known. All of these women are afforded privileges that generate successful careers and, as a result, their images are burnished in the minds of the American public. Their names evoke the kinds of responses my mother and father utter on seeing Lena Horne cross Fred Sanford's threshold.

Horne's appearance on the sitcom is all that matters. What my parents see behind her beauty is the history she brings with her into Sanford's home. My knowledge of Kitt's life fuels my more enthusiastic response to her music.

This is what is so very important about the dance of black celebrity autobiography: we see history through the eyes of the entertainer. Certainly, each entertainer's voice comes through a particular moment in time that informs her story: Horne and World War II and the NAACP; Carroll and the civil rights movement and, later, popularity of the nighttime soap in the 1980s; Dandridge and the Great Depression; Kitt and the pioneering dances of Katherine Dunham and the Vietnam War; Wilson and Motown; and Goldberg and contemporary American popular culture. Horne, Carroll, Dandridge, Kitt, Wilson, and Goldberg use the genre of autobiography to tell a story the flashing lights on the stage of entertainment cannot. They refuse to rest on the laurels of privilege. On the contrary, each actress peers into her circumstances and discerns a greater work to be done. Each woman does so at the risk of her career.

Yes, white stars, including Joan Crawford, Lana Turner, Marilyn Monroe, and Elizabeth Taylor survived the trials and tribulations of the studio, and their autobiographies lay bare the joy as well as the angst of being a part of the studio system. Yes, television stars such as Lucille Ball, Hope Lange, and Doris Day challenge television executives. And, yes, white personalities in visual culture as well survived poverty, child abuse, and other atrocities. But the racial dynamics dancing in the United States pre- and post–civil rights movement of the 1960s do not touch white stars. Audiences wait anxiously to see a lavish dress or suit worn by a white guest on the *Ed Sullivan Show*, but whisper whether Sullivan will kiss Dorothy Dandridge. Hotels welcome white performers through the front door while ushering black entertainers in through the back door. White performers enjoy hotel pools; Dandridge dips her toe into one of them, and the management drains and cleans it.

These six acclaimed actresses, Lena Horne, Dorothy Dandridge, Diahann Carroll, Mary Wilson, Eartha Kitt, and Whoopi Goldberg dance on the stage of four powerful communities: the film, television, and music industries, and the black community (actors and the NAACP). From 1940 to 1990, political and popular culture events, including World War II, the McCarthy era, the civil rights movement, and the Vietnam War, altered U.S. society and culture. Some events set in motion the gradual racial integration of the entertainment industry; others usher in a new kind of black female entertainer. As the first distinguished black female stars, Horne, Dandridge, Carroll, Wilson, and Kitt, are expected to satisfy the expectations of the entertainment industry to appeal to predominantly white audiences. At the same time, they also try to satisfy the black community, which looks to them to provide "authentic" representations of black Americans in American visual culture. These audiences expect them to project a type and an image that will make Americans feel positive about them as individuals and as representatives of a group. The dreadlocked single mother Goldberg modifies our preconceptions of how black stars should look in the 1980s and 1990s.

And the Dance Continues . . . Are We Listening to the Footsteps?

Mary Wilson's tell-all, *Dreamgirl: My Life as a Supreme*, drives a pickax into the cemented landscape of black autobiography, and Tina Turner's project *I, Tina* jumps into the crack, and chips away a space for other black women entertainers to strut their stuff in prose. I remind the readers again of the plethora of celebrity autobiographical dance movements published in the 1990s, including Whoopi Goldberg's *Book*: Ronnie Specter, *Be My Baby: How I Survived Mascara, Miniskirts, and Madness or My Life as a Fabulous Ronette* (1990); Diana Ross, *Secrets of a Sparrow: Memoirs* (1993); Martha Reeves, *Dancing in the Street: Confessions of a Motown Diva* (1994); Nichelle Nichols, *Beyond Uhura: Star Trek and Other Memories* (1994); Patti LaBelle, *Don't Block the Blessings: Revelations of a Lifetime* (1996); Kim Coles, *I'm Free, But It'll Cost You: the Single Life According to Kim Coles* (1997); Gladys Knight, *Between Each Line of Pain and Glory: My Life Story* (1997); and Queen Latifah, *Ladies First: Revelations of a Strong Woman* (1999).

The footsteps of the dance on the white page reverberate throughout the twenty-first century as black female celebrities across genres choreograph fresh new autobiographical movements. Each black woman composes more complex yet dazzling literary dance steps, and every movement generates provocative insights of black women in entertainment. In the process, their texts challenge what we, as academics, deem as literature worthy of scholarship and classroom discussion. Contemporary black women celebrities make fluid the meaning of celebrity in popular culture. Their texts destabilize the heavy influence of the slick image of them in magazines and in the powerful domains of family, television, film, music, and radio. Natalie Cole's *Angel on my Shoulder* (2000) ushers in the new millennium and assuredly complements Dorothy Dandridge's story of black female child stardom. While childhood trauma figures in Cole's life in the death of her famous father, Nat King Cole, and not that of child abuse, *Angel on My Shoul-*

der nevertheless tells the story of a young black girl who inherits child stardom from a phenomenal black parent. The theme of black female child stardom also runs throughout the autobiographies of Gladys Knight and Aretha Franklin.

As mentioned, Mary Wilson's and Tina Turner's memoirs popularize for the masses the genre of black celebrity autobiography. Radio personality Wendy Williams's autobiography *The Wendy Williams Experience* (2004); Karrine Stefans's tell-all *Confessions of a Video Vixen* (2005); *American Idol* winner Fantasia Barrino's *Life Is Not a Fairy Tale* (2005); Kimora Lee Simmons's *Fabulosity! What It Is and How To Get It* (2006); Star Jones Reynolds's *Shine! A Physical, Emotional, and Spiritual Journey to Finding Love* (2006); and former soap opera star and thespian Tonya Pinkins's *Get Over Yourself! How to Drop the Drama and Claim the Life You Deserve* (2006) impact *and* nourish the genre's popularity even more. Williams's storytelling has a similar style to that of Goldberg's as she reports of her dance to the top of her profession in radio. Once a top-paid video dancer in the rap video industry, Stefans's text publicizes her physical abuse, rape, and drug use experienced before age twenty-six and explains her reasons for entering that rhapsodized culture. *Confessions of a Video Vixen*, more significant, deromanticizes an industry consumed by projecting a lifestyle of abundant wealth (the bling-bling). Barinno chronicles how she sustains her desire to perform even when she became a single mother as a teenager. Simmons and Jones complement Eartha Kitt's *Rejuvenate!* as both celebrities challenge women to believe in themselves and look fabulous while doing it. Pinkins narrates her journey from an unemployed soap star (Livia Frye in *All My Children*) and a twelve-year custody battle for her two sons, which legal fees throw her on the threshold of welfare. In *Get Over Yourself!* Pinkins grants to her readership her own motivational proverbs on mastering the drama of life. These stories are intriguing not only because each woman has access to some of the top executives and artists in the film, television, theater, video, and rap industries (namely rap moguls Russell Simmons and Sean "P. Diddy" Combs, rappers Jay-Z and LL Cool J), but also more captivating is each woman's dance toward self-preservation in an undercurrent of obstacles.

The technology of writing for black female celebrities is the means to construct again and again their own life stories at different moments in time. By talking about themselves in the literary realm, black female celebrities dance with other black women who, throughout history, have used the genre of autobiography to choreograph themselves onto the stage of U.S. history. When we talk about, for example, Abraham Lincoln, Elizabeth Keckley's autobiography *Behind the Scenes: Thirty Years a Slave, and Four Years in the White House* (1868) reminds us of her close contact with the president, and that her talent as a seamstress allowed both Abraham and Mary Todd to be presented in grand sartorial style to the American people. Now when there is talk about Lady Bird Johnson and president Lyndon Baines Johnson, we will think of Kitt's proximity to the president. Listening to the footsteps of the dance on the white page gives us a kaleidoscope of black women. As griottes of the stories of black women in entertainment, their dance of storytelling widens the circle of black women writing. When we read their stories, we dance with them on the white page. When we listen to their footsteps on the white page, we save them from the ash heap of forgetfulness and carry with us a world of memories to pass on to generation to generation.

We have listened to the footsteps of the dance on the white page.

Selected Bibliography

Abernathy, Ralph David. *And the Walls Came Tumbling Down: An Autobiography*. New York: Harper, 1989.

"After the Fall." *The Steve Harvey Show*. Dir. Stan Lathan. Perf. Steve Harvey, Cedric the Entertainer, and Wendy Racquel Robinson. Episode 105, Season 5. UPN 1. April 2001.

Agins, Michelle V. *Sisterfriends: Portraits of Sisterly Love*. New York: Pocketbooks, 2001.

Agnes of God. By John Pielmeier. Dir. Michael Lindsay-Hogg. Perf. Diahann Carroll, Geraldine Page and Maryann Plunkett. Music Box Theater, New York, 30 Mar 1982.

All the Women are White, All the Blacks are Men, Some of Us Are Brave: Black Women's Studies. Eds. Gloria T. Hull, Patricia Bell Scott, and Barbara Smith. Old Westbury: The Feminist P, 1982.

Anderson, Marian. *My Lord What a Morning*. New York: Viking, 1956.

Andrews, William L. "Dialogue in Antebellum Afro-American Autobiography." *Studies in Autobiography*. Ed. James Olney. New York: Oxford UP, 1988.

Angelou, Maya. *I Know Why the Caged Bird Sings*. New York: Random, 1970.

The Arsenio Hall Show. Dir. Sandra Fullerton and Scott Schaefer. Perf. Phyllis Hyman. Arsenio Hall Communications / Paramount Television. 4 November 1992.

Autobiography of Miss Jane Pittman. Dir. John Korty. Perf. Cicely Tyson, Odetta, and Josephine Primus. Tomorrow Entertainment, 1974.

Bailey, Pearl. *The Raw Pearl.* New York: Harcourt, 1968.

Bailey, Peter. "Dreams Come True on Broadway for Young Stars in *Dreamgirls.*" *Ebony.* May 1982: 91–96.

Baker, Josephine, and Jo Bouillon. *Josephine.* New York: Paragon, 1988.

Baldwin, James. "Many Thousand Gone." *Notes on a Native Son.* 1955. Boston: Beacon P, 1957: 25, 28–29.

Barrino, Fantasia. *Life Is Not a Fairy Tale.* New York: Fireside, 2005.

Barthes, Roland. *Mythologies.* Trans. Annette Lavers. London: Baylis and Son, 1972.

Basie, Count. *Good Morning Blues: The Autobiography of Count Basie as told to Albert Murray.* New York: Random, 1985.

Bataan. Dir. Tay garnett. Perf. Robert Taylor, George Murphy, and Thomas Mitchell. Metro-Goldwyn-Mayer, 1943.

"Battle Over *Citizen Kane,* The" *The American Experience.* Transcript. Prod. Thomas Lennon and Michael Epstein. WGBH Educational Foundation, 1997.

Bennett, Dionne. *Sepia Dreams: A Celebration of Black Achievement through Words and Images.* New York: St. Martin's, 2001.

Bennetts, Leslie. "When New Stars Step Into Old Roles." *New York Times.* "Weekend" 8 Oct 1982: 6.

Birth of a Nation. Dir. D. W. Griffith. Perf. Lillian Gish, Mae Marsh, and Henry B. Walthall. Triangle, 1915.

Bogle, Donald. *Dorothy Dandridge: A Biography.* New York: Amistad, 1997.

———. *Brown Sugar: Eighty Years of America's Black Female Superstars.* New York: Da Capo, 1980.

———. *Toms, Coons, Mulattoes, Mammies, and Bucks: An Interpretive History of Blacks in American Films.* New York: Viking, 1973.

Bond, Julian. *A Time to Speak, a Time to Act: The Movement in Politics.* New York: Simon, 1972.

Bourne, Stephen. "Black Garbo." *Feature Retro. Pride* 1999: 112–13.

Braxton, Joanne. *Black Women Writing Autobiography.* Philadelphia: Temple UP, 1989.

Brooks, Gwendolyn. "Kitchenette Building." *The Norton Anthology of African American Literature.* Eds. Henry Louis Gates, Jr., Nellie McKay, William L. Andrews, et al. New York: Norton, 1997: 1579.

———. "Riot." *The Norton Anthology of African American Literature.* Ed. Henry Louis Gates, Nellie McKay, William L. Andrews, et al. New York: Norton, 1997.

Brown, Peter H., and Pamela Ann Brown. *The MGM Girls: Behind the Velvet Curtain.* New York: St. Martin's, 1983.

Buckley, Gail Lumet. *The Hornes: An American Family*. New York: Applause, 1986.

Cabin in the Sky. Dir. Vincente Minnelli. Perf. Lena Horne, Eddie "Rochester" Anderson, and Ethel Waters. MGM, 1943.

Califano, Joseph. *The Triumph and Tragedy of Lyndon Johnson*. New York: Simon, 1991.

Campbell, Bebe Moore. "Whoopi Talks B(l)ack." *Essence* Jan. 1997: 58.

Campbell, Joseph. *The Hero with a Thousand Faces*. Princeton: Princeton UP, 1973.

Carby, Hazel. *Race Men*. Cambridge: Harvard UP, 1998.

———. *Reconstructing Womanhood: The Emergence of the Afro-American Novelist*. Oxford UP, 1987.

Carmen Jones. Dir. Otto Preminger, Perf. Dorothy Dandridge, Harry Belafonte, Pearl Bailey, Diahann Carroll. 20th Century Fox, 1954.

Carroll, Diahann. "From Julia to Cosby to Oprah: Tuning into 60 Years of TV." *Ebony* Nov. 2005: 101.

———. "Dianahh Carroll." *Arts and Entertainment*, 1996.

———. *Diahann: An Autobiography with Ross Firestone*. Boston: Little, Brown and Company, 1986.

The Classic Slave Narratives: The Life of Olaudah Equiano, The History of Mary Prince, Narrative in the Life of Frederick Douglass, Incidents in the Life of a Slave Girl. Ed. and Intro. Henry Louis Gates, Jr. New York: Penguin, 1987.

Claudine. Dir. John Berry. Perf. Diahann Carroll, James Earl Jones and Lawrence Hilton Jacobs. 20th Century Fox, 1974.

Cleaver, Eldridge. *Soul on Ice*. New York: Dell, 1968.

"Cockroach on Broadway. *Shinbone Alley*." *Newsweek* 22 Apr 1957: 69–80.

Coffy. Dir. Jack Hill. Perf. Pam Grier, Robert DoQui, and William Elliott. American International Picture, 1973.

Cole, Natalie, with Digby Diehl. *Angel on My Shoulder: An Autobiography*. New York: Warner, 2000.

Coleman, Robin R. Means. *African American Viewers and the Black Situation Comedy*. New York: Garland P, 1998.

Coles, Kim. *I'm Free, But It'll Cost You: The Single Life According to Kim Coles*. New York: Hyperion, 1997.

Collins, Patricia Hill. *Black Feminist Thought: Knowledge Consciousness, and the Politics of Empowerment*. New York: Routledge, 1991.

Cooper, Anna Julia. *A Voice from the South*. Introd. Mary Helen Washington. New York: Oxford University P, 1988.

Cooper, Laura. "The Negro Family and the Moynihan Report." *The Black Family: Essays and Studies*. Ed. Robert Staples. Belmont: Wadsworth, 1978.

Coulbourn, John. "The Sun Rises in North York: Diahann Carroll, Cast Magnificent in Webber Musical." *Toronto Sun*. 16 Oct 1995: 43.

Cramer, Richard Ben, and Thomas Lennon. "The Battle over 'Citizen Kane.'" *The American Experience*. 1997. <http://www.pbs.org/wgbh/amex/kane2/kane2ts.html> June 2000.

Crawford, Joan. *My Way of Life*. New York: Simon, 1971.

Cripps, Thomas. *Making Movies Black*. New York: Oxford UP, 1993.

Crowther, Bosley. *Hollywood Rajah: The Life and Times of Louis B. Mayer*. New York: Holt, 1960.

Cudjoe, Selwyn. "Maya Angelou: The Autobiographical Statement Updated." *Reading Black, Reading Feminist*. Ed. Henry Louis Gates, Jr. New York: Meridian, 1990.

Cyril Dandridge v. Ruby B. Dandridge. No. 227764. Cuyahoga Crt of Common Pleas. 19 Nov 1926.

Dance, Stanley. *The World of Count Basie*. New York: Scribner's, 1980.

Dandridge, Dorothy. *Everything and Nothing: The Dorothy Dandridge Tragedy*. New York: Abelard-Schuman, 1970.

Cyril Dandridge v. Ruby B. Dandridge. "Petition for Divorce and 6 June 1933 (et al.).

David, Ron. *Toni Morrison Explained: A Reader's Map to the Novels*. New York: Random, 2000.

Davis, Angela Y. *Angela Davis: An Autobiography*. New York: Random, 1974.

———. "Joan Little: The Dialectics of Rape." *Ms*. June 1975: 74–75.

———. *Women, Culture, Politics*. New York: Vintage, 1990.

———. *Women Culture Politics*. New York: Random, 1990.

Davis, Ronald L. *The Glamour Factory*. Dallas: Southern Methodist UP, 1993.

Dawson, Michael. *Behind the Mule: Race and Class in African-American Politics*. Princeton UP, 1994.

De Leon, Ferdinand M., and Sally MacDonald, "The Politics of Labels: Does It Matter What We're Called?" *Our Times: Readings from Recent Periodicals*. Ed. Robert Atwan. 4th ed. Boston: Bedford, 1995.

Diahann Carroll. Dir. Jeanne Begley. Narr. Harry Smith. Arts and Entertainment Home Video, 2000.

Dirlik, Arif. "Culturalism as Hegemonic Ideology and Liberating Practice." *The Nature and Context of Minority Discourse*. Ed. Abdul R. Jan Mohamed and David Lloyd. New York: Oxford UP, 1990.

"Diva to Duse." *Newsweek* 1 Nov. 54: 61.

The Divine Secrets of the Ya-Ya Sisterhood. Dir. Callie Khouri. Perf. Sandra Bullock, Maggie Smith, and James Garner. All Girl Productions, 2002.

Do The Right Thing. Dir. Spike Lee. Perf. Ruby Dee and Ossie Davis, Jr. 40 Acres and A Mule, 1989.

Dorothy Dandridge: "An American Beauty." Dir. Ruth Adkins Robinson. Host Obba Babatunde. DVD Passport Productions, 2003.

"Dorothy Dandridge: Hollywood's Fiery Carmen Jones." *Life.* 1 November 1954.

Dougherty, Barry. *New York Friars Club Books of Roasts: The Wittiest, Most Hilarious, and Most Unprintable Moments from the Friars Club.* New York: MJF Books, 2000.

Douglas, Mary. *Purity and Danger: An Analysis of Concepts of Pollution and Taboo.* New York: Praeger, 1966.

Douglass, Frederick. *Douglass Autobiographies.* New York: Library Classics, 1994.

Drake, Sylvia. "'Same' with a Difference." *Los Angeles Times* 31 May 1977 IV:10.

Drcher, Kwakiutl. "Children." *The Toni Morrison Encyclopedia.* Ed. Elizabeth Ann Beaulieu. Connecticut: Greenwood, 2003.

The Duke Is Tops. Dir. William L. Nolte. Perf. Lena Horne and Ralph Cooper. Million Dollar Productions, 1938.

Dunbar, Paul Laurence. "We Wear the Mask." *The Norton Anthology of African American Literature.* Eds. Henry Louis Gates, Jr., Nellie McKay, William L. Andrews, et al. New York: Norton, 1997: 896.

Dunham, Katherine. *A Touch of Innocence: Memoirs of a Childhood.* New York: Harcourt Brace, 1959.

Dyer, Richard. *Heavenly Bodies: Film Stars and Society.* London: Macmillan, 1986.

———. *White.* New York: Routledge, 1997.

———. *Stars.* London: BFI, 1998.

Eagleton, Terry. *Ideology: An Introduction.* London: Verso, 1991.

Early, Gerald. *One Nation under a Groove: Motown and American Culture.* Ann Arbor: U of Michigan P, 2004.

Eastside/Westside. Dir. John Berry and Marc Daniels. Perf. Cicely Tyson and George C. Scott. CBS 23 Sept 1963.

Edwards, Audrey. "An Appreciation: Why Whoopi?" *Essence* Jan. 1997: 58.

Elliott, Emory. *Power and the Pulpit in Puritan New England.* Princeton UP, 1975.

Ellison, Ralph. *Shadow and Act.* New York: Random, 1964.

Equiano, Olaudah. *The Life of Olaudah Equiano. The Classic Slave Narratives: The Life of Olaudah Equiano, The History of Mary Prince, Narrative in the Life of Frederick Douglass, Incidents in the Life of a Slave Girl.* 1791. Ed. and Intro. Henry Louis Gates, Jr. New York: Penguin, 1987.

Estés, Clarissa Pinkola. *Women Who Run With the Wolves.* New York: Ballantine, 1992.

———. "Vasalisa and the Baba Yaga." *Theater of the Imagination.* Boulder: Sounds True Recording, 1995.

Eve's Bayou. Dir. Kasi Lemmons. Perf. Diahann Carroll, Lynn Whitfield, and Debbie Morgan. Lions Gate, 1997.

"Ex-boyfriend of Phyllis Hyman was among last to talk to her; said she was 'happy' with decision to commit suicide." *Jet.* 24 July 1995: 60.

"Fans and friends mourn the tragic death of singer Phyllis Hyman." *Jet.* 24 July 1995: 60.

Father Knows Best. Dir. William D. Russell and Peter Tewksbury. Perf. Robert Young and Jane Wyatt. CBS 3 Oct 1954.

Fauset, Jessie Redmon. *Plum Bun: A Novel Without a Moral.* 1929. Introd. Deborah McDowell. Boston: Beacon Press, 1990.

Fiske, John. *Television Culture.* London: Metheun, 1987.

Florence Ballard Chapman v. Ross, et al. No. 12949. Crt of App of Michigan. 22 May 1973.

"Focus." *Dynasty.* Dir. Don Medford. Perf. Diahann Carroll, John Forsythe, and Joan Collins. Episode Number 151, Season 7. ABC Aaron Spelling Productions. 15 October 1986.

Fowles, Jib. *Starstruck: Celebrity Performers and the American Public.* Washington: Smithsonian Institution P, 1992.

Foxy Brown. Dir. Jack Hill. Perf. Pam Grier, Antonio Fargas, and Peter Brown. American International Pictures, 1974.

Franklin, Aretha, and David Ritz. *From These Roots.* New York: Crown, 1999.

Frazier, E. Franklin. *The Black Bourgeoisie.* New York: Free Press, 1997.

"Fredi Washington 1903–1994." <http://www.africanpubs.com/Apps/bios/0214WashingtonFredi.asp?pic=none> 9 Jan 2003.

Gabriel, Teshome. "Third Cinema as Guardian of Popular Memory: Towards a Third Aesthetics." *Questions of Third Cinema.* Ed. Jim Pines and Paul Willemen. London: BFI, 1989.

Gates, Henry Louis, Jr., ed. *Classic Slave Narratives.* New York: Penguin, 1987.

Genovese, Eugene D. *Roll, Jordan, Roll: The World the Slaves Made.* New York: Random, 1976.

Giddings, Paula. *When and Where I Enter. The Impact of Black Women on Race and Sex in America.* New York: Morrow, 1984.

Gilman, Sander L. "Black Bodies, White Bodies: Toward an Iconography of Female Sexuality in Late Nineteenth-Century Art, Medicine, and Literature." *Critical Inquiry* 12 (Autumn 1985): 212.

Gilman, Sander L. *Difference and Pathology: Stereotypes of Sexuality, Race, and Madness.* Ithaca: Cornell UP, 1985.

Giovanni, Nikki. *The Selected Poems of Nikki Giovanni.* New York: Morrow, 1996.

"Girls From Motown, The." *Time* 4 Mar. 1966: 84.

Goldberg, Whoopi. *Book.* New York: Weisbach, 1997.

Gone with the Wind. Dir. Victor Fleming. Perf. Vivien Leigh, Hattie McDaniel, and Clark Gable. Selznick International Pictures, 1939.

Gordy, Berry. *To Be Loved: The Music, the Magic, the Memories of Motown.* New York: Warner, 1994.

Grosz, Elizabeth. *Volatile Bodies: Toward a Corporeal Feminism.* Bloomington: Indiana U, 1994.

Hagen, Uta. *Respect for Acting.* New York: Macmillan, 1973.

Hale, Thomas. *Griots and Griottes: Maters of Words and Music.* Bloomington: Indiana U P, 1998.

Hallelujah! Dir. King Vidor. Perf. Daniel L. Haynes, Victoria Spivey, and Nina Mae McKinney. MGM, 1929.

Hall, Stuart. "What Is This 'Black' in Popular Culture?" *Critical Dialogues in Cultural Studies.* Ed. David Morley and Kuan-Hsing Chen. London: Routledge, 1997. 468.

Hampton, Henry. *Voices of Freedom: An Oral History of the Civil Rights Movement from the 1950s through the 1980s.* New York: Bantam, 1990.

Harrison, Daphne Duval. *Black Pearls: Blues Queens of the 1920s.* New Brunswick: Rutgers UP, 1988.

Hartman, Saidiya V. *Scenes of Subjection: Terror, Slavery, and Self-Making in Nineteenth-Century America.* New York: Oxford UP, 1997.

Haskins, James, with Kathleen Benson. *Lena: A Biography of Lena Horne.* Chelsea: Scarborough House, 1991.

Hawthorne, Nathaniel. *The Scarlet Letter.* 1850. New York: Vintage, 1990.

The Hazel Scott Show. DuMont Television Network. 3 Jul 1950.

"He Works Hard for the Money." *Living Single.* Episode 3.8. 19 October 1995.

Hearts in Dixie. Dir. Paul Sloane. Perf. Stepin Fetchit, Clarence Muse, and Eugene Jackson. Fox Film Corp., 1929.

Herskovits, Melvin J. *The Myth of the Negro Past*. Boston: Beacon Hill, 1990.

Hill, George. *Black Women in Television: An Illustrated History and Bibliography*. New York: Garland, 1990.

Holiday, Billie, with William Dufty. *Lady Sings the Blue*s. London: Barrie, 1973.

Hollywood: An Empire of Their Own. Writer/Dir. Simcha Jacobovici. Exec. Prods. Michael A. Levine and Monty Montgomery. Arts and Entertainment Home Video. 1998.

"Hollywood and Walter White." *Chicago Defender*. 23 Feb 1946. C2: 14.

Holte, James Craig. "The Representative Voice: Autobiography and the Ethnic Experience" *MELUS* 9.2 (Summer 1982): 28–29.

hooks, bell. *Ain't I a Woman?* Boston: South End P, 1993.

———. *All about Love: New Visions*. New York: Morrow, 2000.

———. *Black Looks: Race and Representation*. Boston: South End P, 1992.

———. *Killing Rage: Ending Racism*. New York: Holt, 1995.

———. "Loving Blackness as Political Resistance." *Black Looks: Race and Representation*. Boston: South End P, 1992. 9–21.

———. Talking Back: thinking feminist, thinking black. Boston:

———. "The Oppositional Gaze: Black Female Spectators." *Movies and Mass Culture*. Ed. John Belton. New Brunswick: Rutgers UP, 1996.

———. *Yearning: Race, Gender, and Cultural Politics*. Boston: South End P, 1990.

Horne, Lena, with Helen Arstein and Carlton Moss. *In Person, Lena Horne*. New York: Greenberg, 1950.

———, with Richard Schickel. *Lena*. New York: Doubleday, 1965.

Horne, Lena. *Lena Horne: The Lady and Her Music*. LP. Qwest, 1981. <http://www.Aphrodite.com>

Houston, Norman O. Letter o Mr. Walter White. 16 Sept. 1943, NAACP mf p18 r20 f257.

Howse, Beth. E-mail to the author. 28 Aug 2003.

———. E-mail to the author. 10 Nov 05.

Hurston, Zora Neale. *Dust Tracks on a Road*. Fwd. Maya Angelou. New York: Harper Perennial, 1991.

———. *Dust Tracks on a Road: An Autobiography*. 1942. New York: Harper Perennial, 1996.

Hyman, Phyllis. *Living All Alone*. Capital, 1986.

———. *I Refuse to be Lonely*. Zoo/Volcano, 1995.

Imitation of Life. Dir. John M. Stahl. Perf. Louise Beavers and Fredi Washington. Universal, 1934.

Introducing Dorothy Dandridge. Dir. Martha Coolidge. Perf. Halle Berry, Brent Spiner, and Loretta Devine. HBO Pictures, 1999.

"Jackie O: In a Class of Her Own." *A&E Biography.* Exec. Prod. Pattie Hassler. Legendary Women Series, CBS News Prods., 1995.

Jackson, Carlton. *Hattie: The Life of Hattie McDaniel.* Lanham: Madison, 1990.

Jacobs, Harriet. *Incidents in the Life of a Slave Girl.* New York: Penguin, 2000.

Janken, Kenneth Robert. *The Biography of Walter White: Mr. NAACP.* New York: New Press, 2003.

Jefferson, Thomas. *Notes on the State of Virginia.* 1787. Chapel Hill: U of North Carolina P, 1955.

Jewell, K. Sue. *From Mammy to Miss America and Beyond: Cultural Images and the Shaping of U.S. Social Policy.* London: Routledge, 1996.

Johnson, Barbara. "Writing." *Critical Terms for Literary Study.* Ed. Frank Lentricchia and Thomas McLaughlin. Chicago: U of Chicago P, 1995. 48.

Johnson, Erskine. "Lena laced her long, thin fingers together and said 'Doggone it' when I asked her if she would ever make another movie in Hollywood." *Daily News* [Los Angeles] 29 May 1951: 19.

Johnson, James Weldon. *The Autobiography of an Ex-Colored Man.* New York: Dover, 1912.

Johnson, Lady Bird. *A White House Diary.* New York: Holt, 1970.

Johnson, Sam Houston. *My Brother Lyndon.* Ed. Enrique Hank Lopez. New York: Cowles Book, 1970.

Jones, G. William. *Black Cinema Treasures Lost and Found.* Denton: U of North Texas P, 1991.

Jones, Kenneth. "Carroll shows us a 'Sunset Boulevard' that's not just black or white." *Showtime! The Detroit News.* 11 Jul 1996: 4C.

"Julia Television Network Introduces First Black Family Series." *Ebony.* Nov. 1968: 56–62.

Jungle Fever. Dir. Spike Lee. Perf. Wesley Snipes, Samuel L. Jackson and Annabella Sciorra. 40 Acres and a Mule, 1991.

Kanter, Hal. *So Far, So Funny: My Life In Show Business.* Jefferson: McFarland & Co., 1999.

Keckley, Elizabeth. *Behind the Scenes: Thirty Years a Slave, and Four years in the White House.* 1868. Urbana: University of Illinois P, 2001.

Keenan Ivory Wayans Show, The. 16 Jan. 1998.

Kempton, Arthur. *Boogaloo: The Quintessence of American Popular Music.* New York: Pantheon, 2003.

Kent, George E. "Maya Angelou's *I Know Why the Caged Bird Sings* and Black Autobiographical Tradition." *African American Autobiography: A Collection of Critical Essays.* Ed. William L. Andrews. Englewood Cliffs: Prentice, 1993.

Khosla, Dinesh, and Patricia Williams. "Economies of Mind: A Collaborative Reflection." *Nova Law Journal* 10 (1986): 621.

"Kid Star Parents Exposed." *VH1 News Presents.* Prod. Dan Adler. VH1, 6 Apr 2007.

King, Coretta Scott. *My life with Martin Luther King, Jr..* New York: Holt, Rhinehart and Winston, 1969.

King, Martin Luther. *I Have a Dream.* 1963–1993 anniversary edition. Forward Revered Bernice A. King. San Francisco: Harper, 1993.

King, Wilma. *Stolen Childhood : Slave Youth In Nineteenth-Century America.* Bloomington: Indiana UP, 1995.

Kinney, Katherine. *Friendly Fire: American Images of the Vietnam War.* New York: Oxford UP, 2000.

Kitt, Eartha. *Alone with Me.* Chicago: Regnery, 1976.

———. *The Best of Eartha Kitt.* Collectibles. MCA, 1985.

———. *I'm Still Here: Confessions of a Sex Kitten.* London: Sidgwick, 1989.

———. *Rejuvenate!: It's Never Too Late.* New York: Scribner, 2001.

———. *Thursday's Child.* New York: Duell, 1956.

———, with Tonya Bolden. *Rejuvenate! (It's Never Too Late).* New York: Scribner, 2001.

Knight, Gladys. *Between Each Line of Pain and Glory: My Life Story.* New York: Hyperion, 1997.

Koenen, Anne. "The One Out of Sequence." *Conversations with Toni Morrison.* Ed. Danille Taylor-Guthrie. Jackson: UP of Mississippi, 1994.

LaBelle, Patti, with Laura B. Randolph. *Don't Block the Blessings: Revelations of a Lifetime.* New York: Riverhead, 1996.

Latifah, Queen. *Ladies First: Revelations of a Strong Woman.* New York: William Morrow, 1999.

Leave It To Beaver. Dir. Norman Abbott and Charles Barton. Perf. Jerry Mathers, Barbara Billingsley, and Tony Dow. ABC 4 Oct 1957.

"Lena Horne Joins Singer Harry Belafonte, Psychiatrist Dr. Alvin Poussaint and Poet-Playwright Larry Neal on the *Mike Douglas Show* in a Discussion on the Topic 'Bias in the Media.'" *Ebony* July 1968: 134.

"Lena Horne, Officially Retired From Showbiz, Turns 90 in June." *Jet.* 23 April 2007: 58.

"Lena Horne Turns 80." *Online Focus Online Newshour*. 30 June 1997. <http://www.pbs.org/newshour/bb/entertainment/june97/horne_6–3 0.html> June 2000.

Lewis, John, with Michael D'Orso. *Walking with the Wind: A Memoir of the Movement*. New York: Simon, 1998.

Lifeboat. Dir. Alfred hitchcock. Perf. Tallulah Bankhead, William Bendix, and Canada Lee. 20th Century Fox, 1944.

Life is not a Fairytale: The Fantasia Barrino Story. Dir. Debbie Allen. Perf. Loretta Devine, Fantasia Barrino, and Viola Davis. Lifetime, 2006.

Lionnet, Françoise. "Authoethnography: The An-Archic Style of *Dust Tracks on a Road*." *African American Autobiography: A Collection of Critical Essays*. Ed. William L. Andrews. Englewood Cliffs: Prentice, 1993.

Living Single. Dir. John Bowab and Henry Chan. Perf. Queen Latifah, Kim Fields, and Kim Coles. Fox 22 Aug 1993.

The Long Walk Home. Dir. Richard Pearce. Perf. Whoopi Goldberg and Sissy Spacek. New Vision Pictures, 1990.

Lorde, Audre. "Eye to Eye: Black Women, Hatred, and Anger." *Sister Outsider*. Freedom: Crossing, 1996.

Lupton, Deborah. *Food, the Body and the Self*. Thousand Oaks: Sage, 1996.

Malcolm X, and Alex Haley. *The Autobiography of Malcolm X*. New York: Ballantine, 1992.

Mapp, Edward. *African Americans and the Oscar: Seven Decades of Struggle and Achievement*. Lanham: The Scarecrow P, 2003.

Maxwell, Elsa. "Glamor v. Prejudice." *Bitter Fruit: African American Women in World War II*. Ed. Maureen Honey. Columbia: U of Missouri P, 1999.

"Meet the Real Lena Horne: Hollywood Star in Private Life Is Far Different from Glittery Glamour Girl of Films." *Ebony* Nov. 1947: 10, 14.

Merriam-Webster Collegiate Dictionary. 10th ed. Springfield: Merriam-Webster, 1996.

Miller, Alice. *For Your Own Good: Hidden Cruelty in Child-Rearing and the Roots of Violence*. Trans. Hildegarde and Hunter Hannun. New York: Farrar, 1983.

Miller, Edwin. "Off the Record with the Supremes." *Seventeen* Aug. 1966: 280, 424.

Mills, Earl. *Dorothy Dandridge: An Intimate Portrait of Hollywood's First Major Black Film Star*. Los Angeles: Holloway House, 1999.

More, Thomas. *Care of the Soul: A Guide for Cultivating Depth and Sacredness in Everyday Life*. New York: Harperennial, 1994.

Morrison, Toni. *The Bluest Eye*. New York: Plume, 1994.

———. "It Is Like Growing Up Black One More Time: Rediscovering Black History." *New York Times Magazine* 11 Aug. 1974: 14.

———. *Paradise*. New York: Knopf, 1998.

———. *Sula*. New York: Knopf, 1974.

"Motown Sound, The." *Ebony* Aug. 1966: np.

Moynihan, Patrick. *The Negro Family: The Case for National Action*. Office of Policy Planning and Research / United States Department of Labor, March 1965.

Mulvey, Laura. "Visual Pleasure and Narrative Cinema." *Feminism and Film Theory*. Ed. Constance Penley. New York: Routledge, 1988.

Muse, Clarence. "Muse Presents the Other Side of Film Pictures. Noted Screen Actor Thinks Performers Have Been Ignored." *Pittsburgh Courier* 12 Sept. 1942: 20.

Negro Soldier. Dir. Stuart Hiesler. Perf. William Broadus, Clarence Brooks, and Norman Ford. War Department/U.S. Army/Columbia TriStar, 1944.

Nelson, Jill. *Straight, No Chaser: How I Became a Grown-Up Black Woman*. New York: Penguin, 1999.

Nichols, Nichelle. *Beyond Uhura: Star Trek and Other Memories*. New York: Putnam, 1994.

Nobles, Wade W. "Africa American Family Life." *Black Families*. Ed. Harriette Pipes McAdoo. Thousand Oaks: Sage P, 1997: 90.

Nugent, Frank. *Liberty* 7 Apr. 1945: 54.

Nugent, Frank. "Ten years ago she was a nobody, going nowhere. Today the lovely Lena Horne is one of our top entertainers. But you'll never catch her whipping up spoon bread and spirituals in an Aunt Jemima rig, because She's Nobody's Mammy." *Liberty* 7 Apr 1945: 54.

Olney, James. *Autobiography: Essays Theoretical and Critical*. Princeton: Princeton UP, 1980.

Peck, Seymour. "The Star of *Jamaica* Reflects on Career and Marriage." *New York Times*. 27 Oct 1957: X3.

Peller, Gary. "Race Consciousness." *Critical Race Theory: The Key Writings that Formed the Movement*. Ed. Kimberlé Crenshaw, Neil Gotanda, et al. New York: New P, 1995.

"People." *Time* 30 Nov. 53: 48.

Petry, Ann. *The Street*. 1946. Boston: Houghton Mifflin, 1974.

"Phyllis Hyman Says, 'The Man I Wanted I Made Him Not Want Me and Now I'm All Alone.'" 16 December 1991: 58.

"Phyllis Hyman Wants Love to Match Records, Stage Success." *Jet.* 1 October 1981: 60–62.

Pinkins, Tonya. *Get Over Yourself!: How to Drop the Drama and Claim the Life You Deserve.* New York: Hyperion, 2006.

Posner, Gerald. *Motown: Music, Money, Sex, and Power.* New York: Random, 2002.

Prince, Mary. "The History of Mary Prince." *The Classic Slave Narratives.* Ed. Henry Louis Gates, Jr. New York: Penquin, 1987.

"Promised Land (1967–1985), The" *Eyes on the Prize II: America at the Racial Crossroads.* Prod./Dir./Writer Paul Stekler and Jacqueline Shearer; Narr. Julian Bond. Blackside, 1989. PBS Video.

Reeves, Martha, and Mark Bego. *Dancing in the Street: Confessions of a Motown Diva.* New York: Hyperion, 1994.

Regester, Charlene B. "Hazel Scott and Lena Horne: African-American Divas, Feminists, and Political Activists." *Popular Culture Review* 7.1 (1996): 81.

Reynolds, Star Jones. *Shine! A Physical, Emotional, and Spiritual Journey to Finding Love.* New York: Collins, 2006.

Richardson, Joe Martin. *A History of Fisk University 1865–1946.* Tuscaloosa: U of Alabama P, 1980.

Rippy, Marguerite H. "Commodity, Tragedy, Desire: Female Sexuality and Blackness in the Iconography of Dorothy Dandridge." *Classic Hollywood Classic Whiteness.* Ed. Daniel Bernardi. Minneapolis: U of Minnesota P, 2001.

Rookies on Parade. Dir. Joseph Santley. Perf. Bob Crosby, Ruth Terry, and Gertrude Niesen. Republic, 1941.

Ross, Diana. *Secrets of a Sparrow: Memoirs.* New York: Villard, 1993.

Russell, Jan Jarboe. *Lady Bird.* New York: Scribner, 1999.

Sahara. Dir. Zoltan Korda. Perf. Humphrey Bogart, Bruce Bennett, and J. Carroll Naish. Columbia Picture Corp., 1943.

"Salty Eartha." *Time* 9 June 1952: 61–62.

Same Time Next Year. By Bernard Slade. Dir. Warren Crane. Perf. Diahann Carroll and Cleavon Little. Huntington Hartford Theatre, Los Angeles. Apr 1977.

Sampson, Henry T. *Blacks in Black and White: A Source Book on Black Films.* Metuchen: Scarecrow P, 1995.

The Scar of Shame. Dir. Frank Peregini. Perf. Harry Henderson, Ann Kennedy and Norman Johnstone. Colored Players Film Corp., 1927.

Schomberg, Arthur. "The Negro Digs Up His Past." The Survey Graphic. Mar. 1925. 670. < http://etext.virginia.edu/harlem/SchNegrF.html> May 2006.

Scott, Joan W. "Experience." *Feminists Theorize the Political*. Ed. Judith Butler and Joan W. Scott. New York: Routledge, 1992.

Simmons, Kimora Lee. *Fabulosity: What It Is & How to Get It*. New York: HarperCollins, 2006.

Simone, Nina, with Stephen Cleary. *I Put a Spell on You: The Autobiography of Nina Simone*. New York: Pantheon, 1991.

Singleton, Raynoma Gordy. *Berry, Me, and Motown: The Untold Story*. Chicago: Contemporary Books, 1990.

Sister, Sister. Dir. John Berry. Perf. Diahann Carroll, Rosalind Cash, and Irene Cara. 20th Century Fox/NBC, 1982.

Skolsky, Sidney. "Close-Up of Lena Horne." *Motion Picture* Oct. 1944: 82.

Smith, Barbara. "Toward a Black Feminist Criticism." *All the Women Are White, All the Blacks Are Men, Some of Us Are Brave: Black Women's Studies*. Eds. Gloria T. Hull, Patricia Bell Scott, and Barbara Smith. Old Westbury: Feminist P, 1982.

Smith, Darr. "She expects to be finished with her MGM contract next April and then she will be off for a singing tour of Europe and South America." *Daily News* [Los Angeles] 15 Aug. 1949.

Smith, Suzanne E. *Dancing in the Street: Motown and the Cultural Politics of Detroit*. Cambridge: Harvard UP, 2000.

Smith, Valerie. *Self-discovery and Authority in Afro-American Narrative*. Cambridge: Harvard UP, 1987.

Snead, James. *White Screens Black Images: Hollywood from the Dark Side*. Ed. Colin MacCabe and Cornel West. New York: Routledge, 1994.

Somé, Malidoma Patrice. *The Healing Wisdom of Africa*. New York: Penguin, 1998.

Sounder. Dir. Martin Ritt. Perf. Cicely Tyson, Paul Winfield, and Kevin Hooks. 20th Century Fox, 1972.

Specter, Ronnie, with Vince Waldron. *Be My Baby: How I Survived Mascara, Miniskirts, and Madness, or My Life as a Fabulous Ronette*. New York: Harmony, 1990.

"Spike Lee Slams Clooney's Acceptance Speech." <http://femalefirst. co.uk/entertainment/Spike+Lee+Slams+Clooney+s+Oscar+Acceptance+Speech-15376.html> 20 Mar 2006.

Spillers, Hortense. "'Mamma's Baby, Papa's Maybe' An American Grammar Book." *Diacritics* 17 (Summer 1987): 65.

Spoto, Donald. *Marilyn Monroe: The Biography*. New York: Cooper Square P, 2001.

Stampp, Kenneth. *The Peculiar Institution: Slavery in the Ante-Bellum South*. New York: Random, 1956.

Stefans, Karrine, and Karen Hunter. *Confessions of a Video Vixen*. New York: Amistad, 2005.

Steve Harvey Show, The. "After The Fall." Dir. Stan Lathan. Perf. Steve Harvey, Cedric "The Entertainer," and Wendy Racquel Robinson. UPN. 1 Apr 01

Stormy Weather. Dir. Andrew L. Stone. Perf. Bill "Bojangles" Robinson, Lena Horne, and Cab Calloway. 20th Century Fox, 1943.

Story, Rosalyn M. *And So I Sing: African American Divas of Opera and Concert*. New York: Warner, 1990.

Stuckey, Sterling. *Going through the Storm: The Influence of African American Art in History*. New York: Oxford UP, 1994.

——. *Slave Culture: Nationalist Theory and the Foundations of Black America*. New York: Oxford UP, 1987.

Studio System. American Cinema. Video series produced by the New York Center for Visual History in association with KCET/Los Angeles and the BBC. Annenberg/CPB, 1995.

Summers, Anthony. *Goddess: The Secret Lives of Marilyn Monroe*. New York: Penguin, 1986.

Sunset Boulevard. By Andrew Lloyd Webber. Dir. Trevor Nunn. Perf. Diahann Carroll, Rex Smith, and Walter Charles. Toronto, Ford Centre for Performing Arts, 15 Oct 1995.

"Supremes Are Tops, The." *Ebony* Aug. 1966: 153.

"Supremes Make It Big, The" *Ebony* June 1965: 81.

Takiff, Jonathan. "Phyllis Hyman: Phyllis Hyman's Posthumous Final Album Reflects Hauntingly on Her Life." 11 June 1995 <http://www.geocities.com/Heartland/Meadows/2318/phyllis_article.html>. Sept. 2000.

"Talk with the Star." *Newsweek* 22 Apr. 57: 70.

Tamango. Dir. John Berry. Perf. Curd Jürgens, Dorothy Dandridge. CEI Incom, 1958.

Taubman, Howard. "'No Strings' Opens at the 54th Street." *New York Times Theater Reviews 1920–1970*. Vol. 7. New York: Arno P, 1971. 10 vols. 1960–1966.

Truth, Sojourner. *The Narrative Sojourner Truth*. 1850. New York: Penguin, 1998.

Turner, Lana. *Lana: The Lady, the Legend, the Truth*. New York: Dutton, 1982.

Turner, Tina. *I, Tina*. New York: Avonbooks, 1987.

Ulanov, Barry. "How Lena Learned to Sing." *Negro Digest* Dec. 1947: np.

"Verdict, The." *Dynasty*. Dir. Jerome Courtland. Perf. Diahann Carroll, John Forsythe, and Joan Collins. Episode 94, Season 5. ABC Aaron Spelling Productions. 7 Nov. 1984.

VH1 News Presents: Kid Star Parents Exposed.

Walker, Alice. *The Color Purple.* 1982. Florida: Harvest, 2003.

———. *In Search of Our Mother's Gardens: Womanist Prose.* New York: Harcourt, 1983.

Waters, Ethel, with Charles Samuels. *His Eye Is on the Sparrow.* New York: Doubleday, 1951.

Wells, Ida B. *Crusade for Justice: The Autobiography of Ida B. Wells.* Ed. Alfreda M. Duster. Chicago: U of Chicago P, 1970.

West, Cornel. *Race Matters.* New York: Vintage, 1993.

"White House: A Word From Miss Kitt, The." *Newsweek* 29 Jan. 1968: 23.

White, Walter. *A Man Called White: The Autobiography of Walter White.* New York: Viking P, 1948.

"Why Negroes Don't Like Eartha Kitt." *Ebony* Dec. 1954: 29, 32, 37.

Wigglesworth, Michael. *The Diary of Michael Wigglesworth: 1653–1657: The Conscience of a Puritan.* Ed. Edmund S. Morgan. Gloucester: Peter Smith, 1970.

"Will, The." *Dynasty.* Dir. Nancy Malone. Perf. Diahann Carroll, John Forsythe, and Joan Collins. Episode 102, Season 5. ABC Aaron Spelling Productions. 9 Jan. 1985.

Williams, Myrlie Evers. *Watch Me Fly: What I Learned on the Way to becoming the Woman I was meant to be / Myrlie Evers-Williams with Melinda Blau.* Boston: Little, Brown, 1999.

Williams, Patricia J. *The Alchemy of Race and Rights: Diary of a Law Professor.* Cambridge: Harvard UP, 1991.

Williams, Wendy. *The Wendy Williams Experience.* New York: Dutton, 2004.

Wilson, Mary. *Dreamgirl: My Life as a Supreme.* New York: Cooper Square P, 1999.

Within Our Gates. Dir. Oscar Micheaux. Perf. Evelyn Preer, Flo Clements, and James D. Ruffin. Micheaux Book and Film Co., 1920.

Wiz, The. Dir. Sidney Lumet. Perf. Lena Horne, Diana Ross, and Michael Jackson. Motown Productions, 1978.

Wolcott, Victoria. *Remaking Respectability: African American Women in Interwar Detroit.* Chapel Hill: U of North Carolina P, 2001.

"Word From Miss Kitt, A." *Newsweek* 29 Jan 1968: 24.

Wright, Richard. *Black Boy.* New York: Harper, 1945.

Young, Andrew. *An Easy Burden: The Civil Rights Movement and the Transformation of America.* New York: Harper Collins, 1996.

Index